KU-615-983

OPERATION FORTITUDE

THE STORY OF THE SPY
OPERATION THAT SAVED D-DAY

JOSHUA LEVINE

Collins

First published in 2011 by Collins
HarperCollins Publishers
77–85 Fulham Palace Road
London W6 8JB

www.harpercollins.co.uk

1 3 5 7 9 10 8 6 4 2

Text © Joshua Levine 2011

The author asserts his moral right to
be identified as the author of this work

All images © The National Archives UK except for: page 2, top left © Getty
Images, top right and middle © Spanish police courtesy of the Churchill
Archives Centre, bottom left and right © Imperial War Museum;
page 3, bottom right © Time & Life Pictures/Getty Images; page 5, middle
left © Getty Images, middle right © Time & Life Pictures/Getty Images,
bottom © Imperial War Museum; page 8, top left © Popperfoto/Getty Images,
top left © Getty Images, middle © Bettmann/CORBIS

A catalogue record for this book is
available from the British Library

HB ISBN: 978-0-00-731353-2
PB ISBN: 978-0-00-743323-0

Printed and bound in Great Britain by
Clays Ltd, St Ives plc

All rights reserved. No parts of this publication may be
reproduced, stored in a retrieval system or transmitted,
in any form or by any means, electronic, mechanical,
photocopying, recording or otherwise, without the prior
permission of the publishers.

Mixed Sources

Product group from well-managed
forests and other controlled sources
www.fsc.org Cert no. SW-COC-001806
© 1996 Forest Stewardship Council

FSC

FSC is a non-profit international organisation established to promote the
responsible management of the world's forests. Products carrying the FSC
label are independently certified to assure consumers that they come
from forests that are managed to meet the social, economic and
ecological needs of present and future generations.

Find out more about HarperCollins and the environment at
www.harpercollins.co.uk/green

STOCKPORT LIBRARIES	
C2001798982	
Bertrams	13/05/2011
940.5486	LEV
CLL	£16.99

CONTENTS

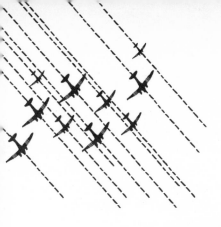

ATLANTIC WALL

As the rain poured down in the English Channel on the night of 19 May 1944, a British motor torpedo boat headed for the French coast. On board were two officers – a Commando and a Royal Engineer. Their mission was to investigate a new type of German mine and to take infrared photographs of the obstacles dug into the beaches to resist the coming Allied invasion. The Germans, aware that the Allies were planning to attack 'Fortress Europe', had fortified the entire length of the Atlantic and Channel coasts. For the Commando officer, Lieutenant George Lane, this would be the third night in a row that he was being delivered to the same spot to carry out the same reconnaissance.

Lane was a Hungarian who had been studying at London University when war broke out. After a spell in the Pioneer Corps he was invited to join the Special Operations Executive (SOE), before transferring to the Commandos, where he helped to form a special unit of refugees from occupied Europe. These were men who had already suffered at the hands of the Nazis and they felt a hatred for the enemy far greater than that felt by the average British soldier. They had assumed British identities on joining the unit, but their accents betrayed their origins and as Commandos and nationals of

1

occupied states they could expect to be handed over to the Gestapo if captured. For Lane – whose real name was Dyuri Länyi – the current mission was merely the latest in a string of secret and highly dangerous raids on the enemy coast.

This particular raid came about as a result of a recent RAF strafing attack on the French coast. A Spitfire had fired a rocket which fell short of its target but set off a series of under-water explosions. The aircraft had been mounted with a camera and, to the analysts studying the film, the sequence of events suggested the existence of a previously unknown type of German mine. Lane was therefore to comb the beach for unknown varieties of pressure mine, release mine or magnetic mine. Over two tense and tiring nights he scrutinized numer-ous mines and decided that they were nothing more than ordi-nary landmines fixed to stakes driven into the sand. They were, he noted, underwater at high tide, and so designed to destroy landing craft on contact. But Lane's report had been doubted and so on the third night Lieutenant Roy Woodridge, a mine expert from the Royal Engineers, was sent beachcomb-ing with him.

The two men were transferred from their motor torpedo boat into a smaller dory. They landed on the beach and began studying the mines as the dory's crew waited. Woodridge quickly confirmed Lane's previous findings. The landmines, he decided, hadn't been properly waterproofed, their firing mechanisms had been corroded, and the pressure of the rock-et's explosion had set them off in unison. The mystery solved, Lane ordered the dory's crew back to the motor torpedo boat and told them to return in an hour, once he and Woodridge had taken their infrared photographs.

Minutes later the two men were surprised by the sound of gunfire. They lay down in the sand dunes as a pair of German patrols opened fire on each other, each believing the other to be a raiding party. When the firing stopped, they picked themselves up and hurried back to the water. The dory's crew had left a small rubber dinghy behind. Lane and Woodridge knew that if the Germans found them on the beach they would be shot as saboteurs, so they climbed into the dinghy and paddled furiously. By the time it was light they were a mile out to sea.

As they paddled they became aware of a motorboat heading towards them from the shore. After a quick discussion they decided to feign helplessness in the hope that they could overpower the boat's crew when it drew alongside them. But as the boat came into focus out of the gloom they could see that it was full of soldiers pointing Mauser rifles. There seemed little point in resistance. With what Lane later described as 'a theatrical gesture', he and Woodridge raised their arms and surrendered. They had already thrown away their cameras, mine detectors and any other evidence that they had been ashore, and would now have to convince their captors that they were neither saboteurs nor Commandos.

On land they were separated and interrogated. In a dark cellar Lane was repeatedly told that he would be executed as a saboteur, but he stuck to the story that he and Woodridge were the remnants of a naval battle and had not been anywhere near the beach. Woodridge, fortunately, was telling the same story in a nearby cellar. The next morning they were blindfolded, their hands were tied, and they were led outside to a car. Lane was placed in the front seat, but his blindfold was slightly askew; by tilting back his head he could catch glimpses through the window and he tried to memorize the signposts that flashed past him. He had no idea where they were going. Presumably to their deaths. The car stopped soon after passing a sign which read 'La Roche-Guyon'. Neither man was aware of the fact, but they were arriving at a twelfth-century château to meet a man who had expressed a desire to meet them and who had the power to save their lives. He was the man chosen by Hitler to defend western Europe from Allied invasion, as well as the most famous German soldier of them all: Field Marshal Erwin Rommel.

La Roche-Guyon is a pretty village nestled in a loop on the River Seine between Mantes and Vernon. It is not far from Giverny, where Monet obsessively painted his waterlilies. Lane remembers, when his blindfold was removed, being faced by a striking château set against grass-rimmed cliffs and, above it, a half-ruined Norman tower. The ancestral home of the Rochefoucauld family, the château now served as the headquarters of Rommel's Army Group B. Rommel had chosen the château for three reasons. First, for its security; centuries-old tunnels dug into the soft limestone cliffs were enlarged to provide secure living quarters for officers and men. Secondly, for its proximity to Paris. Thirdly, and most crucially, for its central position between the Pas de Calais and Normandy, the two most likely sites of the forthcoming Allied invasion. Rommel's Army Group B was made up of the Seventh Army, charged with defending the coast from Brittany up to the River Orne, and the Fifteenth Army, responsible for the sector from the Orne further up to Belgium. For all their preoccupation with the approaching invasion, and despite the fact that the Allies were feverishly preparing for it less than 100 miles away, the Germans did not actually know where or when it was coming.

Having arrived at the château, Lane was marched through the front door and placed alone in a brightly gilded room. Intrigued by events, and relieved to be in civilized surroundings, he became curious. He spotted a door slightly ajar and opened it. He was instantly confronted by the most ferocious dog he'd ever seen, which growled unpleasantly as it was pulled back by a guard. Curiosity quelled, he sat down. He was joined by an elegant German officer who brought him a sandwich and a cup of coffee. This was Lieutenant Colonel Hans-Georg von Tempelhoff, Rommel's chief operations officer, and one of his most trusted companions. Von Tempelhoff addressed Lane in fluent English, a language native to neither of them. This was a concern to Lane, who spoke English with a noticeable Hungarian accent, which, with a few tweaks, he attempted to pass off as a Welsh lilt. He had done much of his Commando training in Wales, but was his accent plausible enough to fool the German, a cultured officer with an English wife?

'I've got something important to tell you,' said von Tempelhoff. 'You are going to meet a very important person, and I must have your assurance that you will behave with the utmost dignity.' 'I happen to be an officer and a gentleman,' replied Lane in his best Welsh-Hungarian, 'and I can't behave in any other way. Who am I going to meet?' 'You're going to meet His Excellency Field Marshal Rommel!' Lane was delighted; Rommel had earned a great deal of respect among British soldiers. Von Tempelhoff wondered whether there was enough time for Lane to tidy himself up, but decided that there wasn't. 'But would you like to clean your nails?' he asked, offering Lane a nail file. So, his accent having passed muster, Lane made his nails presentable for the field marshal.

Lane was taken into Rommel's study, at the far end of which the field marshal was sitting behind a huge inlaid desk. Lane was sure that Rommel would try to unnerve him by making him walk the entire length of the room, but instead he walked towards him and said, 'Setzen Sie sich.' An interpreter was present and Lane played his part by asking what Rommel had just said, even though his German was probably as good as the Swabian Rommel's. Referring everything to the interpreter gave Lane extra time to think – an important consideration given that the next few minutes would decide his fate.

The meeting began tensely. Rommel asked Lane whether he realized that he was in a very tricky situation. 'Why, sir?' 'Because everybody seems to think that you're a saboteur.' Instead of flatly denying the charge, Lane used his charm on Rommel: 'If the field marshal thought I was a saboteur, he wouldn't have invited me here!' Rommel laughed. 'So you think this is an invitation?' 'Yes, naturally,' said Lane, 'and I'm delighted to be here.'

Rommel was now smiling broadly, and when Rommel smiled so did the men around him. The mood in the room was transformed. 'Well,' said the field marshal, 'we've had a lot of trouble with gangster Commandos!' Lane's professional pride was piqued by this and he replied huffily, 'Commandos are Commandos and gangsters are gangsters. The two words don't go together!' Rommel smiled again and asked, 'How's my friend Montgomery doing?' 'Unfortunately I don't know him,' answered Lane, 'but he's preparing the invasion, so you'll see him fairly soon.'

The banter between the two men bubbled along. 'I only read about these things in *The Times*,' said Lane, referring to the invasion, 'but it's a very good newspaper and I think you ought to read it.' 'We do,' replied Rommel. 'We get it from Lisbon.' 'Well, then,' said Lane, 'you'll see that they'll be here shortly fighting you.' 'That'll be the first time the English have done any fighting,' said Rommel. 'I beg your pardon? What happened at El Alamein?' 'It wasn't the English!' laughed Rommel. 'The English always get others to do their fighting for them. The Canadians, the Australians, the South Africans …' Rommel neglected to add 'the Hungarians' to his list of English surrogates. 'I'm afraid we have to differ on that,' said Lane. 'I don't think that's the case.'

Rommel then made a remark that surprised his guest. 'The great tragedy,' he said, 'is that you, the British, and we, the

Germans, are fighting each other, instead of combining our strength and fighting the real enemy, the Russians.' Lane gave a considered reply: 'Well, it would be very difficult for the Germans and British to get together because we think so differently about so many things.' 'What sort of things?' asked Rommel. 'Well, for instance, the Jews,' said Lane. 'We abhor the way you treat the Jews.' Rommel's reply amounted to a meaningless fudge: 'Ah, that's something that is very, very difficult to make the English understand. People have different ideas about it all and it's impossible to talk about it – because everybody has different ideas.' 'Well, there you are,' struck back Lane, 'we can't agree on that, so we can't fight against the Russians together.' Rommel laughed again.

Now feeling that he had the upper hand, Lane became bold. He asked whether he could put a question to Rommel. The field marshal said he could and Lane asked how the French people felt about being occupied by the Germans. Rommel's answer was striking for its casual German self-importance: 'The French were always in a bad way because there wasn't anybody to lead them. They were all rushing about heedlessly. And now we are occupying them and we look after all the necessary things like water and electricity and food supplies. And, for the first time, the French are relaxed and happy because they know where they are.' 'I'd like to see that,' said Lane, 'but every time I travel with your boys they blindfold me and tie my hands behind my back – so I don't think I'll have the chance ...' Rommel turned to one of his officers and asked whether such treatment was really necessary. 'Oh yes,' he was told, 'these are very dangerous people. We can't take any risks.' 'They have the experience,' Rommel said to Lane. 'I can't argue with them.'

Lieutenant Woodridge was also brought before Rommel, but he refused to speak other than to give his name, rank and number. Throughout his life Lane remained convinced that their lives were spared by Rommel's intervention, and in essence this was true. The two men had been brought to La Roche-Guyon at the direct request of Hans Speidel, Rommel's chief of staff, when the Fifteenth Army would otherwise have handed them over to the Gestapo. After La Roche-Guyon they were sent, with Rommel's express consent, to a prisoner-of-war camp. Rommel would later tell his naval adviser, Vice-Admiral Friedrich Ruge, that Lane had asked the name of the château so that he could find it again after the war. When nobody would tell him, he said that he would search all of France after the war until he found the spot. Lane, who had managed to conceal his Hungarian identity from his captors, survived the war. He died in March 2010.

The obstacles that Lane had been trying to photograph represented just one tiny section of Rommel's massive Atlantic Wall. Rommel decorated 3,000 miles of coastline with gruesome obstacles with names like Czech hedgehogs, Belgian gates and nutcrackers. He blocked beach exits with trenches and concrete pyramids known as dragon's teeth. He floodlit beaches to dazzle the enemy as they landed. He flooded flatlands to make them impassable. He placed a Death Zone behind the beaches, tightly mined and reinforced by infantry and artillery. He pleaded with Hitler to have entire Panzer divisions dug in behind the Death Zone. And he handed out accordions as a reward to members of units who had shown particular zeal during the construction of what the Allies called the 'Rommelbelt'.

Rommel's obsessive focus on shore defence reflected his firm belief that the enemy must be defeated on the beaches. The Luftwaffe had lost control of the air and many of the soldiers at Rommel's disposal were ageing, unfit or simply exhausted from their exertions on the Eastern Front. If the

Allies succeeded in gaining a bridgehead, battered German supply lines would fail to deliver troops, tanks, fuel and weapons to the battle zones. Rommel was sure that the overstretched Germans would be defeated in open warfare. But if the Allies could be thrown back into the sea within the first twenty-four hours, it might be a very long time before they attempted to return, and the full strength of the Wehrmacht could be unleashed on the Eastern Front. At this point, envisaged Rommel, a peace could be sought with the Anglo-Americans, and his fond wish, as expressed to George Lane, might be realized: German and British soldiers fighting together against a common Soviet enemy.

A negotiated peace was not a hope shared by Hitler. The Führer knew that the Allied invasion would be decisive for the outcome of the war, and he believed – or allowed himself to believe – that it would be triumphantly resisted. But, unlike Rommel, he had no interest in peace deals. He was aware, for one thing, that the Allies would have little interest in seeking a peace with him. While both Hitler and the war were still alive, he would pursue it aggressively on every front.

Future strategies aside, the immediate concern of both Hitler and Rommel was to defeat the imminent invasion. But where and when was it coming? During their meeting Rommel asked Lane whether he knew the answer. 'I can only tell you what I would do if it was up to me,' Lane replied. 'I would arrange it across the shortest possible route – that's the best way of doing it.' 'That's interesting,' said Rommel. 'The Führer seems to think the same.'

Actually this was not quite true. Hitler's belief in late May and early June, as he told the Japanese ambassador in Berlin, was that the Allies would attack first in Normandy, where they would attempt to establish their bridgehead. After this, he thought, they would launch a second front on the Pas de

Calais, Lane's 'shortest possible route'. And Rommel's words to Lane seem to mask his own view. In a report he sent to Hitler at the end of 1943 he had stated his firm belief that the Allied assault would be directed against the Pas de Calais.

Five months later Rommel's belief was confirmed when he was visited by General Hans Cramer. Cramer, a captive of the British for the past year, had just been released in an exchange of prisoners. He told Rommel that on his release he had been driven through south-east England and it was crowded with troops and invasion activity. He knew where he was thanks to road signs and the loose tongue of a soldier guarding him. Clearly the invasion was going to be launched from Dover, to an area north of the Somme estuary. Two days later, on the eve of D-Day, Rommel repeated Cramer's warning to the commander of the 116th Panzer Division.

But even as Hitler and Rommel were trying to predict the Allies' intentions, a small number of individuals, working for Allied intelligence and for Britain's Security Service, were trying to influence those predictions. A remarkable deception operation, codenamed 'Fortitude', was being carried out, its aim to confuse the Germans as to when and where the invasion would take place, and once it had, to make them believe that a larger invasion was coming elsewhere. Operation Fortitude involved double agents, fictional armies and fake wireless transmissions. It involved lies being told to neutral diplomats, a General Montgomery lookalike – and it involved General Hans Cramer.

The eagle-eyed general might have believed that he was being driven through south-east England, but he wasn't. The road signs he spotted were fakes. The garrulous soldier he questioned was playing a role. Cramer was actually being driven through the south-west of England to Portsmouth. As he ran to Rommel with his story of an invasion force in south-east England aimed at the Pas de Calais, he was acting just as the Fortitude deceivers had hoped he would. He must have congratulated himself on the importance of the information he was bringing the field marshal. But, unknown to either of them, Hans Cramer was serving the other side.

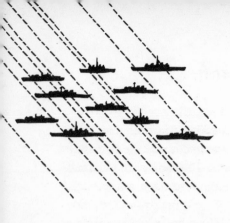

THE PILLARS OF FORTITUDE

Operation Fortitude was not an act of isolated inspiration. It was the culmination of years of rigorous logic, hard-slogging effort and a few near-catastrophic errors. And it was built upon two solid pillars which had to be constructed almost from scratch: strategic deception and the Double Cross system.

The comprehensive system of strategic deception was developed – more or less single-handedly – by Lieutenant Colonel Dudley Wrangel Clarke. Clarke was a dynamic little man with carefully slicked blond hair and haunting blue eyes who had already made a valuable contribution to the war effort before he turned his unorthodox mind to deception. In the days following the evacuation of Allied soldiers from Dunkirk in mid-1940, he had been chatting with General Sir John Dill, the Chief of the Imperial General Staff. 'We must find some way,' said Dill, 'of helping the Army to exercise its offensive spirit once again.' Clarke had grown up in the Trans-vaal and he thought back to the Boer Commandos, loose-knit bands of horsemen used as guerrillas to strike against the British during the Boer War. He suggested the formation of a modern equivalent which could 'hit sharp and quick, then run to fight another day'.

One of Clarke's first Commandos was actor David Niven, who recalled being summoned to the War Office, where Clarke explained to him the concept of cut-and-thrust raids on the enemy coastline. A little while later Niven met Winston Churchill and cheerfully described to him the Commandos' prospects. 'Your security is very lax,' said the Prime Minister. 'You shouldn't be telling me this.' Niven had no idea whether Churchill was serious or not.

Clarke himself led the first Commando raid on 24 June 1940. He claimed to have been unaware of receiving any injury during the raid, until he returned to the depot ship, where the petty officer in charge of the sick bay stared at his ear and exclaimed, 'Gawd almighty, sir! It's almost coming off!' Clarke was subsequently posted to the staff of General Sir Archibald Wavell, Commander-in-Chief Middle East. Wavell appreciated Clarke's 'puckish sense of humour', which, in his eyes, made Clarke ideal for a very particular task: heading a section with the sole purpose of misleading the enemy.

Clarke had served as a fighter pilot with the Royal Air Force at the tail end of the Great War. This set him apart from the mainstream. Individualistic and questioning, airmen had offered a challenge to traditional military thinking. In the years after the war Clarke's superior officers reported on his 'initiative, originality and energy'. He had an instinctive understanding of display and performance born of a love of the theatre, which he had put to good military use in organizing an exuberant Royal Tournament featuring camels, oxen, and tribesmen. Yet while these obvious qualities may have led Clarke to the unusual work of deception, it was other, less showy traits which brought him success. He was a slightly detached man, a laconic observer who had, novelist and fellow deceiver Dennis Wheatley noted in his memoirs, an 'uncanny habit of suddenly appearing in a room without anyone having noticed him enter it'. This allowed Clarke to observe the foibles and weaknesses of those around him. He had what have sometimes been described as feminine sensibilities: empathy, imagination and subtlety. These – coupled with a superior intellect – were the real qualities needed to get inside the mind of an enemy.

Clarke's first deception plan for General Wavell was Operation Camilla, an attempt to make the Italians think that an attack was to be mounted on occupied British Somaliland by troops based in Egypt, when in fact the real attack was to be made on Eritrea by troops in the Sudan. Clarke spared no effort in thinking up ways of misleading Italian intelligence. Raids were launched on Somaliland by air and sea to make it seem as though an assault must follow. Campaign maps and pamphlets relating to Somaliland were issued to British troops. The airwaves were bombarded with fake wireless traffic and the Japanese consul in Port Said was tipped off that an attack on Somaliland was imminent. In the event, the plan managed to succeed – and simultaneously to fail utterly. The Italian commander certainly believed that Wavell was intending to attack Somaliland. But, deciding that the attack could not be resisted, he removed his troops from Somaliland and sent them to Eritrea, where their presence made the actual assault far more difficult than it would have been without the deception plan.

This misfortune proved to be a valuable learning experience for Clarke. His response was to formulate his first rule of strategic deception: to make your opponent act as you want him to. It doesn't matter what he thinks. In this case the Italian commander was led to expect an attack on Somaliland, but Clarke hadn't considered what he would do as a result. The deceiver, he realized, had to get inside the mind of the enemy commander. On this occasion he had failed. In future Clarke would make a point of asking his commander, 'What do you want the enemy to do?' And very often, to his surprise, the commander would be unable to answer. 'So,' Clarke said, 'I developed the trick of asking them to imagine that I had a direct telephone line to Hitler, and that he would do anything I told him to do. And this proved quite successful ...' During Operation Fortitude Clarke's golden rule would sit above all others as the one to be obeyed.

Clarke was also coming to appreciate the value of playing on his enemy's fears. It takes relatively little effort to convince an enemy commander of a false notion he already believes. After all, people like to be proved right. Clarke learned – through deciphered wireless traffic – that the Italians expected the deployment of British paratroops in Libya. It was a groundless fear, but Clarke took advantage of it. He invented a unit which he named the Special Air Service Brigade. This brigade of 500 paratroops – so Clarke's story went – was being trained to take the Italians by surprise. Rumours were spread about its existence. Pictures of men with parachutes were published in a Cairo magazine. Dummy gliders were built and ostentatiously concealed on airfields. Soldiers wearing 'SAS' armbands and badges were planted in Middle Eastern cities, where they spoke, apparently reticently, about their future activities.

This imaginary 1 SAS Brigade was not created to assist any specific military action. Its role lay in the longer term. It was the first link in a chain of notional units which, added together, would make the British army in the Middle East appear far greater and deadlier than it really was. These notional units would be called upon, at a future stage, to deceive the enemy on a truly impressive scale. This 'Order of Battle' deception was Clarke's long-war innovation and it reflected his belief that effective deception needed time to work. It required a great deal of systematic planning and time-consuming maintenance.

'Once started,' warned Clarke, 'it remains a standing dish which can never be neglected or abandoned.' Yet its rewards could be great. General Wavell once asked Clarke, 'What is your deception work worth to me?' 'On the evidence of captured documents,' replied Clarke, 'three divisions, one armoured brigade and two squadrons of aircraft.' The Order of Battle idea, transplanted to Britain, would form the basis of Operation Fortitude.

The SAS, of course, did not remain a notional unit for long. Major David Stirling sought Clarke's assistance in forming a streamlined version of the Commandos, to be made up of teams of four men trained in the use of parachutes. Clarke agreed to help – so long as Stirling named the new unit after his own made-up brigade. Aside from his deception work, Clarke had therefore been instrumental in the creation of both the Commandos and the SAS. And once the enemy had evidence of the genuine SAS in action, they simply assumed it to be Clarke's imaginary unit, and so his Order of Battle deception gained added credibility.

In March 1941 Clarke's deception service became known as 'A' Force and a month later it moved to offices beneath a Cairo brothel. This in itself was clever. Clarke did not want attention drawn to his unit, and little would be paid to a succession of army figures entering a bordello. He continued to deceive, with impressive results, and by now was building up a system of double agents entirely independent of the system that was simultaneously under development in London. His first, and most important, double agent went by the codename *Cheese*. As early as June 1941 *Cheese* was the channel for a strategic deception – targeting Rommel, who was commander of Panzer Group Africa – which helped to achieve total surprise for the Eighth Army when it advanced into Libya in November. Just as Rommel was absent from his command post during the Normandy landings, so he was absent – in Athens – during this advance.

Clarke had begun to surround himself with laterally thinking assistants. These included an officer to advise on building dummy tanks, an expert in faking documents, a locally born officer responsible for recruiting informers, and a celebrated West End magician, Jasper Maskelyne, who served as one of Clarke's camouflage experts. Clarke's own uncle had been president of the Magic Circle, so it is not surprising that he was drawn to a conjurer. Maskelyne's previous military inventions had included exploding sheep, which were actually woollen fleeces stuffed with explosives and placed in fields where enemy gliders were likely to land. In the Middle East he set to work on creating fake battleships, fake submarines, and even a fake Alexandria Harbour several miles from the real thing, which was duly attacked in error by the enemy.

The more varied the deception tools available to him, and the more complex his Order of Battle deception became, the better Clarke was able to put each cover story across through small, unconnected details from which the enemy could piece the story together for himself. This was commonsense: a cover story deduced from many apparently unconnected sources must be more trustworthy than one from a single uncorroborated source. It was also psychologically shrewd, for the enemy was much keener to believe something that he had 'cleverly' worked out for himself. And if one element of the deception failed, the whole cover story was not necessarily blown, whereas, conversely, if the deception succeeded, the enemy might well blame himself for reaching a false conclusion from perfectly accurate bits of information.

This tactic of putting a story across in small pieces would become a rule of strategic deception. It would bring good results when employed on the members of the German

Intelligence Service, and it was used to put over the Fortitude cover story. Yet there was one wartime enemy who seemed unable to draw the desired conclusions from a drip-feed of information: the Japanese. Peter Fleming, the head of MI5's 'D' Division (and the brother of fellow intelligence man and creator of James Bond, Ian Fleming), noted that throughout the war the Japanese 'could in no circumstances be relied upon to make the necessary deductions from even the most obvious hints'. This, he concluded, 'must be ascribed to the folly and ignorance of the average Japanese Intelligence Officer'. Or perhaps, rather than folly and ignorance, it reflected a hierarchical society where an individual was not encouraged to think laterally or act instinctively. At any rate it seems to sweep away the dusty stereotype of the wily Oriental.

Clarke, however, was wily. The conflicts within him, between the conventional military man and the lover of flamboyance and artifice, between the dynamic high achiever and the laconic, amused spectator, made him an innovative deceiver; deception, after all, was a game played on many levels. And perhaps these conflicts also explain a particularly odd – and almost disastrous – episode which took place in October 1941. Clarke was arrested in Madrid while apparently attempting to pass misinformation concerning the *Cheese* strategic deception to the German military attaché. His arrest alarmed the British authorities – but his state of dress positively bewildered them. 'At the time,' records the diary of Guy Liddell, the chief of MI5's 'B' Division, 'he was dressed as a woman complete with brassière. Why he wore this disguise nobody quite knows.'

Spanish police took a photograph of Clarke in his flowery dress with a kerchief covering his military short back and sides. His lips are full and red, while three small strings of pearls, gloves and very high heels complete the outfit. A small clutch purse nestles in his lap. His face may look masculine, but his posture is really rather convincingly feminine. So what on earth was he doing? Was he indeed making contact with German agents? If so, were they supposed to fall for his drag act? Was this part of a more complicated story? Or was the get-up not work-related at all? To this day nobody quite knows.

Clarke was fortunate to be released from custody. The doyen of strategic deception – with his vast knowledge of current operations as well as deceptions – could very easily have found himself handed over to the Germans. Liddell's diary records that Clarke was probably released on the word of an enemy agent who believed that he was a British agent willing to work for the Germans. Whether it was a shadowy German or the British naval attaché to Madrid who ultimately secured his release, Clarke was escorted safely to Gibraltar. He eventually resumed his duties in Cairo, but not before the Governor of Gibraltar, Lord Gort, had been asked to deliver a report on the incident to be put before the Prime Minister. Gort concluded that Clarke was 'mentally stable' and that 'this escapade and its consequences will have given him sufficient shock to make him more prudent in the immediate future'. But Liddell's diary underlines the general confusion caused by the incident: 'Nobody can understand why it was necessary for him to go to Spain … It may be that he is just the type who imagines himself to be the super secret service agent.'

Irrespective of what he decided to do once he got there, Clarke was passing through Spain on his way back from London to Cairo. He had been summoned to London by the Chiefs of Staff to report on his experience of strategic deception. A small amount of deception was already being carried out in Britain under the auspices of the Inter-Service Security Board, but this was small-scale 'defensive' deception, aimed at concealing the real reasons for activities such as the movement of troops or the departure of convoys. There was as yet no strategic deception.

While in London Clarke met with the Joint Planning Staff, who recommended that strategic deception should be given a central controlling body based in London. They also recommended that Clarke's 'A' Force should be used as the model for this controlling body. At a subsequent Chiefs of Staff meeting the First Sea Lord, Dudley Pound, asked Clarke to head the new worldwide organization. Clarke declined, pointing out that he was on the staff of General Wavell, who was alone in conducting active operations at the time. 'You can't pinch a man's butler,' said Clark, 'when he has been lent to you for the night.' To Clarke's amusement this comment went down very well with the Chiefs.

Two days later, on 9 October 1941, the Chiefs of Staff offered the role of 'Controlling Officer' to Colonel Oliver Stanley, a distinguished member of the House of Commons who had been Secretary of State for War until the Norway fiasco of April 1940. Once Stanley had been appointed, Clarke set off back to Cairo. He may have been an 'exasperating genius', as his personal assistant, Rex Hamer, once described him, but he had single-handedly turned strategic deception from a twinkle in Wavell's eye into a valued instrument of war with its own controlling section in London.

It seems that before Clarke left London nobody had thought to ask him to provide any useful information about what he had actually been doing in Cairo, and so Colonel Stanley had to start his job without any assistance from the master. He quickly realized that if he was to make a success of the controlling section he would have to maintain 'very close contact with the planning side' and be 'absolutely conversant with the general run of strategic thought and operational possibilities'. This assessment tallied with Clarke's own view that deception was really a matter for the Operations branch of the staff, and not for the Intelligence branch. 'There was a popular misconception,' explained Clarke, 'that because deception involved cloak-and-dagger business, it must be under the control of Intelligence.' This was not the case. 'Deception,' he stressed, 'often had to be implemented by the movements of real troops and ships, and was as much a function of Operations as was the real plan.'

In the Middle East, however, Clarke was in the privileged position of being able to meet his commander and planning staff on equal terms. This was not an option for Stanley. For all his good intentions, there was very little that he could actually do. The operations staffs with whom he had dealings did not understand the concept of strategic deception. He was promised representatives from each of the services. The Naval representative did not even turn up. The Army representative, Lieutenant Colonel Fritz Lumby, arrived in December. The Air Ministry declared that as the RAF was fighting the war it could not spare a Group Captain for such a speculative venture. Instead the author Dennis Wheatley received a quick commission into the RAF Volunteer Reserve and suddenly found himself working alongside Stanley as the RAF's representative. It is a measure of the value placed on the new controlling section that Stanley and Wheatley were not even informed of the existence of the Double Cross system. They were simply told that MI5 had a 'special means' of passing information to the enemy intelligence service.

In his memoirs Wheatley recalls that in the early days there was very little for him to do. His overriding memory is of the Army representative 'doing his crosswords and me twiddling my thumbs'. But in mid-January 1942 Stanley's steady pressure on the Chiefs of Staff bore fruit when they agreed to let him mount a deception: a notional attack on Stavanger in

Norway. It had no real purpose, so it broke Dudley Clarke's cardinal rule: the motley crew of deceivers had no concept of what they wanted German High Command to do. They were simply planning a deception because they had been told that they could.

Wheatley chose the codeword for the operation. The Inter-Service Security Board kept a book of possible codewords and from it he chose 'Hardboiled'. When Stanley asked, 'Who was the bloody fool who chose such a silly codeword?', Wheatley had to explain that codewords were meant to be chosen for their irrelevance to the operation in hand. His boss had not been aware of the fact. Being privy to neither the wealth of knowledge built up by Clarke, nor the existence of the Double Cross system, the deceivers began running the deception as a real operation. The Royal Marine Division was to be sent for training in mountain warfare before carrying out an embarkation exercise. Ships and troops were to be diverted from their usual activities. Officers were to be sent on special courses about Norway. Hundreds of maps of Stavanger would be printed. Cold-weather clothing would be issued to troops who would never really need it. The intention was that these measures would provide material evidence of preparation for an operation, which would then be reported to the enemy by its spies.

There were some non-literal measures taken by the deceivers, of which Clarke might have approved. Rumours were spread about the invasion both in Britain and in neutral countries, feelers were put out for Norwegian interpreters, supplies of Norwegian currency were set aside, and Norwegian refugees were interrogated about possible landing grounds in the Stavanger area, in the hope that word would reach German sympathizers who would pass it on to the enemy. Crucially – and unknown to the deceivers – double agents began passing information regarding the invasion to their German handlers.

Wheatley was to encounter great hostility from the services as he tried to implement his plans. 'To get what we wanted done,' he later wrote, 'meant putting these people to a great deal of trouble, and very few could be persuaded that it was worth it. Some of them took no pains to hide their view that this newfangled business of strategic deception was a crackbrained idea upon which there was no justification for wasting the time of busy men like themselves.'

Many of the troop preparations were never actually carried out owing to the intervention of actual events for which real soldiers were needed. In the end, however, rumours of a proposed assault began to circulate in neutral Sweden and the German press published articles concerning a forthcoming British invasion of Norway. Most importantly, Hitler reinforced his Norway garrison in April and May 1942. It cannot be said with any certainty that this was a direct result of Operation Hardboiled. Hitler consistently displayed a near obsession with the defence of Scandinavia. All the same, the deceivers had been given some practice, and it could be positively claimed that British strategic deception was under way.

But strategic deception was only one pillar of Operation Fortitude, only one foundation upon which the most important deception of the war was built. The other pillar was the Double Cross system. It was all very well formulating a plan to deceive German High Command, but an effective vehicle was needed for bringing the plan to the Germans' attention. And by the time of the Normandy landings, that vehicle – a trusted stable of double agents – was in place.

A double agent is someone who pretends to spy for one side when he is really under the control of another. At the outbreak of the Second World War the British Double Cross system consisted of a hard-drinking Welshman and a wireless transmitter buried in his garden. Yet from this unpromising beginning a thriving structure would grow. MI5's 'B' Division was responsible for counter-espionage, and subsection B1a, headed by 'Tar' Robertson from late 1940 onwards, took responsibility for running double agents. Lieutenant Colonel Tommy Argyll Robertson was 'immensely personable and monstrously good-looking, with a charm that could melt an iceberg', recalled his colleague Christopher Harmer. A Ronald Colman type, Robertson was conspicuous for his quirky habit of walking around in the tartan trews of the Seaforth Highlanders, and his team came to embrace an equally quirky band of intellectuals and individualists, from the future Vice-Chancellor of Oxford University to the impresario of the Bertram Mills Circus. Most had no previous experience of intelligence work. Christopher Harmer, a solicitor before the war, recalls being given two Norwegian double agents (whom he codenamed *Mutt* and *Jeff*) to run on his third day in the job. 'We were complete amateurs,' he says, 'not much more than overgrown schoolboys playing games of derring-do.'

Double Cross work was a largely unexplored area in which Harmer and his fellow newcomers were pioneers. Their first job was to establish a close relationship with their agents. This was not necessarily straightforward. 'No one who has not worked in this field,' says Harmer, 'can comprehend the practical problems associated with looking after a captured and turned agent, whose true loyalty and motives must still be suspect, and who therefore needs round the clock watching and supervision.' 'You had to know the agent's background, his antecedents, how he was recruited, and so on,' explained B1a case officer Hugh Astor in an interview he gave the

Imperial War Museum. 'That was absolutely basic. Only then could you ask yourself how you wanted to use him.'

But what were the agents to be used *for*? An MI5 memorandum of December 1940 (the work of J. C. Masterman, the future Vice-Chancellor of Oxford University) clarifies the early objects of the system. One particular role – counter-espionage – was stressed above others. Double agents could be used to learn about the personalities and methods of the German Intelligence Service. They could be a device for catching new spies who would use them as contacts on arrival. And they could amass significant funds for the MI5 bank account, as the Germans paid them in cash. The second role, noted Masterman, was cipher work. Double agents would send messages which the Germans would repeat in code, allowing, it was hoped, new codes to be broken. Thirdly Masterman wrote of the operational objects. A great deal could be learned about the enemy's plans and intentions from the information they asked double agents to gather. Lastly – and most presciently – he underlined their potential for misleading the Germans as to large-scale military operations. Strategic deception might still have been a long way off in 1940 – but it was already the spymasters' goal.

Whatever MI5's hopes for them, the double agents were an even more varied bunch than their handlers. 'Some of them,' says Hugh Astor, 'were very anxious to help the Allied war effort, either because they were pro-Allied, or because it suited their own political outlook.' Others were not at all anxious to help the Allies, but ended up doing so anyway. The agents' contrasting attitudes reflected their varied paths to B1a's door. Some had been recruited as spies by the Germans in neutral countries, before freely offering their services to the local British authorities. Others had been sent to spy in Britain, before handing themselves in on arrival. A significant number had come – by boat, by parachute or as refugees – with the full intention of spying, but had been caught. They were given a stark choice: serve a new master or be hanged. There were plenty of captured spies who were not considered double-agent material – and so plenty of work for the hangman and the jailers at Camp 020 at Ham Common in Surrey, Britain's spy prison.

However the double agents came on board, their newly acquired role was to pass information to German Intelligence. This was done by coded wireless transmissions, by messages written in secret ink or by rendezvous on neutral territory. Of course, had they been real German agents, they would have been passing on real information which they had themselves discovered. But they weren't real German agents – so what ought they to be saying to their German handlers? They were trying to build up their credibility in the enemy's eyes for the important work ahead, but, in the meantime, should their reports be made up substantially of the truth? Or was the truth too precious to be divulged?

It may be surprising to learn that a great deal of the information they passed on was entirely accurate. It was known as 'chickenfood' and it had to be accurate because the Germans would quickly suspect an agent who was sending them inferior, evasive or dubious information. At the same time, however, the information mustn't be allowed to damage British interests. Secrets and lives were at risk. A difficult balancing act resulted, and in July 1941 the Germans sent the double agent *Tate* this request: 'It would be of extraordinary interest to us if you could find out which factories in Coventry have been hit and what the production still is.'

Tate and his case officer prepared a message to be transmitted to the Germans. It was full of detail and calculated to reassure the Germans as to *Tate*'s reliability. It began: 'I have been in Coventry. The centre of the town looks very bad. Many streets completely disappeared, many roads are up, very many police … the outskirts have suffered less …'

The message went on to name and accurately describe twenty factories, giving details of the bomb damage sustained by each, their levels of activity, and the state of their camouflage. *Tate*'s note on one factory read: 'ROOTES SECURITIES LTD. (Aircraft Division) Number 1 Engine Factory in Aldermoor Lane. A huge factory very well camouflaged – bomb damage not important – very great activity – hundreds of lorries of all kinds coming and going.'

This level of accuracy alarmed Sir Findlater Stewart, the chairman of the Home Defence Executive, who was responsible for vetting the message. In his view it provided the Germans with 'a valuable bombing plan'. While accepting that agents had to return satisfactory answers in order to retain the confidence of the enemy, he urged that *Tate*'s answers be redrafted. In the end a much blander message was sent: 'I have been in Coventry but had to stop operations after my first preliminary run round because I found the police were conducting an Identity Card drive … I found much less activity than I had expected … the authorities were so frightened by the raid of last November that they have put into operation a large-scale dispersal policy …'

Having made his excuses for the limited information he could give, *Tate* proceeded to name only two factories, both of which he described as being out of action owing to bomb damage. From a reality of thriving factories to a fiction of bombed-out shells, the censored message offered a pale, diluted version of the original. And while a balance was clearly required between the need for security and the need to provide the enemy with a steady stream of chickenfood, MI5 was often left groping in the dark to find it.

In an attempt to cast some light for MI5, two secret bodies were created. One was the W Board, made up of high-powered Intelligence figures with knowledge of the double-agent system. They were Guy Liddell (Director of 'B' Division), Stewart Menzies (Chief of MI6), John Godfrey (Director of Naval Intelligence), Archibald Boyle (Director of Intelligence at the Air Ministry) and Frederick George ('Paddy') Beaumont-Nesbitt (Director of Military Intelligence). The W Board could clear chickenfood for use so that B1a didn't have to seek permission from military authorities who were not privy to the double agent secret – and who might well refuse the request. In addition the W Board was intended to give guidance on matters of policy. In other words, it could advise B1a, off the record and in broad terms, what it should be saying in order to assist the war effort.

The other body created at about the same time was the Twenty Committee. In Roman numerals twenty is a double cross, which may make it the only wartime committee whose name doubles as a joke. It was chaired by J. C. Masterman, who struck many as a dry, donnish type. He would, it was said, examine each side of an argument with logic and lucidity, before coming down with a dull thud on the side of doing nothing. All the same, his autobiography reveals a rather touching figure who suspected that his weekly meetings were well attended mainly because he served up tea and buns. Whereas the W Board concentrated on offering policy guidance, the more hands-on Twenty Committee supervised the daily running of the Double Cross system. It selected and granted approval for the material to be sent and decided in practical terms how agents were to be used.

It cannot be said, however, that the existence of these bodies entirely solved the problems faced by case officers. In May 1942 the Home Defence Executive once again stymied *Tate*'s efforts to report on the details of two factories. Not only did it delete a considerable part of Tate's report, but Sir Findlater Stewart refused to suggest any alternatives. Ian Wilson of B1a noted that HDE seemed to be rejecting all proposed traffic. 'It seems quite impossible to keep agents alive,' he said, 'unless they are more cooperative and imaginative.'

The excessive caution of the civil and military authorities may have made life difficult for MI5, but the same authorities had it in their power to improve B1a's lot by providing a regular supply of chickenfood. Yet they rarely bothered. In January 1943 Wilson's colleague M. C. B. Grimaldi complained to 'Tar' Robertson that HDE, the War Office, the Foreign Office and GHQ Home Forces were systematically failing to provide B1a with any material at all. Case officers, Grimaldi grumbled, were having to rely on their own imaginations, on newspaper cuttings, and even on bits of information gathered by B1a's secretaries. The root of the problem was set out squarely in a letter from GHQ Home Forces to the Twenty Committee in July 1942. 'We cannot supply information an enemy can use against us,' wrote the unimaginative author, 'unless we are absolutely certain we will get a high return for the risk run. If double agents cannot be maintained without this, then it is for consideration whether the system is worthwhile.'

But if case officers could not rely for help on the military and civil authorities, some chose to rely even less on their own agents. There has been a tendency in books and films down the years to romanticize the agents as the authors of their own traffic, but this was not usually the case. 'The agent provided the channel of communication,' says Hugh Astor,' but beyond that he or she might have a very small role to play.' For the most part it was the case officer, inhabiting his agent's persona, alert to the single error that could jeopardize the whole network, who alone had the perspective and knowledge to carry out the difficult job in hand.

Yet the story of one of Astor's agents, *Brutus*, suggests that, so long as the agent was trusted, his role could be significant. For the first year of his existence *Brutus* wrote much of his own material and operated his own transmitter. After a security scare he was provided with a wireless operator and his method altered. But his case officer (initially Christopher Harmer and subsequently Astor) would still send him on espionage missions to see what he could find. The results were impressive. *Brutus* was an accomplished spy. He would return after a few days in the field with a map showing the locations of units as well as their identification signs and commanding officers' names. Harmer or Astor could then use *Brutus*'s observations – with names and identities changed – as the basis of a report to the Germans.

Occasionally *Brutus* would be allowed to operate his own radio transmitter – but always under supervision. Every agent was presumed to have a security code, given to him by the Germans, to indicate that he had been caught and was working under control. One day, while operating his transmitter, *Brutus* sent the Germans the word 'Londres' – only he missed off the 's'. Astor was fairly sure by now that he could trust *Brutus*, but what if this omission was his security code? *Brutus* – and possibly other agents – would be blown. Astor asked *Brutus* to write letters and to address envelopes to a number of people living in London. It soon became clear that *Brutus* sometimes spelled 'Londres' with an 's' and sometimes without. A relieved man, Astor noted that spelling was a matter of complete indifference to his Polish double agent.

Even when *Brutus* wasn't on reconnaissance or operating his transmitter, Astor still needed him close by. Questionnaires would regularly arrive from the Germans and Astor would often seek his advice on how to tackle an assignment. *Brutus* would explain his method and Astor would follow his procedure. 'And every now and then,' says Astor, 'they'd send us a trick question. What is the name of your mother-in-law? When was she born? I'd have to give the answer immediately. So I'd ring *Brutus* up ...'

If *Brutus* took an active role in his own traffic, the role taken by B1a's master double agent, *Garbo*, was even more involved. The Lisbon-based *Garbo* had managed to fool the Germans into thinking he was spying for them in Britain before he had ever set foot in the country. They had accepted his reports at face value, including one which assured them that Glasgow men would do anything for a litre of wine. It wouldn't have taken a Clydebank welder to spot the error in that statement. When *Garbo* finally arrived in London, and came under the control of B1a, he had already created three imaginary sub-agents. His case officer, Tomás Harris, was an imaginative man, and rather than reining *Garbo* in, he allowed his audacity to fly. 'I would never have had the nerve,' admitted Christopher Harmer years later, 'to allow any of my agents to be as audacious as he was.' By the end of the war the *Garbo*–Harris partnership had invented a network of twenty-seven fictional characters – including a cell of Welsh nationalists, a Portuguese commercial traveller and an Indian poet called 'Rags'.

In this chapter we have glanced at the practicalities of MI5's Double Cross system. We have encountered a few of its central characters, key concepts and thornier problems. But none of this explains how, in a very short period of time, an idea brewing in the minds of a few mavericks turned into a solid structure capable of fooling the German intelligence service, and – when it mattered in the summer of 1944 – Adolf Hitler and German High Command. It doesn't explain how double agents came to stifle the German spy network in Britain – so that by the time of Operation Fortitude the Germans had no effective means of countering the deception. And it doesn't explain how the system came to assume its leading role in Dudley Clarke's vision of strategic deception.

To make sense of Fortitude, one must first make sense of Double Cross. And the story begins with a narcissistic little Welshman who spent most of the war locked up, but without whom Fortitude would not have deceived anybody at all.

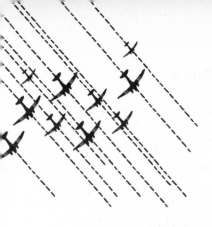

THE GAME'S AFOOT

The first British double agent of the war, Arthur George Owens, didn't fit the debonair archetype of a storybook spy. He was a short and scrawny electrical engineer from Wales, with oddly shaped ears, small bony hands and a shifty, uncertain manner. Yet all of these shortcomings masked – and probably contributed to – an uncompromising urge to turn himself into the central character in his own spy drama. Like many of the most interesting double agents, Owens was neither forced into the role nor motivated by conviction, but rather chose to enter the game for his own more obscure reasons. An MI5 report on the activities of *Snow* – as Owens was codenamed by the British – describes his principal traits as vanity, untruthfulness and self-deception. 'At times in his complicated career,' says the report, 'he has, most likely, genuinely seen himself as a patriot doing dangerous and valuable work for his country; at other times, not less genuinely, as a daring spy, clever enough to outwit the British Intelligence.' It was out of one man's rampant desire for melodrama that the Double Cross system was created.

Born in South Wales in 1899, Arthur Owens moved to Canada before returning to Britain in 1933. He was hired as a consultant with the Expanded Metal Company, on whose behalf he travelled regularly to Holland, Belgium and Germany. On these trips he came across a mass of technical information, and his espionage career began – long before the outbreak of war – when he started passing some of it to the Admiralty. In 1936 he applied to MI6 to work as a paid informant and was accepted. But almost straight away a problem arose: he took a dislike to his MI6 case officer, Edward Peal; and if Peal's condescending description of Owens as 'a typical Welch underfed Cardiff type' is anything to go by, his feelings may have been justified. All the same, a simple personality clash cannot fully explain Owens's subsequent behaviour. He began attending a German social club in Bayswater, in the hope of being introduced to members of the Abwehr, Nazi Germany's Intelligence Service. He was not disappointed. He became friendly with the club's manager, Peter Brunner, explaining that he frequently made lonely trips abroad and wanted to meet some new 'friends'. Brunner understood Owens perfectly well and arranged for him to meet an engineer named Konrad Pieper in Brussels. Pieper introduced him to Hans Dierks of the Abwehr's naval branch, who passed him on to a man known as 'Dr Rantzau' – in fact Nikolaus Ritter, a senior member of German Air Intelligence.

Owens's motivation for approaching the Germans while engaged by the British was probably a blend of Welsh nationalism, financial greed and a near-pathological desire to complicate his own existence. Ritter took Owens to dinner, where spy and spymaster struck a deal. Owens neglected to tell Ritter that he already had a job with MI6, but Ritter was wise to the possibility that Owens might be a British plant, so he decided to test him on one element of his story: his claim that he could not speak German. While debriefing Owens, Ritter turned to his secretary and told her in German that he was going to knock a lamp from the table onto the Welshman. Owens made no reaction. Ritter stood up suddenly and, as if by accident, carried out his threat. It was clear from Owens's astonished and foul-mouthed outburst that he had been telling the truth – about his language skills at least.

On the other side, meanwhile, the condescending Peal of MI6 was becoming suspicious of Owens and asked Scotland Yard's Special Branch to keep an eye on him. In September 1936 a letter from Owens to Ritter, addressed to 'Box 629' in Hamburg – a known Abwehr cover address – was intercepted. It became clear to the British, if not to the Germans, that Owens was working for both sides at once. Other equally incriminating letters followed. In one the Abwehr drily acknowledged, in response to some out-of-date details Owens had sent them about British tanks, that they were not running a museum. In spite of the evidence the British decided not to confront Owens straight away. They were going to give him an opportunity to come clean, although they terminated his work for MI6 on the grounds that his reports 'were no longer of interest or value'.

Owens continued to meet Ritter and correspond with the Abwehr, but he suspected that the British would be watching him, and on one trip to Germany, in November 1936, his suspicions were confirmed. When he returned to Britain – and just as Scotland Yard was finally about to arrest him – he contacted Peal, saying that he needed to meet him urgently. He dictated a statement admitting that he had agreed to act as an agent for the Germans, but only, he said, because it gave him the opportunity to gather intelligence about the Abwehr. Peal didn't accept this story and threatened Owens with prosecution as a spy. But Owens called his bluff; his defence to any charge, he said, would be that he was really a British agent. He knew very well that MI6 would not be keen for its methods and personnel to be exposed in court.

For many months Owens and the British authorities danced awkwardly around each other while the Welshman continued to work for Ritter, who was paying him increasing sums of money and offering him generous hospitality on Hamburg's Reeperbahn. Owens particularly enjoyed one club in the city's red-light district, the Valhalla, where each table was fitted with a telephone so that the keen punters – and no punter was keener than Owens – could call up likely looking girls at other tables. In the meantime Owens was making regular contact with British Intelligence to offer up bits of information, but each time he did so he was sent away with a warning that he was no longer a British agent. He was even made to sign a document to that effect. And so Owens was spying for the Germans, with the full knowledge of the British, who declined to either employ him or prosecute him. An internal Royal Naval Intelligence report from April 1938 reveals the absurdity of the situation. Owens turned up at the Admiralty with photographs of German warships that he had taken in Hamburg harbour, but was turned away. 'He was conducted out of the Admiralty,' the report concludes, 'and told not to return.'

In September 1938 Owens approached MI5's chief interrogator, Edward Hinchley-Cooke, and asked to be allowed to resume his activities on Britain's behalf. 'I think it is my duty,' he righteously declared. 'You have been in touch with the German Secret Service?' asked Hinchley-Cooke. 'Yes, I have. At least they have been in touch with me.' 'With whom were you in touch?' 'Let us get away from this,' said the Welshman. 'I have done everything I can. I have always had one object in view – and that was to help this country when I could. I risked my life, at least I deserve a little thanks.' Hinchley-Cooke said nothing. 'I am prepared to go on and take further chances if you wish it, provided you are not suspicious of me all the time,' continued Owens, before throwing down a very vague warning: 'You have got to realize what is going on!' 'I have a shrewd suspicion,' said the MI5 man. Owens carried on dodging direct questions, but he announced that the Germans were going to send him a wireless set, as well as the names of other agents who were to work for him. And so Arthur Owens, Britannia's noblest patriot, pleaded with Hinchley-Cooke to be reinstated as a British agent. War seemed likely, after all, and Owens was determined not to be left stranded as a known traitor at its outbreak. He may have been an opportunist, playing a self-seeking game, but he needed the protection of the British authorities to play it. Yet the authorities were playing a game of their own. There was still no Double Cross system in existence, and neither MI6 nor MI5 was yet sure what to do with Owens – if anything at all. Hinchley-Cooke did not grant Owens his wish. He was not brought back into the fold.

In January 1939 the promised wireless transmitter was smuggled into London in privileged German diplomatic baggage, and placed in a cloakroom locker at Victoria Station. The Abwehr sent the locker ticket to Owens, who gingerly passed it on to MI6, who examined the radio set before giving it to Owens. Two months later Owens contacted Special Branch, claiming that he was using the set regularly to contact Hamburg. This was a lie. He also claimed that his set was the only one of its kind in Britain, which was true. He was implying that if the British were to bring him onside, they would have instant control of the German espionage network. And the British did not seem to be discounting him from their future plans; why else let him have the wireless set? Unless they were setting a trap for him …

Such confusion was not confined to Owens's espionage life. His private life was equally fraught. He had just left his wife for a young woman of German origin, Lily Funnell, who began accompanying him on his trips to Germany. In early August 1939 Owens, Lily and a man named Alexander Myner – whom Owens intended to offer Ritter as a sub-agent – visited Hamburg. While there, Owens agreed to start using his transmitter on his return to London. He would do so on hearing the song 'Du, du liegst mir im Herzen' played twice in succession on a German propaganda radio station. But while Owens was in Hamburg his long-suffering wife showed up at Scotland Yard to report her husband as a German spy. She had, she said, known for some time of his espionage activities but had not betrayed him 'for the sake of the children'. But now that he had left her – and also tried to recruit their son into 'this despicable business' – she was prepared to inform on him. She was unaware that British Intelligence already knew as much about Owens's duplicity as she did.

On 23 August, Owens returned from Germany. His arrival was monitored, but he managed to evade his observers as he left the port, and he did not return home. Five days later he heard 'Du, du liegst mir im Herzen' played twice on German radio and he went ahead with his first transmission to Hamburg. Less than a week later Prime Minister Neville Chamberlain announced that Britain was at war with Germany. Owens was now playing a very dangerous game. He was spying for the enemy.

The outbreak of war presented Britain's Security Service with the pressing task of protecting the country from enemy agents – although, unknown to British security officers, the Germans had actually made little effort to infiltrate spies into Britain. This omission reflected the Nazis' belief that the British were highly unlikely to proceed with a costly and ultimately futile war against more powerful racial equals. The immediate spy threat therefore consisted only of Owens and a small handful of others, but the Home Office took necessary precautions. The arrest was ordered of 415 'enemy aliens', and the remainder were required to report to the police. The work of actively sifting the spies from the chaff expended much of MI5's early wartime energy, and the organization was forced to expand its personnel. 'When the war broke out,' wrote MI5 chief Sir David Petrie, 'each officer "tore around" to rope in likely people; when they knew of none themselves, they asked their acquaintances.' This was how MI5 began gathering together the diverse crew of intellectuals and individualists who were to run the Double Cross system.

Now that a state of war existed, Owens more than ever needed the protection of the British authorities. They had allowed him to keep his transmitter, but was this simply in the belief that he would incriminate himself? Fearing a trap, he contacted Special Branch on 4 September 1939 to arrange a meeting at Waterloo Station. Two inspectors showed up and Owens told them, once again, that he wished to offer his services to the British government. And then, to his surprise, he was arrested. A Detention Order had been issued against him.

In Wandsworth Prison Owens asked to see his former MI6 case officer, Edward Peal, and an MI5 officer – 'Tar' Robertson, the trews-wearing Ronald Colman lookalike – to whom Owens had taken a liking during a previous encounter. Owens offered Robertson a deal. He would tell him where his wireless set was hidden, in return for his release from prison. The set could then be used – under the control of MI5 – to transmit information to the Abwehr. Robertson was quick to agree. By a stroke of good fortune the man with the imagination to develop a Double Cross system had crossed paths with the man who could help him to do so.

Owens revealed his new address, a flat in Surbiton, just south of London, that he was sharing with Lily Funnell. He told Robertson that the transmitter was to be found in the bathtub. And there was indeed a wireless set in the bathroom, but it wasn't the set that Ritter had given him. It was one that Owens had built himself. He had buried the German set in the garden. The Welshman was never one to tell the whole truth when a pointless lie could offer him the merest hint of control. The real set was found and brought to Wandsworth Prison, where attempts were made to send a message to the Germans from Owens's cell. The first attempt failed when Owens pushed a switch on the transmitter and blew a fuse. The next attempt also failed, causing an MI5 operative to note that Owens was being uncooperative. Owens was warned that it was in his interests 'to use his best endeavours to get in touch with Germany'. In truth he was perfectly happy for his set to be used – he just didn't want to remain in Wandsworth Prison.

On the evening of 11 September 1939 Owens was granted his freedom. Robertson and a Special Branch inspector escorted him out of the prison and together the men went 'flat hunting'. Having found a suitable apartment, they rigged up the transmitter, with the aerials concealed in the roof. At 11.30 the next night a message was successfully sent to Germany: 'Must meet you Holland at once. Bring weather code radio town and hotel. Wales ready.'

This message was only sent once Owens had explained its meaning to Robertson. Owens was to go to Holland, where Ritter would give him a code to describe the state of the weather in areas the Germans intended to bomb. The mention of Wales related to the fact that Owens was supposed to find a sympathetic Welsh nationalist to be used as a link for the supply of German sabotage materials. Owens asked Robertson to find a suitable Welshman to fill the role, who could accompany him to Holland. An enthusiastic Robertson agreed. Through Owens he could now create a network of double agents which would be accepted without question by the Abwehr. And so, late in the evening of 12 September 1939, the Double Cross system was truly born – thanks to the overlapping interests of a two-faced Welshman and a far-sighted Scot.

The immediate result of Owens's first message under British control was an invitation from Ritter to meet him, not in Holland but in Antwerp. At the meeting Owens informed Ritter that he had recruited a member of the Welsh Nationalist Party as requested. Ritter was curious as to how Owens was able to travel so freely; Owens explained that his engineering business was considered crucial to the British war effort. Reassured that his agent was still genuine, Ritter asked for another meeting in a fortnight's time, to which Owens was to bring his Welsh recruit. 'Tar' Robertson meanwhile had found the perfect man for the role. Gwilym Williams, a retired police inspector from Swansea, was a Welsh nationalist who had had dealings with the Security Service while working as a court interpreter. He is said to have spoken seventeen languages – remarkable for a man who had been illiterate on leaving school. Williams was, declared MI5, 'an extremely determined type of individual'.

Owens and Williams met for the first time just before their trip to the Continent. Williams came away from the meeting with an impression of Owens as a quick-witted man with tremendous will power. But he was also offered brief access to the Welshman's fantasy world. Having told Williams what to expect at the meeting with Ritter, Owens said, 'And don't be surprised if I am addressed as "Colonel". I hold the rank of colonel in the German Army.' 'It must be difficult being a German colonel who can't speak German,' teased Williams. 'Oh, they call me "Colonel"!' insisted Owens, annoyed that his 'recruit' should doubt him. 'Tar' Robertson was becoming used to dealing with Owens's fabrications. He had recently written 'Oh Yeah' in an MI5 memo next to Owens's claim that he knew the whereabouts of every German submarine.

Even so, Robertson seems to have accepted Owens's account of a visit made to his house by a thin, bespectacled stranger with an American accent, who had asked him whether he was in touch with Ritter. The stranger, according to Owens, had told him to expect to be contacted in a pub or in the street. The implication was that Owens was being watched by the Abwehr. But did this incident ever really take place? It seems unlikely that the Germans had the agents available to make house calls on Owens or to keep an eye on him. This story may have been Owens's crafty attempt to keep Robertson and MI5 off his back; for if Robertson tried to interfere with Owens too much, his efforts now risked being observed by the Germans – which would have meant the end of Owens as a double agent. The story has the hallmarks of a bluff.

On 21 October, Owens and Williams met Ritter in Antwerp as planned. With Ritter were Kapitänleutnant Witzke, in charge of sabotage operations in Britain, and Major Brasser of Air Intelligence. Ritter gave Owens detonators disguised in blocks of wood for use in sabotage and explained that from now on Owens would be provided with money by a female German agent living in Bournemouth. He also handed him three 'microdots'. These were full-sized photographs which had been reduced to the size of tiny ink dots and could be properly viewed under a microscope. They were to be hidden under postage stamps on innocuous-looking letters and sent to agents. Owens was told to deliver the microdots to a Liverpool man in the pay of the Germans, a Fellow of the Royal Photographic Society. Finally Ritter handed Owens money and told him that he would be informed of the appointment of future agents. A delighted Owens reported all of this to Robertson on his return to England.

In his diary entry for 2 October, Guy Liddell gives a rather optimistic assessment of Owens's character. 'There seems no reason,' he writes, 'to doubt his loyalty at the moment. He is acting entirely under our orders.' And on their return from Antwerp, Gwilym Williams, who had been present throughout the meeting with Ritter, Witzke and Brasser, was able to confirm Owens's account of the meeting. But Owens was not playing a simple game: there had been another meeting between Owens and Ritter, which Williams did not attend. At this encounter Owens gave Ritter a large amount of information that he had personally gathered, including a drawing of a Royal Navy oil refinery near Swansea, a report on conditions at Croydon Airport, and the detailed conversations of RAF officers overheard on a train. This was not the harmless chicken-enfood provided by MI5. Owens had certainly passed that to Ritter, but he was supplementing it with the best genuine information he could offer. Yet, whatever its short-term contribution to the German war effort, Owens's personally gathered intelligence probably damaged the Germans in the long run, by reinforcing Ritter's trust in the Welshman, or *Johnny* as the Abwehr codenamed him.

While Owens was still in Antwerp, two letters arrived for him at home, each containing £20 in £5 notes. The notes had all been stamped 'S. & Co. Ltd'. This was short for Selfridges, the London department store. And so R. J. Stopford, Robertson's assistant, was able to visit the store, where he spoke to two members of staff who recalled serving an elderly lady with grey hair and glasses who had asked them to exchange her own £1 notes for the £5 notes in question. One of them, a cashier, remembered taking the same woman's name and address in connection with a separate order and so Mrs Mathilde Krafft, a German woman living in Bournemouth, was traced as the source of the letters. This was clearly the female agent described by Ritter. Married to an Englishman, Krafft had been a British national for the past fifteen years and had therefore escaped MI5's round-up of aliens. She was duly interned in Wandsworth Prison.

MI5 had also to locate the Liverpool agent, the Fellow of the Royal Photographic Society, whom Owens was instructed to contact. This turned out to be a man named Eschborn, who was interviewed by Robertson. Along with his brother, Eschborn had been recruited as a German agent the year before, but he now assured Robertson that he had only agreed to work for the Abwehr for fear of what the Germans would do to another brother still living in Germany. Terrified by his predicament, Eschborn told his interrogator that he was entirely British in his sympathies. He had lived in Britain nearly all his life, he said, and would do anything that MI5 asked. Robertson chose to trust him and, codenaming him *Charlie*, recruited him as MI5's third double agent, after Owens and Williams. Robertson found Eschborn's brother and fellow German agent less trustworthy, however, and he was interned.

Unwittingly, therefore, Nikolaus Ritter of the Abwehr had provided 'Tar' Robertson of MI5 with enough information to ensure the arrest of every German agent who had not already been apprehended in MI5's round-up operation. He had also offered him the perfect means of picking up those yet to arrive in the country. It seems little wonder that counter-espionage, in the early days of the Double Cross system, was considered its primary function.

But, even as the system was establishing itself, Robertson was waking up to the sorts of problems it was likely to present, for double agents were, by their very definition, disposed to disloyalty. One evening Robertson and his wife June arranged to meet Owens and Lily in a pub in Richmond, near London. As Robertson waited outside in his car, June went into the pub, where she noticed a young man at the bar behaving suspiciously. When Robertson drove away, the young man got into his own car and began following him closely. Robertson had to accelerate sharply on Richmond Hill to lose his pursuer. If Robertson was disturbed by the incident, he was even more disturbed when Owens treated it with utter indifference, causing the MI5 man to wonder whether Owens was double-crossing him. But it takes a lot to shake a handler's faith in his agent, particularly one as important as Owens, upon whose shoulders an entire system was being constructed. Robertson's belief in Owens survived the incident. 'He is a stupid little man given to doing silly things at odd times,' he reflected, 'but I am perfectly convinced that he is quite straightforward in the things which he gives me and the answers to my questions.' Owens would have been reassured by this hopeful, if not exactly flattering, vote of confidence.

Such qualified confidence meant that Owens continued to be allowed to travel freely and to gather his own intelligence. On 14 January 1940 Robertson gave him coupons for thirty gallons of petrol and sent him off to the north of England with instructions to visit as many aerodromes as possible and to try to discover the headquarters of 13 Group Fighter Command. Owens was instructed to telephone Robertson every night with an update on his progress. The plan was to turn Owens's report into harmless chickenfood to be passed on to Ritter at their next meeting. But the danger of trusting Owens with valuable information was soon to become apparent.

In February, Owens met Ritter again in Antwerp and told him of a valuable new source of intelligence. William Rolph was a retired MI5 agent in dire financial straits who had agreed to sell information to the Abwehr using Owens as an intermediary. Robertson knew nothing of this, but on his return to London Owens did his corresponding bit for the British by repeating to Robertson some news that Ritter had offered him: the 'real war' was going to start in the middle of April. This was a clear warning that the anticipated German offensive was due to be launched. In order to discover more about German strategic intentions, Robertson told Owens to send a message requesting another meeting with Ritter as soon as possible. In his reply to the message, Ritter said that there could be no meeting as 'major operations are expected to take place between 1 April and the end of the month'. Owens was instructed by MI5 to ignore the warning, and he travelled to meet Ritter.

At the meeting Ritter asked Owens to provide him with another agent. The Abwehr, he said, was hoping to relocate Owens to Germany soon and in the meantime he wanted him to find 'a thoroughly reliable individual' who could take over as the Germans' chief spy in England. Ritter also confirmed that the German offensive was imminent, which meant that Holland and Belgium, the countries where the pair usually met, might soon be occupied and therefore off limits to Owens. He suggested that their next meeting should take place on a boat in the North Sea. This idea had been brewing in Ritter's mind for some time. Several months earlier he had asked Owens to find a reliable fisherman on the east coast of England whose trawler could be used to smuggle sabotage equipment into the country. Now it would be used to convey Owens and his new recruit to a seaborne conference, to which Ritter would show up by seaplane or submarine.

Ritter asked Rear Admiral Karl Dönitz for the loan of a submarine for the mission. Dönitz was not interested, but Vice-Admiral Otto Ciliax offered him the use of a Dornier Do-18 aircraft. He then contacted Owens, saying that he intended to take Owens's chosen recruit back to Germany with him for training. Robertson meanwhile was securing the loan of a Grimsby trawler, the *Barbados*, to bring Owens and the recruit out to the meeting place, near Dogger Bank. The trawler's crew was to be paid a bonus to keep quiet about the 'funny things' they would see. Owens's recruit was to be Sam McCarthy, a petty villain, codenamed *Biscuit*, who was already working for MI5 within the British underworld. Owens, crucially, was led to believe that McCarthy was *not* working for MI5. Robertson wanted McCarthy to monitor an unguarded Owens – and he was to receive quite a surprise.

Owens was on particularly melodramatic form when he met up with McCarthy the day before the trawler was due to depart. McCarthy asked him how much money he would be paid by the Germans. 'Don't worry a bit,' said Owens, 'the Germans will look after you a hundred per cent. They are all very fine people.' But he went further. 'I've decided,' he told McCarthy, 'to introduce you to them as a member of MI5.' McCarthy was alarmed; wasn't this a very dangerous course to take? 'You need not worry about that,' smiled Owens. 'They know all about my connection with Robertson. They know exactly what I am doing.' McCarthy was astonished: Owens was claiming to be a triple agent working for the Germans. 'Robertson is in for it,' exclaimed the Welshman, 'when the Germans start landing in England!'

By the time the two men were on board the London to Grimsby train, Owens was warming to his theme. 'I'm so pleased we're on our way,' he said. 'It won't be long before I can get my own back on the bastards in MI5.' He showed McCarthy a dinner card which he had brought with him, on which were printed the names of MI5 men who had attended a 1939 function. 'When our advanced guard gets here,' he said, 'they will know who to get, and where to get them.' 'I'm having you trained in sabotage and espionage,' he continued, 'and you will be brought back here without *them* knowing.'

The anxious McCarthy took an opportunity to phone Robertson that night and repeated all that Owens had said. Robertson decided that it would be far too dangerous to go ahead with the meeting as planned. The trawler would still set off with Owens and McCarthy on board, but it would now fail to keep its rendezvous and instead would return to port. In the meantime a submarine would be in position nearby to capture Ritter if possible. And so, early in the morning of Monday, 20 May, Owens and McCarthy boarded the *Barbados* at Grimsby harbour and set out to sea. Owens had soon installed himself in the captain's wheelhouse, where McCarthy noticed that he was staring up at the sky, even though the meeting with Ritter was not due to take place for another two days. Owens then asked the captain whether the boat was fitted with flash lamps and it suddenly dawned on McCarthy that the Welshman was expecting Ritter to show up early.

Sure enough, when Owens was briefly below deck a seaplane appeared and made a low circle over the trawler, sending Morse signals for it to stop. Convinced that Owens was intending to hand him over to the Germans, McCarthy asked the boat's captain and master for help; the three men grabbed Owens, tied him up, and locked him in a cabin. The Welshman was taken by surprise. 'So you are a German agent!' he shouted at McCarthy. 'I am a mug! I thought so. My man in London warned me about you.' He then took a different approach, saying, 'It's not me you want. It's the other fellow – my agent in London. If you let me go, we will get him.' McCarthy ignored Owens's pathetic protests as the trawler put out its lights and returned to Grimsby.

On hearing of these latest developments Robertson hurried north to confront his troublesome agent. Owens flatly denied that he was double-crossing the British. He had become certain, he told Robertson, that McCarthy was really a

German spy who was leading him into a trap, so he had had no option but to pretend that he was also a German agent. When Owens was searched the dinner card containing the names of MI5 personnel was found. Robertson demanded an explanation. Owens said that the card had belonged to William Rolph, the impecunious former MI5 agent, who, he explained, bore a grudge against Robertson for refusing to allow him to work as a British spy in Germany. Rolph had given him the card and told him to sell it to the Germans for £2,000. But Owens insisted that he had never intended to do any such thing. He had shown it to McCarthy in order to convince him that he was a fellow German agent and was going to show it to Ritter merely to convince him of his loyalty to Germany.

What was Robertson to make of these ready answers? Why would Owens think that McCarthy was working for the Germans? If he did believe that McCarthy was a German spy, why was he agreeing to take him to Germany, and why didn't he warn Robertson of his suspicions? Whatever hindsight offers up as answers, at the time Robertson decided that Owens's mind was 'a very odd affair' which 'does not work on logical lines' and that, while Owens's answers 'had not been exactly convincing', they 'seemed to hold a certain amount of water'. By underestimating the Welshman's cunning and speed of thought, Robertson was about to let him off the hook. But the adventure was not yet played out. Robertson told Owens that he was to be sent straight back out to sea in the *Barbados*, accompanied by a crew of armed naval ratings. The purpose was to intercept Ritter at the appointed meeting time – which had not yet arrived – and to capture him. If Owens gave any sign that he was double-crossing, Robertson warned, he would never see England again.

With this unambiguous threat hanging over him, Owens played his part and 'appeared most anxious' to get hold of

Ritter 'either alive or dead'. As well as the trawler, a British submarine was put on standby. But the North Sea was now thick with fog and Ritter's aircraft was nowhere to be seen. When questioned by Robertson on his return to Grimsby, Owens repeated his excuses and begged to be given another chance to catch Ritter. He was quite confident, he said, that he could do it. And it was little wonder he was keen: he had come very close to losing the game, his freedom, perhaps even his life. Robertson, for his part, was now much warier of Owens and gave orders that he was not to be allowed out in the future without specific instructions. A message was sent to Ritter saying that Owens had been at the rendezvous point at the planned hour but that conditions had been poor. Ritter accepted the excuse and asked to meet him again, this time in neutral Lisbon. But it would be much safer, Robertson concluded, to send McCarthy. He could cultivate his own relationship with Ritter, independent of Owens, and could give the German a satisfactory explanation of the North Sea fiasco.

And so, in early August, McCarthy travelled to Portugal. The Double Cross system was no longer reliant on one man. Ritter struck McCarthy as being an 'exceedingly common' man who was 'fond of telling filthy stories'. McCarthy was able to reassure Ritter that he and Owens had been waiting to meet him on the trawler at the appointed time but had missed him in the fog. Ritter confirmed that it had been his aircraft which circled the trawler, and he gave McCarthy the strong sense that Owens had known all along that he was going to show up early. When Ritter expressed concern about the quality of Owens's recent work, McCarthy explained that the Welshman had far too much to do, implying that the Germans should send another agent to Britain to assist him. Ritter said that an agent was already waiting in Belgium to be brought across. Finally McCarthy passed Ritter false information about British anti-invasion measures, giving him the impression that the country was better defended than it really was. McCarthy came home from Lisbon with another wireless set and a large amount of Abwehr cash. But from Robertson's point of view the most positive outcome of the meeting was the certain knowledge that *this* agent was acting wholeheartedly in Britain's interest.

Yet, as if to highlight the risks of working with double agents, no sooner had McCarthy returned than he began behaving oddly. Within the space of a few days he threatened to murder Owens and his family, visited Eschborn to question him about Ritter, and started getting ostentatiously and boastfully drunk in his local pub. 'He is succeeding in upsetting everyone, which is not adding to the smooth running of the case,' Robertson was informed by a concerned MI5 employee.

In the meantime Robertson had to deal with the problem of William Rolph, the ex-British agent whose intelligence Owens had hoped to sell to Ritter and whose dinner card he had shown to McCarthy. Rolph was currently working as the manager of Hatchett's restaurant in Piccadilly, where he received a surprise visit from Robertson and Stopford. Visibly agitated, Rolph claimed to have no idea how Owens had got hold of the dinner card. He thought he could recall meeting Owens for a coffee, but he wasn't sure. He corrected his story repeatedly, before admitting that Owens and Lily had indeed come to his office together one evening. His story was so shaky that Robertson decided to have Owens brought to the restaurant, to confront him. As the MI5 men were waiting for Owens, Stopford noticed Rolph picking something out of his desk drawer and surreptitiously tearing it up before walking out of the room and dropping it into a bin.

When Owens arrived he explained – once again – that Rolph had given him the dinner card and asked him to sell it to Ritter for £2,000. Owens was calm and matter-of-fact; he seemed to have absolutely no qualms about betraying his former associate. Rolph, on the other hand, seemed desperate as he groped for an explanation that might hold water. Owens, he said, must have stolen the dinner card from him when his back was turned. But then Owens told Robertson that he and Rolph had jointly created a secret code. And when the bin was searched and bits of torn card were found, Rolph was forced to admit that these bits were indeed the pieces of a key to a code. But he could not explain what this code was for and he continued to deny every aspect of Owens's story.

Rolph was clearly lying. But what was Robertson to do about him? Should he call in Special Branch? If Rolph was arrested the Germans would guess that Owens was also compromised. And an espionage trial threatened to shed unwanted light on the embryonic Double Cross system. Robertson, Stopford and Owens left the office, watched by Rolph, who was aware that his fate was in MI5's hands. Later that day, however, he seized it back. He placed his head in a gas oven and took his own life. And in order to prevent the Abwehr from interpreting Rolph's suicide as the consequence of being unmasked as a spy, MI5 influenced the Coroner for London, Bentley Purchase, to return a verdict of death by natural causes. To the world at large, Rolph died of a heart attack.

And so the melodrama of Arthur Owens, the unprepossessing little man with an inflated sense of himself, ran on. He had received an almighty scare, but he was still fooling both sides as to the sheer extent of his deceit. It is clear that Owens's motivation for becoming a double agent was not loyalty to the British, even though his work ultimately advanced the British cause. It is also highly unlikely that he ever really saw himself as a triple agent working in the German cause, even though he often attempted to deliver valuable information to Ritter at their meetings. In reality Owens was only ever an agent in his own cause. He wanted to be important, and so long as he could remain the hero of his own frenzied narrative, he never really minded whom he was serving or whether anybody else was being harmed.

While Robertson and MI5 might not yet have appreciated Owens's full capacity for treachery, there is a sense within this tale that, by allowing him so much latitude, the British intelligence services – both MI6 and MI5 – were consciously exploiting his corrupt instincts to help them to find a new way of working. Once it had been found, only the most trusted agents would be granted anything like the freedom Owens had received. But in the meantime he was serving a purpose. He had brought a new system into being, he had helped to uncover the existence of German spies, and he had brought MI5 directly to the door of Nikolaus Ritter. And Ritter was an important man. In the summer of 1940 he was put in charge of Operation Lena, the Abwehr's attempt to infiltrate Britain with a new wave of spies in advance of the proposed German invasion. The Double Cross system was about to face its first major challenge.

THE GERMAN INVASION

Dudley Clarke was always keen to stress that the ultimate target of his strategic deceptions was the enemy commander. The commander was the man, after all, who made the decisions that Clarke was trying to influence. But the commander was not his immediate 'customer'. That was the enemy intelligence services which would receive, sort and assess the deception material before it ever reached the commander. It was crucial, therefore, for deceivers to understand the workings of the intelligence services thoroughly. And for Double Cross to function properly, MI5 needed an intimate understanding of the individuals to whom its agents were reporting – and an understanding of the chain of command along which its information would pass. Arthur Owens was doing sterling work in this regard: by developing a personal relationship with the unsuspecting Nikolaus Ritter, he was opening a window onto the workings of the Abwehr.

The Abwehr, unlike MI5 and MI6, was a part of the army. Under the leadership since 1935 of Admiral Wilhelm Canaris, it was responsible for running Germany's spy network. Hitler had personally chosen Canaris for the job, but he was a surprising choice. Canaris was undoubtedly a patriotic German, but he was never a member of the Nazi Party and he came to fill the ranks of the Abwehr with others who shared his scepticism about Nazi ideology. And not only were some of the Abwehr's members of dubious loyalty, but Canaris gave them a large measure of autonomy. 'In effect,' wrote Hugh Trevor-Roper in a postwar MI5 internal analysis, 'the operational officers of the Abwehr sat in Paris and Athens, in Biarritz and Estoril, enjoying the opportunities for self-indulgence provided by these resorts, undisturbed so long as a quota of reports was sent in. Whether these reports were true or false was unimportant, since there was no centralized evaluation.'

Even the best case officers – British as well as German – wanted to believe in their agents, and as a result they might have overlooked the odd warning sign. The scrupulous 'Tar' Robertson, after all, was sometimes willing to overlook Arthur Owens's erratic behaviour. Robertson's close colleague J. C. Masterman once explained to the Twenty Committee that 'anyone running an agent will defend that agent against criticism through thick and thin'. But some members of the Abwehr went further than this: they were apparently unconcerned as to their agents' loyalty. 'It was better,' said one after the war, 'to have a controlled agent than none at all.' Such attitudes could explain how *Garbo* retained his handlers' trust as he informed them of the Glaswegians' love of wine. And when a handler's prospects were tied to those of his agent, his job could become untenable. One German case officer, under Allied interrogation in 1945, explained that he had not been able to share his suspicions about an agent with his chief, for fear of being shot for defeatism. It is hardly surprising that some members of the Abwehr would end up having to conceal the success of Allied deception.

But it was not, strictly speaking, the Abwehr's job to collate or analyse the information gathered by its spies. That was the task of another division of the intelligence service: Fremde

Herre West (FHW). FHW was a branch of Wehrmacht High Command with responsibility for assessing the resources and intentions of the Allies. It compiled its assessments from the Abwehr's spy reports, and from reconnaissance reports, signals intelligence, interrogation of prisoners and seized documents. But as the Wehrmacht had little direct contact with its western enemies for most of the war, much of FHW's source material came from spies. And since MI5 maintained effective control of the Abwehr's spy network in Britain, many of FHW's assessments were effectively drafted by the British.

This fact was to prove crucial during Operation Fortitude, as FHW was responsible for assessing the overall strength of Allied forces. Dudley Clarke had first demonstrated the importance of creating an exaggerated Order of Battle, after which deceivers in Britain closely followed his lead. And the deceivers' lies – which were fed to the Abwehr and passed on to FHW – were unfailingly believed. Every single British or Mediterranean-based unit invented by 'A' Force or the London Controlling Section found its way onto FHW's Order of Battle. This was partly due to the ingenuity of the deceivers; but it was also thanks to the sheer determination of FHW's head, Lieutenant Colonel Alexis von Roenne, from early 1943 onwards, to attribute the maximum possible strength to the Allies in the west. Like Canaris, Roenne was a patrician with an instinctive dislike of the Nazis. He would be executed after the 1944 attempt on Hitler's life for his – very tangential – part in the plot. But it is unlikely that he deliberately inflated the Allied Order of Battle as some measure of anti-Nazi resistance. Rather, in his role as chief of FHW, he was concerned with the defence of the west, and he was aware of the risk of western units being diverted to the Sisyphean struggle in the east. Roenne was simply behaving pragmatically by stressing the existence of every apparent enemy unit or partial unit.

But for all the assistance – more inadvertent than deliberate – that MI5 and the Allied deceivers received from the ineptitude and disloyalty of the German intelligence service, an even greater advantage came from the breaking of the German Enigma and Japanese Magic codes. To give a single example, from 1943 onwards updates on the existence and strength of Allied units were set down in FHW's Lagebericht West, a weekly situation report, which also gave details of specific Allied activity. The Allies were able to read these reports with the assistance of Ultra – the codebreaking operation at Bletchley Park in Buckinghamshire which decrypted German Intelligence signals – and to gain a very vivid picture of how much of their deceptive information was believed by the Germans.

Yet MI5 had been taking advantage of deciphered German codes even before Enigma was cracked. Codebreaking, after all, was one of the objects of the Double Cross system – and the codes supplied to Owens by Ritter gave the codebreakers at Bletchley Park a solid start in identifying Abwehr techniques. In March 1940 the British Radio Security Service (RSS) intercepted traffic between the Hamburg Abwehr and a North Sea spy ship, which led to the breaking of the Abwehr hand cipher used to communicate with agents in the field. Once this had been broken, MI5 had the ideal system for locating newly arrived spies – so long as the spy's traffic could be picked up by the RSS. Intelligence from this source was named ISOS (Intelligence Section, Oliver Strachey) after the head of the Bletchley section dealing with Abwehr traffic.

Throughout the war Abwehr communications within the German Reich itself were by landline, which could not be intercepted. But messages between Berlin and Abwehr stations in occupied and neutral countries were coded using Enigma, and these codes were broken in December 1941. And so, as the war drew on, MI5 and the deceivers knew that for almost everything they did, the results were there to be observed. The Germans were marking their homework.

But as Britain waited for invasion in the days before Enigma was broken, the war's ascendancy lay very much with the Germans. One of the few sources of comfort to the British might have been that Double Cross was under way – had it not been for the fact that the first double agent, Arthur Owens, was an amoral fantasist. The Germans now proposed to increase their stable of British-based spies, but their plans, fortunately for MI5 and for Britain, were very hastily conceived. In July 1940 Admiral Canaris was called to see General Alfred Jodl, the Chief of Operations Staff at Wehrmacht High Command. 'Do you have any agents in Britain?' Jodl asked. 'Yes,' replied Canaris, thinking of Owens and his growing network. But Jodl explained that he now needed a different kind of network. He wanted spies who could act as scouts in advance of the invasion: Operation Seelöwe. He wanted spies able to provide detailed information about the state of British defences, who could identify suitable beaches for the landings, and who could guide the invading troops inland once they had fought their way off the beachheads. The invasion, said Jodl, would take place by mid-September, and Canaris's spies must be in place a month before that date.

This operation to send spies to Britain was codenamed 'Lena'. Canaris placed Nikolaus Ritter in charge, alongside Hans Dierks, the Abwehr man who had passed Owens on to Ritter in 1936. Their task was not an easy one: to find and quickly train up likely young candidates already possessed of some measure of technical knowledge. The man charged with selecting a shortlist was the charming Walter Praetorius, known as 'The Pied Piper' for his conspicuous success in recruiting agents. Praetorius was an Anglophile and one of the more unlikely alumni of Southampton University, where he had studied for a year in the twenties. Working on the logic that the British authorities would not be suspicious of sudden arrivals from countries recently occupied by the Germans, he began looking for recruits in Holland and Belgium. He had soon assembled his list of candidates, from whom Ritter and Dierks chose their favourites. But these favourites were hardly fortunate: they were being selected for a mission of such danger that it would come to be known as 'Himmelfahrt', 'the journey to heaven'.

Four men were chosen as the very first batch of invasion spies: Sjoerd Pons, an unemployed ex-Dutch army ambulance driver, Charles van den Kieboom, a half-Dutch, half-Japanese YMCA receptionist, Carl Meier, a German-born Dutchman, and Jose Waldberg, a German born in France. Only Meier and Kieboom could speak decent English and Waldberg spoke none at all. Waldberg was a relatively experienced agent who had spied for the Germans in France before its fall, but the others had no experience of espionage. Pons and Kieboom were not even willing volunteers: they had been offered a choice between spying or being sent to concentration camps for smuggling jewels between Holland and Germany.

Before the four men were sent to England they were housed in lodgings in Brussels and given a month of very basic training. They were taught Morse code, how to use their transmitters, and simple cryptology. They would be expected to report about coastal troop positions, frequency of patrols and the location of landmines. They would be looking out for the names of ships in harbour and sounding out the morale of the population. They were taught about the units and structure of the British army. But their lessons was patchy and rudimentary.

As the men prepared to cross the Channel, many in Britain believed that the country was already full of enemy agents and fifth columnists. Spy fever was widespread. The Imperial War

Museum Sound Archive contains examples of the kinds of Chinese whispers that did the rounds in 1940. One story describes a spy posing as a wounded British army officer in a ward at Barnet Hospital, north London; another recalls fifth columnists flashing lamps at low-flying Dorniers in Herefordshire. Sometimes these stories contain a grain of truth. One relates that Reverend H. E. B. Nye, the rector at Scampton in Lincolnshire, was arrested for transmitting messages to Germany from his vicarage. In fact Nye, a pre-war fascist, was arrested and interned under Regulation 18B, but he was not a spy and he was quickly released following a protest from his parishioners.

But it is too easy simply to blame spy fever on the credulity of the British public. The authorities contributed heavily to the anxiety. The Ministry of Information, for example, published a leaflet which declared that 'There is a fifth column in Britain' and explained that anybody who thought otherwise had 'simply fallen in to the trap laid by the fifth column itself'. Still, as Joseph Heller wrote in *Catch-22*, 'just because you're paranoid doesn't mean they aren't after you'. The country may have been a little too alive to the spy threat – but it was probably as well that it was. The 'Four Men in a Boat' – as Pons, Kieboom, Meier and Waldberg would be known by MI5 – were on their way.

And, as well as preconceptions about the scale of the threat, the British public had existing ideas – fostered by writers and filmmakers – about the kinds of people who would be spying for Germany. John Buchan's popular novels contained agents with aristocratic names like Graf Otto von Schwabing, who uttered grandiose remarks such as, 'I am not the least of the weapons that Germany has used to break her enemies.' Sapper's Bulldog Drummond stories, meanwhile, were introducing readers to a baser kind of German, the sort who wore a sneer and took delight in horsewhipping decent types. But the Four Men in a Boat were another sort again. They were not pompous and superior, nor were they sneery and brutal. They did not amount to a literary cliché. They were unsophisticated, poorly trained and barely even German.

At the end of August the four men were driven from Brussels to a villa on the outskirts of Boulogne. A few days later they were taken to a house in Le Touquet, where an officer explained to each in turn precisely where he was to land. They were given a celebratory lunch, and that night were placed onto fishing smacks moored in the estuary. The smacks sailed first to Boulogne, where they were attached to minesweepers, and then they were towed to within five miles of the English coast. Finally the men boarded dinghies, Pons and Kieboom in one, Waldberg and Meier in the other, and they began rowing ashore. They landed in Kent before daybreak on the morning of 3 September 1940, Pons and Kieboom near the Dymchurch Redoubt and Meier and Waldberg at Lydd. They had with them binoculars, wireless transmitters, cases containing clothes, cigarettes and brandy, £30 in banknotes, and enough food for a fortnight, by which time, they had been assured, the invasion would be under way. They were in effect its advance guard – and the first Germanic invaders of England since the fifth century, when the Saxons, Angles and Jutes arrived and Hengist became chieftain of Kent.

Private Sidney Tollervy Pearce of the Somerset Light Infantry was on patrol near Dymchurch early on the morning of 3 September. When a beached dinghy with its oars still in its rowlocks was noticed by a member of his platoon, a search was ordered of the surrounding area. A short while later Pearce spotted a man crossing the coast road in the gloom. 'Halt, who goes there?' he called out. The man threw himself down and shouted back, 'I don't know your codeword!' Kieboom had been ashore for less than an hour, but his espionage career was already over. 'I have come across the water,' he told Pearce. 'I am a Dutch refugee, and if I can see one of your officers I can explain the situation.' Kieboom was taken to battalion headquarters before being handed over to the police. While he was waiting for the police to take him away, he asked to use the battalion headquarters toilet – down which he flushed his map, code and secret ink.

Half an hour later another man was spotted in a nearby field. 'Who are you? What are you doing there?' shouted Lance Corporal Robert North. 'I am a Dutchman!' shouted back Sjoerd Pons. He told the lance corporal that he had travelled from Brest with a companion who had come ashore before him. He didn't know where his companion was, or whether he was alive or dead. Pons was also taken to battalion headquarters, and then delivered to the police. His arrest might have been unremarkable, but it is worth noting the name Sjoerd Pons; his story would have a surprising conclusion.

Carl Meier and Jose Waldberg meanwhile had landed a few miles to the south. They had pushed their dinghy back into the water, hoping that it would drift back out to sea. It stayed where it was. They had buried their wireless transmitter in the sand, stashed their food and brandy in a wrecked lifeboat, and gone to sleep for a few hours against the wall of a pumping station. They slept unobserved, and when Meier woke he wandered into Lydd in search of refreshment. What followed should stand as a salutary lesson to budding spies.

At 9 a.m., Meier walked into the Rising Sun pub on New Street. He was nervous and unclear about the services on offer in the English pub. In his American-tinged accent, he asked the landlady, Mrs Mabel Cole, for a bottle of champagne cider – and a bath. Taken aback, Mrs Cole explained that he couldn't take a bath, and that he should come back in an hour for a drink. As he turned to leave, he banged his head on – and broke – a light fitting. The coastal village of Lydd was no hub of cosmopolitan activity and Mrs Cole's suspicions had been truly aroused by this agitated and ignorant foreigner. On his return, Meier ordered half a pint of mild and sat down to drink it. Mrs Cole went into the private bar, and told two local men that there was a 'strange man' next door whom she was sure was 'up to no good'. The two men stepped into the public bar and watched Meier for a while. Aware that he was being observed, Meier said, 'Good morning, gentlemen,' and left the pub. The men followed him outside, and asked to see his identity card. Meier said that he didn't have one yet, and showed them his passport. He said that he was a Dutch refugee who had escaped to England through France. The men asked him to get into their car; they wished to take him to the police station. Meier put up no resistance. 'You've caught me, I guess,' he said. 'And I don't mind what happens to me – but I refuse to go back to Germany.'

Jose Waldberg – the only one of the four with espionage experience – was the only one actually to carry out any espionage activity in England. That evening, as he waited in vain for Meier to return to the pumping station, he dug up the wireless set, rigged up an aerial between a tree and a bush, and transmitted a message to his handlers. It read: 'Arrived safely. Document destroyed. English patrol 200 metres from coast. Beach with brown nets and railway sleepers at a distance of 50 metres. No mines. Few soldiers. Unfinished blockhouse. New road. Waldberg.'

Several hours later Meier had still not returned and Waldberg's mood was darkening. He sent another message: 'Meier prisoner. English police searching for me. Am cornered. Situation difficult. I can resist thirst until Saturday. If I am to resist send aeroplanes Wednesday evening 11 o'clock. Am 3 kilometres north of point of arrival. Long live Germany. Waldberg.'

Meier was indeed a prisoner. Not only that, but he had informed the police that another member of his group was still at large, and he had told them where to look for him. Between five and six o'clock on the morning of 5 September a policeman spotted Waldberg walking near the railway line, a little over a mile from the shore. When the policeman asked him where he was going, Waldberg, who spoke no English, replied in French. The policeman, described in a contemporary report as being 'no great French scholar', gathered that Waldberg was asking to be taken to an English officer. The policeman said, '*Coucher?*' with an upward inflection, and Waldberg pointed in the direction of the pumping station. The two men walked together to the station, where the policeman found the wireless set. Waldberg was then escorted to the police station, where he joined his colleagues. When he was searched, another message was found written in his notebook. He had not yet had time to send it: 'This is exact position yesterday evening 6 o'clock. 3 Messerschmitts fired machine guns in my direction 300 metres south water reservoir painted red. Meier prisoner.'

As inept as the invasion spies had proved, Meier had only been caught as the result of a chance encounter with a civilian, and Waldberg as a result of information provided by Meier. But all four men were now in custody and MI5 policy, as underlined in the diary of B Division chief Guy Liddell, was 'to get the prisoner to Latchmere House at the earliest possible opportunity'. And so Pons, Kieboom, Meier and Waldberg were transferred on 6 September to MI5's new spy prison and interrogation centre, Latchmere House, which would soon become known as Camp 020.

It may have been only a short walk from suburban Richmond Underground Station, but Camp 020's unattractive buildings and spacious grounds, ringed by barbed-wire fences, gave it an air of secluded menace. Once a Victorian private residence, it had later been a Great War asylum for officers suffering from neurasthenia, the technical name for shell-shock. And it is still in government hands today, in use as an open prison.

Camp 020's commandant was a fierce Indian Army veteran named Lieutenant Colonel Robin Stephens. Known behind his back as 'Tin Eye' for his ever-present monocle, Stephens inspired strong reactions. 'He was disliked by most of the people he came into contact with,' writes the author Nigel West, 'because of his almost Nazi behaviour and vile temper.' After the war Stephens wrote a history of Camp 020, intended as an internal MI5 document, and his prejudice and bluster pervade every page. A Belgian spy who spoke quietly during interrogation is described as a 'low-voiced snivelling creature', whose execution moved Stephens to write, 'of all the spineless spies who ever had their spinal cords broken by the hangman's rope [he] was the most craven'.

In Stephens's robust worldview Spaniards are 'stubborn, immoral and immutable', Frenchmen are 'volatile' and Italians are 'undersized, posturing folk'. Southern Europeans are not Stephens's least favourite people, however. 'For all their confounded tantrums,' he writes, 'the Latins are less detestable than the Huns.' But Stephens isn't always so predictable in his prejudices. In 1941 he interrogated an Irish republican named Lenihan who, he says, had 'no love for the British government' but 'much less love for the Germans'. Lenihan was an IRA gun-runner, captured by the Germans in Jersey, who agreed to work as a German agent in return for his freedom. But on his return to Ireland he made his way to Ulster, where he handed himself in to the British authorities. At Camp 020 Lenihan 'told his story frankly and fully without prompting'. He was duly released, writes Stephens, 'probably to continue in his home land the legitimate struggle against the English oppressor'.

Throughout his history of Camp 020 Stephens displays a straightforward sense of right and wrong which offers no succour to those who fall short of his standards. He praises Lenihan for being 'true to his ideals'. A spy who shows no fear at his execution is 'a brave man'. These are the manly ethics of Kipling, like whom Stephens spent his crucial formative years in India. He served in the Peshawar Division of the Indian Army and afterwards remained on the subcontinent, working in the Political Service and as an assistant Judge Advocate General. On his return to England he co-edited a digest of the rules of evidence relating to courts martial and found work as a journalist. At the outbreak of war he was recruited into MI5, for whom he took on the role of interrogator. In the days before Camp 020 he found himself having to interrogate internees in makeshift surroundings. On one occasion he had to delay an interrogation because the designated room doubled as officers' sleeping quarters, in which, he was told, an officer was having difficulty changing his trousers. A permanent interrogation facility was plainly needed and the Home Defence Executive was speedily prompted to establish Camp 020. In his history of the camp Stephens wrote, 'It would be reasonable [in the event of another war] to have an interrogation centre ready at the beginning of the war rather than an improvisation ten months later in the face of invasion.'

So, from July 1940 onwards, suspected spies were brought to Camp 020 to be questioned by MI5 interrogators, and often by Stephens himself. Christopher Harmer, MI5 case officer, remembers him rubbing his hands with glee on hearing that a suspect had been caught. The initial aim was to force a confession in the shortest possible time. Stephens was aware that no spy was proof against relentless interrogation, but equally that no interrogator could guarantee success. Interrogators, he thought, came in two types: breakers, who reduced the spy to the stage of speaking the truth, and investigators, who made order of the broken spy's information. The ideal breaker, he felt, should have an implacable hatred of the enemy, an ability to focus entirely on the spy, and sufficient common sense, experience of life and flexibility to be able to deal with any individual. This list of qualities just happened to reflect Stephens's own opinion of himself. But barristers, in his view, did not make good breakers; their ethics got in the way. A spy, in his view, was guilty until proven innocent. And while the breaker should possess 'a certain aggressive approach', this was not, Stephens makes clear, an invitation to practise violence. For the fact is that Stephens strictly forbade violence against Camp 020 prisoners.

This might seem surprising, particularly as violence amounting to torture *was* carried out by another branch of British Military Intelligence during the Second World War. At its London interrogation centre in Kensington Palace Gardens, MI19 – the intelligence section responsible for gathering information from prisoners of war – was engaged in practices that Stephens would not tolerate at Camp 020. Between 1940 and 1948 over 3,500 enemy POWs passed through 'the London Cage', as the MI19 centre was known. Its commandant was Lieutenant Colonel Alexander Scotland, who stated in the first, unpublished draft of his autobiography: 'If any German had any information we wanted, it was invariably extracted from him in the long run.' By Scotland's own admission the means of extraction included beating prisoners around the head while they were kneeling and making prisoners stand to attention continuously for over twenty-four hours at a stretch.

More comprehensive allegations against Scotland's regime were made by SS Hauptsturmführer Fritz Knöchlein. Knöchlein complained that, while being held in the London

Cage, he was kicked by guards, drenched in cold water, pushed down stairs, beaten with a club and made to run in circles carrying logs. He also claimed that other prisoners were beaten until they pleaded with their captors to be killed. Scotland refuted Knöchlein's assertions, but in 1946 he refused to allow Red Cross Inspectors access to the London Cage. The reason for their exclusion is hinted at in a letter from Scotland to the War Office: 'The Secret Gear which we use to check the reliability of information obtained must be removed from the Cage before permission is given to inspect the building.' Whatever this 'Secret Gear' was, the Red Cross would evidently not have approved.

Fritz Knöchlein, it is worth noting, had his own history of inflicting cruelty, which was known to the guards and officers of the London Cage. On 27 May 1940, at Le Paradis in northern France, he had ordered the massacre of ninety-seven British prisoners. The victims were all members of 2nd Battalion, Royal Norfolk Regiment, who had surrendered to Knöchlein's SS unit on their retreat to Dunkirk. Knöchlein's men marched the prisoners into a field and lined them up in front of a barn, where two machine guns opened up on them. All but two of the prisoners were killed. One of the survivors, Bill Pooley, identified Knöchlein in a refugee camp after the war. Knöchlein was executed in 1949.

So why was violence against inmates forbidden by Stephens at Camp 020, yet allowed by Scotland at the London Cage? The answer has nothing to do with morality or legality. Neither man was an enlightened humanitarian. The contrast in approach relates to the very different natures of their establishments. The purpose of the London Cage was to gather information from soldiers who were invariably protesting that they had been performing their duty. Camp 020, on the other hand, was MI5's interrogation centre for enemy spies and its recruitment centre for double agents. Stephens was responsible for choosing prisoners suitable for Double Cross work, before 'turning' them. This meant being able to win them over. It would be very difficult to win the confidence of a man or woman who had been tortured.

But Stephens's attitude to violence had another rationale. A spy had to confess before he could be turned. It was the breaker's task, as we have seen, to bring about the confession, and violence, felt Stephens, would discourage a true confession. A victim of torture would merely say what he (or she) thought the torturer wanted to hear in order to escape further punishment; and once a false answer had been given, all further information would rest on the false premise. On only one occasion was violence used against a Camp 020 inmate, and it was inflicted by Alexander Scotland. In September 1940 Scotland had been allowed into 020 in his capacity as a military intelligence officer in order to carry out an interrogation. When Stephens discovered what Scotland had done, he was apoplectic. Outside officers were never again allowed to interrogate Camp 020 inmates.

All of which is not to say that new arrivals to Camp 020 were offered a cup of tea and a tour of the facilities. The first interview was crucial, and the prisoner had to be broken. Stephens's favoured approach was 'a driving attack in the nature of a blast that will scare the man out of his wits'. He was to be allowed 'no liberties, no interruptions, no gesticulations'. He was to remain standing throughout the interview. 'Figuratively,' said Stephens, 'a spy in war should be at the point of a bayonet', because 'if the interrogator fails during the first vital hours, trouble untold is in store.'

While Stephens might not have allowed physical violence, intense psychological pressure was applied. Prisoners were left in no doubt that they faced execution if they did not cooperate. The single factor shared by all of his prisoners, stressed Stephens, was the desire for self-preservation: 'To avoid the hangman's rope, that is all important.' In addition a prisoner would be given the impression that more was known about him than was the case – although, thanks to Double Cross and ISOS, a good deal might well be known already.

Stephens developed an interrogation technique familiar to modern-day viewers of television cop shows. 'Blow hot-blow cold' involved bringing a prisoner before an interrogation board where Stephens would behave ferociously towards him. A calm officer would intervene, trying to pacify the commandant. Stephens would react angrily to this interference. After the interrogation the calm officer would apologize to the prisoner for Stephens's behaviour, explaining that he was an unreasonable man who might go to frightening lengths to force a confession. Perhaps it would be better if the prisoner made a statement to the calm officer? Another painful scene could be avoided that way. 'If you want my assistance,' the calm officer would say, 'I will come. I will try to help you.' This technique, claims Stephens, succeeded in a number of cases.

And then there was Cell Fourteen. Just as George Orwell's Room 101 contained 'the worst thing in the world', so Cell Fourteen at Camp 020 was intended to exploit a prisoner's personal fears. Cell Fourteen was actually a perfectly ordinary room around which a legend was created. The prisoner would be told that he was being transferred to a cell that had been padded before the war. It was opposite the mortuary. Men had committed suicide in it. It was remote and dark, and the prisoner would not be spoken to again. A guard would check on him. He would receive food – but he would remain there until he confessed – or until he left 'for the last time'.

According to Stephens, the legend of Cell Fourteen often proved successful as a last resort in breaking a spy. Much

depended on the prisoner's suggestibility, as well as the interrogator's ability to convey menace. 'An Italian gesticulated
wildly for writing materials within the hour,' writes Stephens,
'but an Icelander remained unmoved; between Cell Fourteen
and the land of desolation there was no contrast.'

So this was the regime waiting for Sjoerd Pons, Charles van
den Kieboom, Carl Meier and Jose Waldberg on their transfer
from the police station at Seabrook in Kent to Camp 020 on 6
September 1940. Stephens records that on arrival the men
were already partially broken. As he began the interrogation
process he decided to put the greatest pressure on the weakest
link. In his view this was Waldberg, whose transmitted wireless
messages – containing his name and the words 'Long live
Germany' – seemed to make a full confession inevitable.

In the event, Waldberg did not attempt to deny that he had
been a willing German spy. But he trusted in the imminent
German invasion to rescue him from his predicament. The
general plan of invasion, he told Stephens, was for two simul-
taneous assaults: one on the coast between Rye and Hythe, the
other between Aldeburgh and the Wash. He said that were he
to send his handlers a wireless message reading, 'Weak coastal
dispositions', then the landing between Rye and Hythe would
go ahead; but if he reported that local defences were strong,
then it would be abandoned. He also claimed that he had not
feared capture by the British, as he had been assured by his
handlers that he would be treated as a prisoner of war.

Waldberg was wrong about most of these details. In reality no
assault was planned between Aldeburgh and the Wash, while the
south coast assault front was intended to run from Lyme Regis
in the west to Ramsgate in the east, not from Rye to Hythe. All
the same, his version was sufficiently close to the truth to suggest
that he had decided to cooperate with his captors to a degree.
He actually told his interrogators that he was willing to work

'loyally' for England until the Germans arrived. And perhaps he really did believe that he would be treated as a prisoner of war. After all, on being captured his first words were a request to see an army officer – unlike his companions who all made immediate claims to be refugees. But whatever his beliefs, the fact is that Jose Waldberg never pretended to be anything other than a willing and committed Nazi spy.

Sjoerd Pons, unlike Waldberg, told his Camp 020 interrogators that he was not a spy. He had, he claimed, been coerced into coming to England. Had he not done so, he would have been sent to a concentration camp. But when he was asked whether he would be willing to use his transmitter to send false messages to the Germans, he replied, 'It is difficult.' The interrogator seized on his indecision. 'Difficult, is it? Why? You love Germany, do you?' 'Perhaps the German come ...' replied Pons. 'So you are afraid to send a message in case they come, is that right?' 'Yes, sir.' 'Because they will shoot you?' 'Yes.' 'Suppose we shoot you? Why shouldn't we shoot you? You are a spy.' 'Sir,' said Pons, 'you know I am not really a spy.' The interrogator asked Pons what his intention had been on his arrival in England. 'To take it all to you ... I carry the apparatus under my arm to the soldier.' 'So you were going to tell the police, were you, in this country?' 'Yes.'

Pons had a number of options. He could cooperate fully with the British and agree to send the controlled message. But what would the Germans do to him when they arrived? Alternatively he could refuse to assist the British, and wait for the Germans. But what if they didn't come? He would be executed as a spy. And so he raised a third option with his interrogator: 'I would ask that you help me ... to go away.' Pons wanted MI5 to accept that he had not intended to spy, and to send him to America, where he would be clear of the approaching Nazis. This was not a request to which MI5 was likely to accede.

But one question did concern MI5. Could Pons, Kieboom, Meier and Waldberg be used as double agents? A number of tests governed the decision. First, only spies who had been captured very quickly after their arrival, before they had a chance to communicate with the Germans, could be used. Secondly, a spy's capture must only have been observed by a very few, trusted people. Thirdly, the spy must be able to communicate effectively with the Germans. Fourthly, the spy's whole story must have been extracted, and fifthly, the spy must be willing to work under orders. In this case Waldberg had already transmitted a message to his handlers that Meier had been arrested, and Meier had been seen by several civilians in the Rising Sun pub. The first and second tests were not satisfied.

The result was that all four men were charged with espionage under the Treachery Act. This Act had been hurried through Parliament two months earlier to fill a loophole; the existing Treason Act did not cover foreigners who owed no allegiance to the British crown. They were the first defendants to be tried under the Act, by an Old Bailey jury. If found guilty they would be sentenced to death. But before the case came to trial Waldberg pleaded guilty. He had never claimed to be anything other than a spy and he was prepared to face the consequence.

In truth the prospects for the other three men were not a great deal better. And it is unlikely that their spirits were significantly raised by a visit in custody from the well-meaning Osbert Peake, a Home Office Minister. Peake, it was reported by Guy Liddell, had a pleasant conversation with Kieboom, culminating in the hope that he 'would not be here long'. He then enquired of Meier whether his relatives were sending him clean laundry each week. Neither man's reply is recorded.

The trial of Pons, Kieboom and Meier began on 24 October. Mr Justice Wrottesley advised the jury to keep an open mind. This must have been difficult advice to follow at a time of such national uncertainty. Spies were dreaded, invasion was feared, the Blitz was raging, and Britain and her colonies were standing alone against Hitler. Rarely can a trial have played so acutely on a nation's – and a jury's – collective prejudice.

Once the prosecution evidence had been heard, each of the three defendants, Pons, Kieboom and Meier, took the stand by turns. Pons told the jury that he and Kieboom had been offered a job by a German. This German knew that both men had been smuggling jewels between Holland and Germany and he made it clear that if they refused his offer they would be sent to a concentration camp. When Pons was told that the job involved spying in England, he at first refused, but then he discussed the matter with Kieboom and they decided to accept, but they agreed that when they arrived in England they would report immediately to the police. When they subsequently landed by dinghy in Kent, they took their wireless set ashore. A while later, when Pons saw two people fifteen or twenty yards away, he walked towards them. One shouted, 'Who are you?' Pons shouted back, 'I am a Dutchman!' He was then arrested. Counsel for Pons asked, 'Did you mean to help the Germans when you got to England?' 'No, sir,' replied Pons.

In cross-examination, prosecuting counsel asked Pons why, if it had been his intention to give himself up to the police, he hadn't rowed slowly and landed the boat in the daylight, or if he landed in the dark, he hadn't struck a match and called out to soldiers. Pons replied that it had not occurred to him. The judge then asked why, if he had really intended to surrender, he hadn't come ashore waving a handkerchief. Pons replied that it would have been incriminating because he had the wireless set and other articles on board the dinghy. Counsel suggested that he could have thrown them overboard and come ashore waving a handkerchief. Pons replied that he hadn't thought about it.

The jury retired to consider its verdict at midday on the third day of the trial. They returned to court just over an hour later. The foreman said, 'My Lord, we are not quite clear as to one of the prisoners.' He explained that the jury felt that the prisoner in question had originally conspired with the other prisoners to spy for the Germans 'but when he arrived in England he decided that he would not do anything to help the enemy but he would make a clean breast of it here'. Prosecuting counsel gave the matter some thought. 'I think that would be a verdict of not guilty,' he said.

When the jury later returned with its verdicts, it found Kieboom and Meier guilty and Pons not guilty. 'My Lord, may Pons be discharged, subject, of course, to other powers?' asked counsel for Pons. 'Pons may stand back,' replied Mr Justice Wrottesley. The death sentence was then passed on Kieboom, Meier and Waldberg. When the judge asked what was to be done with Pons, Edward Hinchley-Cooke, the MI5 interrogator who had once sparred with Arthur Owens, quickly came forward and rearrested him under the Aliens Act. Prosecuting counsel explained that Pons had 'landed irregularly without the permission of the Aliens' Officer'. He was taken first to a cell in Pentonville Prison and then to Camp 020, where he remained interned until the end of the war.

The condemned men wrote letters which they hoped would be sent home to their loved ones. They never were. To this day, the letters sit in the case files kept in the National Archives in London. Meier's letter to his fiancée, written in English, ends: 'Darling, keep your chin up! Say goodbye to all our friends from me and here's all the love that my last thoughts will convey. I'm not going to say goodbye, because there must be something after this. Darling. XXXX So long! Carl.

Meier and Waldberg were executed at Pentonville on 10 December. Kieboom was executed a week later, after his appeal against sentence was withdrawn on the advice of his counsel.

A great fuss was made in the British press when the guilty verdicts were announced. Photographs appeared of the spies' wireless sets and possessions, and *The Times* announced that 'the capture of these enemy agents emphasizes still more the need that the public exercise the greatest care when talking among strangers'. The publicity served to highlight the fact that British Intelligence was doing its job. But no mention was made in any of the papers of Sjoerd Pons. His acquittal was an embarrassment to the Secret Service. An internal MI5 memo suggested that he had been acquitted 'because the jury did not feel keen on his execution. Had there been the possibility of a lesser penalty … he would probably have been convicted.'

But this analysis fails to do justice to the trial jury. It appears from the foreman's comments that the jury did not accept Pons's evidence that he and Kieboom had planned to surrender to the police on arrival in England. But it *did* accept his evidence that, once in England, he had no intention of spying and had approached Lance Corporal North with the aim of surrendering. The jury's decision was based not on vague emotion, as MI5 wanted to believe, but on a consideration of the evidence before it. Whether it was a correct decision is a moot point. It is hard to imagine a greater testament to the jury system than that the rule of law still applied at a time of national crisis. And it says much for the decency of twelve ordinary British people that they returned such a brave verdict.

As the Nazis stood poised to invade, a member of their advance guard was acquitted by a British jury. It is hard to imagine a greater symbol of the country's integrity and courage during its darkest hour.

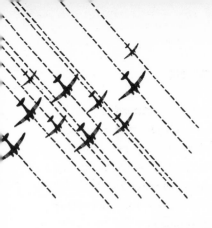

SUMMER'S LEASE

While the four men in a boat were making a hapless stand at spying in Kent (or, as the jury believed in the case of Sjoerd Pons, waiting for an opportunity to surrender), two men, a Swede and a Dane, were preparing to drop into Britain by parachute. Gösta Caroli, the Swede, was a 27-year-old mechanic with, in the words of his Abwehr dossier, 'clear, laughing eyes that inspired confidence'. The Dane was 26-year-old Wulf Schmidt, a slim, dark-blond-haired Danish army veteran who had recently spent time working as a fruit exporter in the Cameroons. They had been discovered by Walter Praetorius, they were enthusiastic Nazis, and they spoke good English.

Nikolaus Ritter spoke plainly with them from the beginning. 'Let's not play games with each other,' he told them. 'You know that you're putting your life in the balance, and that after you land you're completely on your own.' The men were lodged in adjoining rooms of the Phoenix Hotel in Hamburg while they received a much more thorough training than Pons, Waldberg and friends were given in Brussels. They were taught Morse, ciphers, meteorology, aircraft and weapons recognition, and camouflage. An Abwehr man known as Bruhns explained to them that their primary role would be to report back on the details of aerodromes and aircraft. They would also be expected to keep the Abwehr informed about troop movements, national morale, factory production and the British weather. Caroli and Schmidt quickly struck up a close friendship, intensified by the prospect of shared danger. They made swift progress and impressed Ritter, who considered them the cream of his protégés.

Once their training was complete they were driven to Brussels to receive wireless sets and provisions for their respective missions. But they could not set off immediately. The weather had to be right. If it was too clear, their arrival would be obvious; if it was too unsettled, the parachute drop would be hazardous. During the delay Caroli became close to a young woman. Concerned about the extent of his agent's pillow talk, Ritter had the woman taken into 'protective custody', while Caroli and Schmidt were taken to Paris. They stayed on Avenue de l'Opéra and visited the Abwehr's French headquarters in the Hôtel Lutetia. While there, Caroli signed a contract which stated that once his mission was complete he would be entitled to four years of schooling in Germany or the cash equivalent. Schmidt was not offered a contract, but promised work in the colonies and a sum of money. They were then taken to Le Sphinx, a Paris brothel reserved for German officers. The refreshed team returned to Brussels and prepared for work.

Caroli was the first to go. He travelled west to Rennes, where, with his transmitter strapped to his chest, he shook Ritter's hand and boarded a black Heinkel 111. The converted bomber flew across the Channel, before being caught in a searchlight's beam as it crossed the English coast. The pilot turned back and so that same night Caroli was returned to Brussels. Another attempt was made late on 5 September. In the early hours of the morning, after a long and draining wait, Caroli finally found himself falling towards England.

Unfortunately for him, MI5 was awaiting his arrival. The Double Cross system was showing its benefits: Arthur Owens had been informed that another spy was shortly to enter Britain. '*Snow* is in daily contact with the Germans,' writes Guy Liddell in his diary on 27 August, 'and arrangements are being made to land an agent by parachute ... The great difficulty is to get the man down alive and to prevent the Local Defence Volunteers from getting at him.'

In the event, Caroli landed near Denton in Northamptonshire. During his descent the wireless set strapped to his chest struck him on the chin, knocking him unconscious. He was out cold for several hours and when he came to he picked up his equipment, staggered into a ditch and passed out again. This meant that he missed his first scheduled transmission to Hamburg. In the afternoon a farm hand spotted his feet poking out from under a bush. He told the farmer what he had seen and with another two men they went to investigate. They found the dazed Caroli, who told them that he had arrived the previous night by parachute and showed them his pistol and a wallet full of English money. He admitted that he was a German spy and was handed over to the police, but only after a delay was MI5 informed of his arrival. 'Tar' Robertson quickly arranged for him to be taken to Cannon Row Police Station in London. From there he was sent to Camp 020.

And so, in the early afternoon of 7 September, while Nikolaus Ritter was anxiously calling the Hamburg radio station to ask whether 'Agent 3275' had yet made contact, 3275 was already being interrogated by 'Tin Eye' Stephens. By now it had been decided that the Four Men in a Boat would not be used as double agents, but Stephens had high hopes for Caroli – so long as he hadn't yet communicated with Hamburg. 'Did you send any messages?' Stephens barked. 'No,' Caroli replied. 'That's a lie! What is this message?' said the commandant, pointing to a piece of paper found on Caroli. 'I was going to send it at night time,' he replied. 'So the time of sending was past?' 'Yes.' 'Were you arrested before the next time of sending?' 'Yes.' 'So you couldn't send?' 'Yes.'

The first double-agent test seemed to be satisfied, but Caroli was not broken easily. He freely confessed that he was a spy, but admitted little else apart from the fact that the Germans expected him to report on bomb damage in the Birmingham–Oxford–Northampton triangle. He stubbornly refused to betray his oath. 'I liked Germany so much,' he explained, 'I have German blood.' 'You know you are likely to be shot?' asked Stephens. 'Yes.' 'You still intend to keep your oath?' 'Yes.' 'Just consider this very carefully,' bluffed the commandant. 'We have 99 per cent of the whole thing for understanding. The little more necessary we shall discover in a few hours or days. If you tell the rest of it now, we shall be saved the trouble. Is it worth flinging your life away, so that we shall have a few extra hours' work?' 'Yes,' said Caroli.

Stephens continued working relentlessly on his prey. At one point Caroli revealed that another agent was due to arrive shortly – and that he was very friendly with this man. It occurred to Stephens that while Caroli might not be willing to cooperate to save his own life, he *might* do so to save the life of his friend. Stephens promised 'to spare the life of this friend of yours' in return for Caroli revealing everything he knew about his contacts and his mission. The Swede agreed to the bargain. Nikolaus Ritter had made a grave mistake in allowing his spies to become intimate friends during the training process.

Once the deal was done, Caroli began talking freely. He gave Wulf Schmidt's name and described him. He explained approximately where he would be dropped and described the equipment he would bring with him. And he told Stephens something that even Ritter didn't know: the two spies had made an agreement to meet on 20 September outside the Black Boy pub in Northampton. On Caroli went, giving Stephens information that, a little while earlier, he had been prepared to die for rather than reveal.

All the same, Caroli initially refused to work as a double agent when the proposal was put to him. He had already betrayed his masters by giving information; this seemed a betrayal too far. But he was eventually persuaded that the Germans had brought him to England ill equipped and under false pretences. And so, given the code name *Summer*, Caroli agreed to become a double agent. This meant that MI5 had a valuable new man, distinct from the ring of agents that had developed around Arthur Owens. It meant that Ritter would finally receive news from a prize agent. And it meant that 'Tin Eye' Stephens's interrogation strategies were paying off. 'For the first and last time in the history of Camp 020,' writes Stephens, 'a promise was made to a prisoner' and 'upon that promise devolved many of the most spectacular wartime successes of the British counter-espionage services'.

Caroli left Camp 020 on 9 September and sent his first successful controlled wireless message to Hamburg several days later. His transmitter was initially set up in a field near Aylesbury, where Caroli lay tapping out prepared messages under the close scrutiny of a radio operator who ensured that he never wandered off script. But the transmissions failed until the wireless set was moved to higher ground – inside the local police station. When he eventually made contact with Hamburg, Caroli explained the week-long delay by saying that he had been injured on descent and was currently hiding in fields near Oxford. He now intended, he said, to make his way to London, posing as a refugee. The immediate result was unexpected – but gratifying for 'Tar' Robertson and MI5. On receiving the message Ritter decided to call on Owens for help, and sent a message which read, 'Swedish friend in fields near Oxford. How can he contact you at once.' Owens was clearly still trusted by his German spymasters – and MI5 was given an early indication of its level of control over the Abwehr's operations. But as Robertson pondered his next move he was aware of the delicacy of the situation: a mistake now could blow both Owens and Caroli. And Caroli was the potential forerunner of an entire battalion of double agents.

After a discussion with Guy Liddell, Robertson instructed Owens's radio operator to send a message suggesting that Owens should meet 'the Swedish friend' at High Wycombe railway station. Robertson decided that the meeting must really take place in case the Germans had anybody watching. But as Robertson now had doubts about Owens and didn't want him knowing too much about Caroli's true situation, he decided not to send Owens to the meeting. He would instead send Sam McCarthy – *Biscuit* – the sub-agent who had recently met Ritter in Portugal.

And so MI5 double agents *Summer* and *Biscuit* acted out a rendezvous as though they were genuine German spies. The Germans had nobody watching, but MI5 *had*, just in case Caroli decided to make a bolt for freedom. On this occasion he did as he was told. The two men walked together for a while in the direction of London. McCarthy, who had a problem with drink, was instructed not to stop in any pubs as they went. After a time they parted. Robertson decided that the Germans should now be sent a message asking whether they would allow Caroli to spend the winter at McCarthy's house. After all, it now looked as though the invasion wasn't coming, and Caroli needed a roof over his head. Ritter agreed. 'Thanks for help to friend. Won't forget,' he radioed Owens two days later. B1a was playing its hand extremely well.

At 10 o'clock on the night of 19 September, Wolf Nabel took off from Germany for England. Like his colleague Karl Gartenfeld, Nabel was a Luftwaffe pilot who specialized in 'aerial insertion', dropping spies by parachute over their target, and that night his cargo was Wulf Schmidt. An hour and a half later Schmidt jumped out of the Heinkel over Cambridgeshire. As he came down he became tangled in telegraph wires and fell awkwardly, hurting his ankle and hand. For five minutes he lay where he was. Then he got up, cut away his parachute, and did his best to bury it in the hard ground along with his flying overalls. Suddenly he heard a siren. He had landed next to an RAF camp and he stood helpless as a searchlight swept the area. But he was not spotted and he moved away from the camp and hid his transmitter and suitcase in a field by covering them with grass.

In the morning he went into the nearby village of Willingham. Attempting to blend with the locals, he bought *The Times* and a pocket watch to replace one that had been damaged on landing. After taking breakfast in a café he was heading back to the field when he was stopped by a Local Defence Volunteer. He had already attracted suspicion. People were regularly reporting non-existent spies; it is gratifying that they were also reporting those that did exist. Schmidt was handed to the Cambridgeshire Police, who were convinced, despite his protests, that he was a German agent. MI5 received a phone call and the next morning the Dane was on his way to Camp 020. He was driven through central London in order to demonstrate that, whatever he had been told by his handlers and the German propaganda machine, London was withstanding the Blitz.

Schmidt's arrival had, of course, been expected at 020 for some days. In the meantime it had been decided – against the wishes of Stephens – that the Dane's interrogation should be carried out by external officers from the War Office. And one of those officers was none other than Lieutenant Colonel Alexander Scotland. The interrogation began soon after Schmidt's arrival on the morning of 21 September. He put on a stubborn show. He had, he insisted, been in England since 10 July, having arrived by boat from Esbjerg in south-west Denmark. He was escaping the Nazis and hoped to serve with the British army. 'Now look here, my man,' he was told, 'if you don't wish to speak the truth, we have methods to make you speak the truth – which will be very unpleasant for you.'

Schmidt had only to wait until lunchtime for a taste of Scotland's 'methods'. During the break Scotland followed Schmidt back to his cell, where he began punching him in the face. According to Guy Liddell, whose sympathy appears to lie with Schmidt, the spy 'got one back for himself'. This was the incident which so incensed Stephens and which ensured that outside interrogators were thereafter kept away from 020. 'Apart from the moral aspect of the whole thing,' writes Liddell, 'I am quite convinced that these Gestapo methods do not pay in the long run.' The interrogation of Schmidt continued in the afternoon – only now it was performed by Stephens. Scotland and his colleagues had been ordered off the premises.

The fact was that Scotland could not have chosen a more unsuitable spy to assault. It was critical to MI5 that Schmidt be 'worked' as a double agent. If the Germans thought he had been caught, both Caroli and Owens could be compromised. The continued existence of the Double Cross system seemed to depend on the frame of mind of a bruised Danish fruit exporter. Stephens was now in an awkward position. On the one hand, he had to reassure Schmidt that he would come to no further harm; on the other, he had to break him before he could be turned.

Stephens set about the task with his customary zeal. Schmidt claimed that he had been in England for two months and ten days. Why then, asked Stephens, had he not yet surrendered to the authorities? Schmidt replied that he was making his way down to London to see the Danish consul. When Stephens told him to account for his movements since 10 July, Schmidt ran through the amount of time spent on each leg of his journey. Stephens quickly added up the figures and found that Schmidt had badly miscalculated. 'We have caught you out by over a month!' he exclaimed. Schmidt's health was good, he noted, his trousers were creased and his hair was short. How could this be after weeks of sleeping in ditches? 'It is different, my beard does not grow either,' said Schmidt. 'Another bad lie, that,' said Stephens. 'How much longer are you going to go on with this nonsense?'

It went on for a while until Stephens brought it to a halt. He told Schmidt that Caroli had betrayed him. And he proved the fact by reading to him from Caroli's statement: he reeled off Caroli's description of Schmidt, details of their proposed meeting outside the Black Boy pub, and particulars of the training they had received together. He neglected to add that Caroli had only made this statement in return for a promise that Schmidt's life be spared.

At a stroke the Dane's resistance collapsed. 'You have been sold by Caroli,' said Stephens. 'I see so,' replied the spy. 'If you want, shoot me. The man is a *Schwein*.' 'I am sorry for you,' continued Stephens. 'You have been sold by the Germans.' 'I no believe. I am not sold by the Germans.' 'I want the truth and the whole truth from you, Schmidt, before your life is saved. Are you willing to give it?' The broken spy proceeded to give it at length. He drew a map showing where his transmitter was hidden and then Stephens asked him to write a statement summarizing his admissions. 'I think honestly it will help you,' said the commandant. 'I mean that.' 'I no think so,' said Schmidt sadly. But he did as he was asked.

The next morning the incorrigible Scotland returned to 020 with a syringe full of truth serum which he intended to inject into Schmidt. Stephens allowed him nowhere near the spy, who was instead escorted to Willingham, where his transmitter and all his possessions were recovered in precisely the locations described on his map. And so he had now been broken, his story was being extracted, and his capture had been witnessed by only a few trusted individuals. That afternoon Stephens asked him, 'When you landed, did you manage to send off a message?' 'No,' came the reply. Schmidt satisfied the Double Cross criteria. It was now time for Stephens to persuade the keen Nazi to work for the British.

Stephens began the persuasion by flattering Schmidt: 'I respect you because you've got guts.' He praised his integrity: 'You told me you were going to speak the truth – and you have spoken the truth.' He paid him the highest compliment he could offer: 'In many ways I am very much like yourself.' And he prepared the ground for the job to come: 'You say you like playing with danger? That's why you took this up?' 'Yes,' said Schmidt.

Then Stephens changed direction. He stressed how fortunate Schmidt was to find himself in his current situation: 'You are a spy and you've been fairly caught as a spy. If I'd done the same thing as you've had the guts to do in Germany, I'd be shot, and that is your proper reward. *You should be shot.* But there are certain mitigating circumstances in this case … You have forfeited your life – but there's one way of saving your life. You're not bound by any oath to work for us. I am going to ask you *that question* when I've given you sufficient time to answer it properly.' The proposed work, he stressed, would appeal to Schmidt: 'There is adventure in it, and there is danger in it … If we wish to use you for sending messages, we shall come to you from time to time. You will be fairly treated. There are two senior officers here; they will both tell you that if I say a thing like that I can be trusted.' 'Excuse, I must answer now?' asked Schmidt. 'I think it's a good thing to answer now,' replied the commandant. 'I'll do so,' said Schmidt. 'Well, again I respect you because I think you've got guts,' Stephens told him. 'It needs guts to do that. Can you understand what I mean by guts? It means courage … Now I don't want any hesitation from you at all. What is your answer?' 'Yes.' 'You will?' 'Yes.' 'Well done.'

Many years later the author Nigel West tracked Schmidt down and asked him why he had agreed to work his transmitter for the British. Schmidt's answer bears out Stephens's belief that his prisoners were united by a single common factor. 'It was simply a matter of survival, Schmidt explained. 'Self-preservation must be the strongest instinct in man.'

Once Schmidt had sent his first message from Camp 020, Nikolaus Ritter received a late-night telephone call from the Hamburg radio station telling him that Agent 3275 had made contact. 'What does he have to say?' asked Ritter. 'He is only checking in to let us know that he's alive. He'll call again soon,' he was told. 'Good,' said Ritter. 'Call me as soon as you hear from him, please.' Schmidt was subsequently passed from Camp 020 to a house in Radlett in Hertfordshire, under the care of MI5. 'Tar' Robertson gave him the codename *Tate* because of his supposed resemblance to Harry Tate, the music-hall comedian who had died earlier in the year.

For the next fourteen months Schmidt operated his own transmitter, until he was forced to spend time in hospital. At this time an MI5 wireless operator took over and he carried on with his transmissions even after Schmidt was discharged. But

Schmidt always worded his own messages and his style was unmistakable. 'I am beginning to think that you are full of shit,' he once accused Hamburg when payment was not forthcoming. Asked about the standard of British bread, he replied, 'Don't you have anything more important to ask? It tastes all right.' He refused even to consider examining the quality of clothing available to the British public, replying to the request with an invitation to kiss his arse. But requests for important information were always treated seriously and answered carefully. It was Schmidt whose attempt to give a detailed report on bomb-damaged Coventry factories was discussed in an earlier chapter. He was to become the longest-serving of all B1a double agents, still 'loyally' reporting to his German handlers at the end of the war.

During the early part of Schmidt's Double Cross career, however, he was not fully trusted by the British. 'It is not to be supposed that his new-found loyalty to this country would survive any severe strain,' one case officer wrote drily. Schmidt was watched by a full-time guard at his house in Radlett. And had the Germans invaded he would not have survived for very long.

In the event of a German invasion a B1a contingency plan was in place, known as 'Mr Mills's Circus'. Cyril Mills, B1a man and impresario of the Bertram Mills Circus, was in charge of the operation. 'We are dealing,' wrote 'Tar' Robertson, 'with certain individuals who … should not on any account … fall into the hands of the enemy.' And so, when the invasion arrived, it was decided that double agents were to be sent with case officers and guards to a selection of hotels in north Wales. In April 1941 the MI5 representative in Colwyn Bay wrote, 'I have now completed arrangements for the accommodation of the animals, their young, and their keepers, together with accommodation for Mr Mills himself.'

Schmidt's proposed escort was given personal instructions from the head of MI5, Sir David Petrie. Schmidt was to be placed under arrest, handcuffed, and brought to north Wales. 'As it is of vital importance,' Petrie wrote, 'that *Tate* should not fall into the hands of the enemy, *you must be prepared to take any step necessary to prevent this from happening.*' The same unpleasant fate would have awaited Arthur Owens. 'It is highly probable,' surmised an MI5 memo, 'that *Snow* would attempt to join the Germans immediately if invasion occurred.'

By February 1942 Mills was recommending that the plan be scrapped and that, in the event of invasion, double agents should simply be brought to Camp 020. He wrote, 'I do not know what Colonel Stephens's plans are for dealing with the inmates of Camp 020 … but I take it that … he would have power in the event of invasion to liquidate all his charges. If Colonel Stephens does not plan to do anything of this sort, then at least two B1a officers should go and live in Camp 020 so that they are available and ready to deal with our people should the necessity arrive.' Luckily for all concerned, the threat of invasion faded, and in October 1943 Robertson cancelled all contingency plans.

One double agent who was never mentioned in the proposals for Mr Mills's Circus was Gösta Caroli. *Summer*'s lease had already ended by early 1941, brought to a halt by a dark, ultimately comic, train of events. In November 1940 Caroli had been brought back to Camp 020 for reinterrogation after part of his story was found to be false. It was already known that he had spent time in England before the war, but only now did he admit that he had actually been working for the Abwehr at the time. During the interrogation 'Tin Eye' Stephens referred to his case as 'dirty', and Caroli reacted by slashing his wrists when alone in his cell. Dr Harold Dearden, the Camp 020 psychiatrist, found him collapsed but conscious. He was given first aid and treated for shock and loss of blood. A subsequent report concluded that Stephens's remark had caused Caroli to 'think furiously that he was always getting innocent people into trouble and that if he was out of the way he could not continue to cause them harm'.

Caroli recovered fully, but on 13 January, while being held in the more relaxed atmosphere of Hinxton Grange in Cambridgeshire, he tied up his guard and made a bid for freedom. The guard, Paulton, was playing a quiet game of patience when Caroli suddenly sprang at him and wrapped a length of rope around his neck. Paulton blacked out for a moment, allowing Caroli to start tying his hands behinds his back. Caroli tied another rope around the guard's ankles and a third around his upper arms, apologizing all the while. He explained that he 'could not go on'. Paulton complained that he was uncomfortable trussed up on the floor, so Caroli helped him to a sofa and put a pillow underneath him. He emptied Paulton's pockets, took cash out of the safe, gathered up maps, tins of food and a slice of cold beef, and brought Paulton a glass of water. He then left the room. All was quiet for some time. Paulton spotted a penknife on the sofa table and wriggled towards it. With a struggle he cut the rope around his wrists and went to the telephone to report Caroli's escape. At that moment Caroli passed the window pushing a motorcycle, with a canvas canoe strapped to his back. Paulton ducked down and watched Caroli tie the canoe to the motorbike before setting off down the drive. The guard immediately put a call through to B1a.

Caroli did not make a clean escape. Before he had gone far the canoe unbalanced the motorbike and he fell off. A concerned passer-by helped him up and the two men lifted the canoe and threw it over a hedge. A few miles further on, bruised and demoralized, Caroli dismounted and walked into the police station in Newmarket. He handed himself in. He was duly returned to Camp 020, his career as a double agent resoundingly over. 'Tar' Robertson had to decide what to tell the Germans. He could not let it be known that Caroli had been captured, as that would blow Sam McCarthy (with whom he had supposedly been living), as well as Arthur Owens and Wulf Schmidt.

In the end Owens informed the Germans that Caroli had gone on the run and that he had left the transmitter in the cloakroom at Cambridge railway station. The Germans accepted the story and instructed McCarthy to collect the transmitter. Had Caroli's escape succeeded, it would have, J. C. Masterman noted, 'wrecked all our plans'. B1a learned from the experience that double agents must be watched closely and their reactions carefully studied. Fragile tempera- ments and feelings of guilt, solitude and depression had to be anticipated. A single case officer would now be responsible for each agent, willing to constantly monitor, advise, encourage and cajole. Only in this manner could Double Cross hope to succeed. But the system was to suffer two more near- disastrous earthquakes – the second during the implementa- tion of Operation Fortitude.

The first took place just after the *Summer* tremor, when Owens went to meet Ritter in Lisbon. *Snow*'s last trip to meet Ritter had left him tied up in a trawler cabin with a great deal of explaining to do. This trip would cause 'Tar' Robertson even more disquiet. Travelling separately from Owens to the rendezvous was his latest recruit: Walter Dicketts. Dicketts was a once-respectable man, a Great War Royal Naval Air Service officer who had fallen into penury in the years after the war and had accumulated a number of dishonesty convictions. He was, in certain respects, a perfect match for Owens.

Owens and Dicketts had first met in a pub in Richmond. They struck up a conversation, discussing countries they had both visited. Owens paid for Dicketts's drinks and invited him back to his flat to play darts. The drinking carried on until the early hours and began again the following day. In their cups, the two men agreed on a joint business venture: they would market mustard in toothpaste-like tubes. Owens gave Dicketts a cheque for £25 towards the enterprise. But he was playing his old inscrutable game. He signed the cheque with a false name, told Dicketts that his usual business partner was William Rolph (the agent who had committed suicide as a result of the trawler incident), and then informed him that he would not be proceeding with the mustard venture after all. But Dicketts was not to worry, Owens assured him, because they would soon be working together 'in other directions'. Owens went on to boast that he was the 'key man' in the British Secret Service and promptly set about recruiting Dicketts. How much money, he asked, would Dicketts require to 'work for him'? Back at his flat he showed Dicketts his transmitter. And he told him that Germany was certain to win the war and that he and Lily were going to live in Germany as soon as his work in England was complete.

Not unnaturally Dicketts felt sure that Owens was a German spy, which in effect he was. Keen to earn himself a job in British Air Intelligence, Dicketts started monitoring Owens's movements and before long he spotted a clandestine meeting between Owens and a well-dressed man whom he took to be a fellow spy. The man was actually 'Tar' Robertson, but, armed with apparent evidence of a German espionage ring, Dicketts made an appointment to see Air Commodore Boyle at the Air Ministry. As a consequence, and to his surprise and satisfaction, Dicketts was approached to work for MI5. He was assigned the codename *Celery* and told to accompany Owens on his trip to Lisbon. He had two particular objectives. One was to check up on the ever-unreliable

Welshman. The other was more dangerous. He was to do the job that Sam McCarthy had been preparing to do months earlier: to travel into Germany with Nikolaus Ritter. While there, he was to pick up as much information as he could on the Abwehr, its personnel and its training methods.

As it turned out, Dicketts was a natural spy. He had courage, quick wits and a photographic memory. Before Dicketts left England Robertson sent him on a number of espionage missions to gather chickenfood that could safely be passed to Ritter. And Robertson gave him a guarantee that his family would receive a pension were he not to return. At one of his meetings with the B1a chief Dicketts noted that Owens was 'running with the hare and hunting with the hounds'. This was a fair summary of the Welshman's fluid approach to loyalty. At a subsequent meeting Dicketts was blunter: 'He is both mad and double-crossing us,' he told Robertson. Again it is hard to disagree.

Lisbon, the city to which Owens and Dicketts were travelling, had a peculiar wartime atmosphere. Its blend of neutrality and proximity to the war drew agents, adventurers and opportunists. Its open port attracted refugees seeking to escape Europe. Men and women of all nations and loyalties mingled in a paranoid swell. Nightclubs were full, tables were crowded at the Casino Estoril, and the underworld flourished. An expression, 'Lisbon fever', was coined to describe the madness induced by a lengthy stay in this over-heated city. It was a condition to which Arthur Owens would succumb.

Owens arrived in Lisbon before Dicketts, whose ship was delayed. On Dicketts's arrival the two men spoke briefly at the Metropole Hotel. Owens was roaring drunk. They went together to meet Ritter, whom Dicketts found quite unlike the coarse character he had been expecting from McCarthy's description. Instead he found 'a very shrewd American middle-west businessman'. Ritter spoke with an American accent, having lived in the United States for thirteen years, he barely drank, he did not talk excessively, and he seemed to command respect from people around him.

'Owens tells me you want to work for Germany,' Ritter said to Dicketts, 'and he thinks you will be very useful. He says that you would like to come into Germany, and I have arranged for you to come in a day or two – if you want to come.' Owens told Ritter that he wanted to come to Germany as well. 'I don't think this can be arranged,' said Ritter. Owens turned to Dicketts. 'Don't worry,' he promised, 'I *shall* be seeing you in Hamburg in three or four days.' Ritter laughed. He was evidently almost as long-suffering as 'Tar' Robertson. 'If we can arrange it we will,' he said, 'but you know how difficult it is ...'

Before Dicketts set off for Hamburg he was introduced to Lisbon SS chief Johann Döbler, who told him that his loyalty would be rewarded considerably, but that if he was double-crossing it would be 'unfortunate'. This caution was unequivocal, but Dicketts also received a vague one from Owens. 'Don't go unless you want to. I will look after you,' said the Welshman. And just as Dicketts was departing, Owens shook his hand saying, 'You are a very brave man. They have sent you over blindfold, and if it weren't for me, your life would be worth nothing. If you want to change your mind, you can now do so.' There was a genuine reason for Owens's concern, but Dicketts did not know it at the time.

Dicketts was first driven to Madrid. His driver was a staff member of the German embassy in Lisbon, Hans Ruser, who gave the impression of being pro-English and anti-Nazi. 'I do not like travelling with a traitor,' he told Dicketts. Dicketts said that he did not consider himself a traitor; he simply had great admiration for the German system of government and intense disagreement with his own. He was strongly influenced by his Irish mother, he said, and would go to any lengths to stop the war. When Ruser heard this, his attitude changed. He also hoped for an end to the war, he said. While he was anti-Nazi in every way, he stressed that Hitler was the saviour of Germany and could be the saviour of Europe. Hitler, he trusted, would bring peace. Dicketts was to encounter this apparently illogical attitude on a number of occasions in wartime Germany: hatred for the Nazis allied to devotion to the Führer.

While it might appear that Ruser was merely posing as an anti-Nazi in order to test Dicketts's true feelings, this was not the case. In 1942 Ruser would approach British Intelligence to offer himself as an agent. He was given a British codename, although he was never used as a spy. Anti-Nazi feeling was not uncommon in Admiral Canaris's Abwehr and would become more pronounced as the war progressed.

From Madrid Dicketts flew first to Barcelona and then to Berlin. On his arrival in Hamburg he was installed in a suite in the luxurious Hotel Vier Jahreszeiten. Over the next three days he was rigorously interrogated by senior Abwehr members, including a Dr Schwarz who spoke perfect English 'with the pure intonation of a country clergyman'. Dr Schwarz, Dicketts was told, had recently been spying in England and was likely to return in the near future.

On Dicketts's fourth day in Hamburg, Ritter arrived and ran him through his entire story again. The interrogation continued into the night, over a dinner of lobster in the private room of a restaurant. The following day Dicketts was given a long list of questions to answer on the subject of British aviation, which was supposed to be his specialist field. He was able to answer only one, to the utter disbelief of the Abwehr's chief air expert. Ritter, however, calmed the situation. He understood, he said, that Dicketts had been given 'insufficient instruction'. But he followed this encouragement with an alarming question for the Englishman: what knowledge did he have of Owens's connection with British Intelligence? This begged another question: what knowledge did Ritter have? Did he know that Owens was under control? And if so, did he believe that Dicketts was also under control?

This was a crucial moment. Dicketts might be walking into an irresistible trap. He carefully explained that he had been kept apart from Owens's 'other activities', as Owens's view had been that Dicketts would be valuable in 'another sphere', and so the less he knew the better. Dicketts was subtly emphasizing that even if Owens *was* under British control, he was ultimately a loyal German spy, and he had engaged Dicketts in the same capacity. His words seemed to reassure Ritter, who told him that had passed the test. 'I am now prepared to trust you,' the German said.

The lengthy interrogation process over, Dicketts was able to wander freely around the city. Just as MI5 had driven Wulf Schmidt through the centre of London to demonstrate how little of the city had been damaged by Luftwaffe bombing, so the Abwehr wanted Dicketts to see that Hamburg was relatively unscathed. He noted to his disappointment that this was indeed the case. But his experience was an extraordinary one. In the midst of the war Dicketts found himself exploring an enemy city with the freedom of a Baedeker-wielding tourist.

In the evening Dicketts was taken on a tour of nightclubs, including Owens's preferred Valhalla, the place with telephones at the tables. He was caught in a late-night air raid and ordered by police into a shelter, where he struck up a conversation with some German army officers. He claimed to be a repatriated German-American and was assured by his new Wehrmacht friends that Germany's hold on Europe was so strong that America's possible entry into the war would only prolong hostilities; it would not alter the inevitable outcome. Dicketts stayed quiet and let the locals do the talking.

On a subsequent evening he was taken to dinner with Ritter and his wife, a thin-faced woman in her mid-thirties. She gave Dicketts the impression that she was pro-English, desperate for the war to end, and worried about the nature of her husband's work. The next time Dicketts came to Hamburg, Ritter suggested, he should bring his wife with him, and perhaps leave her there so that she would be safe from reprisals if his role was discovered. Ritter later asked Dicketts whether the British public was aware of the U-Boats' success in sinking British convoys. Dicketts replied that German reports were probably exaggerated for propaganda purposes. 'Nothing of the kind!' retorted Ritter. 'We are gradually completely blockading England! We are now building thirty U-Boats a month!' Dicketts asked how the Germans could find sufficient men to crew this number of U-Boats. Ritter replied that Germany relied on the same procedure it used to find bomb-disposal squads: 'We go to the prisons and pick out minor criminal offenders, that is to say money fraud and similar types of crime, and offer these men remission of their sentence if they will undertake the work.'

A few days later Dicketts had a final interview with Ritter, who told him that he had been passed as an agent and that he would now be returning to Lisbon. He would be breaking the journey in Berlin, and Ritter suggested that while there he should have his photograph taken in front of the principal railway stations, in order to show 'his friends in England' that there had been no bomb damage. The two men then discussed Owens. 'I am very fond of him,' said Ritter, 'but he is a goddamn lazy son-of-a-bitch and he won't get going unless someone gives him a good kick in the pants. I am prepared to go on trusting him because I have known him for more than four years and he has never, to my knowledge, let me down.' 'He must have given you some very good information?' probed Dicketts. 'No. He has not given me very much, but I think he is going to be useful to us in other ways.' 'What other ways?' 'Don't ask too many questions. But he is a very clever chemist. In fact, in some ways, he is brilliant.' Even if Ritter was aware of Owens's connection with British intelligence, it appeared as though his ultimate loyalty was not doubted.

When Dicketts eventually arrived back in Lisbon, he found Owens in a nightclub accompanied by two girls. He seemed very relieved to see Dicketts, who was subsequently told by several people that Owens had worried himself to the point of a nervous breakdown in his absence. Owens asked him where he had been and what he had to report. Dicketts replied that, regretfully, he could say nothing. Just before they left Lisbon for England, Owens called Dicketts aside for a private word. 'When you get back,' he said in an undertone, 'you will probably be arrested. I have had a cable from England telling me of this. I think you can trust Robbie ['Tar' Robertson], but no one else. You will have a very bad time. Do you want to go back or not?' Dicketts wisely ignored his companion's latest fantasia of lies.

Back in London on 27 March, Dicketts and Owens were closely questioned. Owens had with him £10,000 in cash provided by Ritter. This was good news for B1a, but Robertson was utterly staggered by one revelation in Owens's report. Ritter, claimed Owens, had challenged him as soon as he arrived in Lisbon, saying that he knew that Owens was in contact with British Intelligence. Owens had not attempted to deny it. He could see by Ritter's expression that there was no point. Instead he told his German spymaster that he had been detected by the British two and a half months previously. Since then he *had* been working under British control, but for all that time he had been attempting to come to Lisbon, to see Ritter. And now he had succeeded.

So what was Robertson to make of this? If Owens was telling the truth, why had Ritter given him £10,000 and allowed him to return to England? Why had Owens allowed Dicketts to go to Germany? Did Owens expect Dicketts to be tortured and murdered in Germany? Why had the Germans allowed Dicketts to return? Or was Owens simply lying?

In B1a's desperation to arrive at the truth J. C. Masterman came up with a number of hypotheses as to what had really happened, although he later suggested that 'the riddle of the Sphinx and the doctrine of the Trinity are simple and straightforward affairs compared with this double inquiry'.

In Masterman's first scenario, Owens was lying. He had not disclosed to Ritter that he was working under control. By telling MI5 that he *had*, he was looking for a way to retire from the game, with, as Liddell put it, 'a foot in both camps'. He could claim to whichever side ended up winning the war that he had done his bit for them.

In the second scenario, Owens was telling the truth. He *had* told Ritter that he was working under control, but Ritter could not openly acknowledge the fact for fear of losing prestige and position. He therefore sent *Snow* back to England with £10,000 as though nothing untoward had happened.

In the third scenario, Owens had told Ritter he was under control – whereupon Ritter converted Dicketts to the German cause. Dicketts was thus now working as a triple agent.

In the fourth scenario, Owens had actually gone over to the Germans previously and so was himself a long-standing triple agent. Either of the last two scenarios could explain why both agents came home safely.

In fact the truth is probably closer to a fifth scenario, set out in *The Game of the Foxes*, a book by Ladislas Farago published in 1971. Farago's version of the story contains some errors – the timing is out by several months and Walter Dicketts is confused with Sam McCarthy – but his portrayal of Nikolaus Ritter is vivid and convincing. As it should be: because Farago spoke to Ritter before writing the book and his version of events is based on Ritter's own memories. In Farago's account Owens admits to Ritter that he is under British control. The British have allowed him to travel to Lisbon, he says, in order to plant false information on the Germans. But Owens persuades Ritter that he is still a loyal German spy. And to prove it he is bringing Ritter a spy whom he has personally recruited, a cashiered British officer.

This, it seems, is essentially what happened. Arthur Owens was, for once, telling 'Tar' Robertson the truth. He *had* been forced to admit to Nikolaus Ritter that he was under British control. But he managed to convince Ritter that he was still a loyal German agent – and Ritter was prepared to believe him. As a result Ritter also believed that Owens had recruited Walter Dicketts in good faith, and that Dicketts was a genuine German agent. This is why Owens said to Dicketts, 'if it weren't for me, your life would be worth nothing' before Dicketts was taken to Germany. But Owens was still concerned that Dicketts might be broken under interrogation in Hamburg. If Dicketts revealed the truth about their mission, Owens would surely be killed. This accounts for Owens's worry while Dicketts was away and his relief on his safe return. And this scenario would explain why Ritter had asked Dicketts about Owens's connection with British intelligence and why he accepted Dicketts's reply that the less he knew the better.

But such an analysis is reliant on hindsight. In the spring of 1941 B1a had no such advantage. At a conference on 10 April attended by Robertson, Masterman and Liddell it was agreed that the only safe course to follow was to assume that Ritter knew that both Owens and Dicketts were double agents. On that reading, Owens could be of little further use. So several days later a message was sent from Owens's transmitter claiming that his health and nerves had collapsed and that he wanted to give up the game. The Germans replied, wishing him better, and hoping that he might one day be able to continue. This German reply could not have come from Ritter. Even as B1a was desperately trying to second-guess him, to work out what he knew and what he didn't know, he had already moved to another job. On 20 March he left the Hamburg Abwehrstelle, or bureau, for North Africa, where he was placed in charge of a special unit whose mission was to infiltrate spies into Egypt.

With the end of *Snow*, so came the end of *Celery* (Dicketts), *Biscuit* (McCarthy) and *Charlie* (Eschborn). As for the real Arthur Owens, he soon found himself interned in Camp 001, the hospital wing of Dartmoor Prison, until the end of the war. A narcissist and fantasist, Owens had been taking liberties with his handlers for almost five years, during which time they had consistently given him the benefit of any doubt. And so there was much irony in the fact that when he was finally interned it was as a result of telling the truth. Perhaps this irony occurred to Owens in Canada after the war when he tried, unsuccessfully, to bring a legal action against the British government for wrongful arrest relating to his internment. He died in Ireland in 1976.

In February 1942 J. C. Masterman presented a paper to the Twenty Committee in which he talked about *Summer*'s end and *Snow*'s fall. 'It was always a dicky period in our career,' he said, 'which we were never anxious to look at too closely.' With the arrival of a James Bond archetype, however, B1a's war was about to bear scrutiny again.

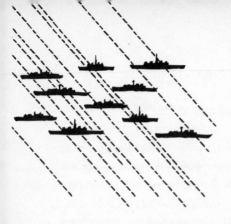

NOBODY DOES IT BETTER

As Dusko Popov left his apartment in the Palacio Hotel in Lisbon one evening in the summer of 1941, the breast pocket of his dinner jacket was bulging with tens of thousands of dollars. It was not his own money. It had been entrusted to him by the Abwehr – for whom he was a spy – to deposit in a New York bank account. But Popov was not going to follow these instructions. Because, unknown to the Abwehr, Popov was ultimately working for the British. He was one of B1a's double agents and his packets of cash were destined for an MI5 bank. In the meantime he felt safer keeping them in his pocket than drawing attention to them by placing them in the hotel's safe.

As Popov walked through the lobby of the Palacio he recognized a British intelligence officer. He paid the man little attention. Wartime Lisbon teemed with intelligence men of every conceivable allegiance. Popov walked to a café for a drink, where he spotted the officer again. He moved on to a restaurant for dinner, and the officer appeared once more. Popov was amused: British intelligence was keeping a close eye on the money.

After dinner Popov walked slowly through the manicured gardens leading to the Casino Estoril. Inside the gaming room he watched the tables for a while, as the officer lurked in the background. Popov soon noticed one of his least favourite characters, an arrogant little Lithuanian, playing baccarat. When the Lithuanian held the bank he refused to set a limit; Popov considered this unsporting behaviour. Sensing an opportunity for fun, he approached the table, reached inside his jacket, and placed down the bulk of the Abwehr money. 'Fifty thousand dollars!' he called out. As chatter in the room died away, he turned to see a look of horror on the British officer's face. But Popov knew that the Lithuanian, for all his bluster, could not meet the bet. And when he failed to do so, Popov feigned indignation with the croupier: 'I trust you'll call this to the attention of the management and that in future such irresponsible play will be prohibited!' He returned the Abwehr money to his pocket, pleased with his performance. The Lithuanian had been publicly shamed and British intelligence had been given a fright. Although when Popov looked again, the officer was smiling knowingly.

In his autobiography Popov claims that the officer was Ian Fleming. Popov was told that this incident had been the inspiration for the baccarat duel at the heart of *Casino Royale*, Fleming's first Bond novel. And perhaps it had. In a 1962 interview Fleming, a wartime Naval Intelligence officer, describes his experiences in the Casino Estoril as 'the kernel of James Bond's great gamble against Le Chiffre'. But whether or not Popov inspired Bond, he certainly shared some crucial traits with 007. They were both courageous and charming connoisseurs of the good life who enjoyed the 'company' of women. Popov was given two codenames by MI5, first *Skoot* and then *Tricycle*, and it has often been said – wrongly, unfortunately – that the name *Tricycle* derived from Popov's fondness for sexual threesomes. But while legends may have grown up around him, Dusko Popov was a very real figure. He was a Yugoslav business lawyer, one of the chief figures in Double

Cross, and the man who would lay much of B1a's groundwork for Operation Fortitude.

Dusko Popov's path to MI5's door can be traced back to his time studying at Freiburg University before the war. While there, he struck up a close friendship with a fellow student, Johnny Jebsen. A wealthy young German of Danish parentage, Jebsen had an ability to enthral others. One man touched by his charisma was Popov, who described him as 'a complete person, fun loving, woman loving, open to all conversations, and intensely curious about human reactions'. The two young men shared similar attitudes, most notably a dislike of Nazism. They enjoyed provoking the profoundly Nazi student body and Popov began openly criticizing the Nazi Party at public meetings. For this he paid the price: in 1937, shortly after completing his doctorate, he was arrested by the Gestapo and imprisoned in Freiburg, accused of being a communist and a defender of Jews. Fortunately Jebsen managed to contact Popov's father in Yugoslavia, who pleaded with the Yugoslav Prime Minister, who in turn approached Hermann Goering, Commander-in-Chief of the Luftwaffe, with the result that Popov was released on condition that he leave Germany immediately. He returned to Belgrade, his mind irreversibly set against Nazism.

Once the war was several months old, Jebsen came to Yugoslavia with news that shocked his friend. He had joined the Abwehr. Jebsen might have been anti-Nazi, but he was a pragmatist. He wanted to both avoid the armed services and be able to pursue his own increasingly dubious financial dealings. Life in the Abwehr offered him the connections and freedom necessary to do so. He attempted to justify his actions to Popov, saying, 'We may have to become part of Hitler's new world – or be crushed.' He also asked a favour of his friend. Would Popov, who was well connected in Yugoslav diplomatic circles, draft a paper for the Abwehr on the French politicians most likely to collaborate with the Nazis? Popov agreed, partly out of loyalty to Jebsen, but mainly because an idea was occurring to him. Once he had delivered the finished paper to Jebsen, he would also deliver it to the British embassy in Belgrade. He agreed to carry out the favour and duly took his report to the British First Secretary, who received it gladly, telling Popov to stay in touch with Jebsen. Popov had eased himself into the Double Cross world.

In the summer of 1940 Jebsen began visiting Belgrade regularly, on both Abwehr and personal financial business. On one visit he invited Popov to dinner with Major Ernst Müntzinger, Jebsen's Abwehr superior. During the meal Müntzinger praised Popov's paper and blamed his 'misadventure' in Freiburg on the zeal of the provincial Gestapo. He went on to make Popov an offer. 'We have many agents in England, some quite excellent,' said Müntzinger not entirely accurately, 'but we would like someone who has entry everywhere. Your connections could open many doors.' In fact Popov had virtually no connections in England, but Jebsen had exaggerated his friend's influence. 'You could do us a great service,' Müntzinger continued, 'and we could do the same for you.'

The major did not demand an immediate answer from Popov. After he had left, Jebsen explained that the Abwehr was desperately in need of an agent who could move in the upper echelons of British society. Evidently Arthur Owens was not being invited to dine with the Duke of Devonshire. Jebsen explained that he had initially suggested Popov for the role and that Abwehr headquarters in Berlin was now ordering him to recruit his friend. 'I hope you'll forgive me, Dusko,' said Jebsen. 'I'm using you. I'm sorry. I can't survive otherwise.' Jebsen needed to maintain his position in the Abwehr in order to continue his own business activities. But as they parted that evening Jebsen uttered a single sentence that suggested to Popov that his old anti-Nazi views were intact. 'If you want to destroy a team,' he said, 'the best way is to become part of it.'

Popov quickly decided that he would accept the offer – so long as the British would engage him as a double agent. And so on 26 July he went back to the British embassy to see the First Secretary. He was handed on to the chief of MI6 for the Balkans, who told him to agree to the German proposition. But Jebsen must know nothing of his connection with the British. 'He'll probably guess,' said Popov. 'Let him,' said the MI6 chief.

The chief also worked out a notional cover story for Popov to present to the Abwehr. In his capacity as a lawyer he would pretend to act for wealthy clients shipping goods from England to Yugoslavia. This would give him reason to move freely between the countries. And he was to suggest the existence of a friendly Yugoslav diplomat in London who could smuggle secret information back in the diplomatic bag. Popov met with Müntzinger again and a deal was agreed. He was now a German agent. Within a few days he was given a supply of secret ink and a long and thorough questionnaire which sought information on British invasion defences and the identities of significant British figures willing to negotiate with Hitler. From now on Popov would be known to the Germans by the code-name *Ivan*.

But as he hurried around Belgrade trying to set up a genuine import organization to serve as convincing cover, Popov's fledgling espionage activities were almost brought to a premature end. His chauffeur, Bozidar, was being surreptitiously paid by Müntzinger to draw up a list of every appointment he attended. And six of these appointments had been at a building known to the Abwehr as the headquarters of British Intelligence. Fortunately for Popov, Bozidar's list was first handed to Jebsen, who stopped it from reaching Müntzinger and rushed to warn his friend. This was only a temporary reprieve, however. Müntzinger was waiting for his list and he might, in the meantime, approach Bozidar directly.

Popov decided to give the chauffeur a chance to admit his betrayal. 'You don't have to drive me any more if you're tired,' Popov told him. 'I'll use taxis …' 'Oh, no, no, no,' said Bozidar quickly, 'I'm glad to be of service.' Satisfied that his man could not be trusted, Popov paid a visit to a rough part of Belgrade, where he found two thugs – both former clients he had represented on assault charges – who were prepared to commit murder. He told them that he was being blackmailed by his chauffeur, paid them well, and asked them to leave Bozidar's body in an obvious spot, as disappearances tended to provoke rigorous police investigations. The two men carried out their job well, making it look as though their victim had been shot dead while robbing a railway yard. The police investigated no further, and Jebsen was able to forward a falsified list of Popov's movements to Müntzinger.

Although Jebsen had seen the list of Popov's appointments and had acted quickly to protect him, Popov still felt that each meeting between them 'took place on a tightrope'. He still could not be *entirely* certain that Jebsen knew of his Double Cross game. For all the suggestions and insinuations, the two men never discussed the issue. It was too dangerous to broach just in case either was mistaken about the other.

In November permission finally arrived from Abwehr headquarters in Berlin for Popov to leave for England. He had first to travel to Lisbon, where he met Albrecht von Auenrode, the chief of the Lisbon Abwehr, who now became his principal spymaster. Auenrode was a charming and intelligent man with whom Popov was to develop a sincere rapport. 'I have been instructed to handle you with loving care,' said Auenrode at their first meeting. He personally instructed Popov in codes, mail drops and photography. One of Auenrode's photography tips was to pose a girl in espionage pictures. A man taking a picture of an installation was suspicious; a man taking a picture of a girl – with an installation in the background – was not. Auenrode also reeled off a list of further questions for Popov to answer in England, relating to the effects of bombing on the morale of the people and the kinds of propaganda which would have most effect on them.

Popov waited in Lisbon for several weeks for a seat to become available on a scheduled flight to England. For the vast majority of the war BOAC, the forerunner of British Airways, flew regular commercial flights between Lisbon and Bristol, using Dutch aircraft and aircrew stranded in England after the fall of Holland. Thanks to Portugal's neutrality, these flights were supposedly safe from Luftwaffe attack, although on 1 June 1943 Flight 777A was attacked and shot down by eight Junkers 88s. All those on board, including the English actor Leslie Howard, were killed.

Popov's flight went off without incident, however, and in December 1940 he landed at Whitchurch, outside Bristol. From there he was driven to the Savoy Hotel, his home for the next fortnight, where he was met by 'Tar' Robertson. Thanks to his dealings with MI6 in Belgrade, Popov was not subjected to the usual Camp 020 welcome. Nevertheless, he would later describe the Savoy as 'a gilded cage'. He might have been free to come and go as he pleased, but he was not yet trusted, and he was rigorously cross-questioned by MI5, MI6, Naval Intelligence and Air Intelligence. The authorities had to be certain that he was not a genuine German agent who had found a devilish way of slipping into the country.

In the event, Popov made an immediately favourable impression on Robertson and the other B1a members he met. 'His manner was absolutely frank,' wrote Robertson's deputy

John Marriott on 21 December, 'and we all considered without question that he was telling the truth.' Marriott's only reservation at this stage concerned Popov's still-shaky grasp of English. On Christmas Day Robertson took Popov to Quaglino's restaurant for a lunch of turkey with all the trimmings. In the afternoon they played billiards at the Lansdowne Club and that evening they went to the Suiva nightclub with a couple they had met earlier. Popov was being received in a very different manner to other double agents. Robertson had yet to take Wulf Schmidt dancing.

On New Year's Eve Popov was invited to a country-house weekend by Stewart Menzies, the chief of MI6, known as 'C'. While there, he was introduced to Friedl Gaertner, a beautiful Austrian singer and MI5 informant. Popov became infatuated with her on sight, which was convenient as Gaertner had been hand-picked to introduce Popov to the high-society figures whom the Abwehr believed he already knew. While Popov was busy flirting with Gaertner, Menzies dragged him off to a small study where he delivered a startling character assessment of B1a's newest double agent, intended as both an encouragement and a counsel. Menzies acknowledged Popov's intelligence and honesty, but noted that his honesty was without scruples. The Yugoslav was ambitious and ruthless, said 'C', but also capable of instinctive cruelty. 'You have the makings of a very good spy,' Menzies concluded, 'except that you don't like to obey orders. You had better learn or you will be a very dead spy.'

Popov was due to fly back to Portugal on 3 January, but before he went he met Naval Intelligence officer Ewen Montagu. Montagu told Popov to mention him to the Germans as one of his well-connected friends, with whom he shared a passion for sailing. He gave him a letter to show to Auenrode, in which Montagu invited Popov to bring his yacht to the

Solent after the war. And in his capacity as naval lieutenant commander Montagu 'told' him that British Atlantic convoys were in future to be accompanied by submarine escorts.

On his return to Lisbon Popov had a set of answers to the Abwehr's questions. From the airport he took a taxi to his apartment at the Palacio Hotel and telephoned Auenrode. The spymaster answered and the two men ran through an elaborate coded ritual which indicated where and when they would meet. At the appointed time Auenrode collected Popov in a borrowed car. With the Yugoslav lying on the back seat, Auenrode drove to one of his several houses, where they had dinner. The following day the full debriefing took place. Over a day and an evening Popov gave Auenrode every detail of his time in England – or at least every detail that was fit for Abwehr ears – as well as the misinformation that he was intended to pass on. To sit for hours under close questioning, passing across a complicated blend of truth and lies, required focus and nerve. But it was to become as routine an event for Popov as boarding the Lisbon to Bristol flight.

The following day Auenrode went to Paris to deliver Popov's report to his superiors. When he returned he delivered their verdict to Popov: his report had lacked detail. Auenrode advised him to report on fewer topics in greater depth. But there was no suggestion that his loyalty was being doubted.

Before Popov left Lisbon to return to London, Auenrode handed him his new questionnaire. It was an extremely long list of questions. 'You'll soon want to know what Churchill had for dinner,' Popov noted drily. The questionnaire – with added notes and observations for MI5's benefit – was still in his jacket pocket the following night when he went for a drink in the Casino nightclub with a French marquise named Pinta de la Rocque. Looking around the crowded club, Popov noticed a familiar face. It belonged to a man who had been tailing him for several days. This shadow might have been British or German, but his persistence frustrated Popov. He had been enjoying his evening with Pinta.

Perhaps unwisely, Popov decided to release his frustration on a drunk woman who, despite being tone-deaf, had decided to get up and sing with the dance band. The woman had arrived at the club with the *Daily Mail*'s Lisbon correspondent, but was now spending far too long at the microphone. Popov called a waiter over, placed a champagne cork on his silver tray, and asked him to deliver it to the singer with his compliments. The waiter did exactly as he was told, but the woman did not use the cork as Popov hoped she would. Instead, fired up with alcohol and indignation, she ran full tilt at Popov's table. Picking up a champagne glass, she thrust it towards Pinta's face. Popov caught the woman's arm in time and pushed her back towards her own table. 'Be a good girl, now,' he said, patting her backside.

This enraged the *Daily Mail* correspondent. He was wearing a plaster cast on his arm, but he came over and swung a punch at Popov with his free arm. Popov ducked out of the way, then knocked the journalist down with a jab to the jaw. Aware of the chaos about to erupt, he slipped the questionnaire into Pinta's purse, and told her to go to the lobby of the Palacio, where he would catch up with her. Meanwhile another member of the *Daily Mail* party, an American, was on his way over. He accused Popov of being a Nazi, and a 'fucking coward' for hitting a man with a broken arm. As the American was speaking, Popov noticed Pinta being followed out of the room by the shadow. Whomever this man was working for, he had obviously seen what Popov had done with the questionnaire. Popov blocked the American's attack by forcing a table at him. The shenanigans continued as Popov dived out of the club and ran towards the hotel. In front of him he could see two people – Pinta and the shadow – wrestling on the ground. The shadow was trying to grab the purse. Just as he was pulling it away from Pinta, Popov hurtled towards him and kicked him in the head as hard as he could. The shadow was out cold, blood everywhere. Popov took back his questionnaire.

The English manager of the Palacio, a man Popov had befriended, was first on the scene and promised to take care of the situation. Popov escorted Pinta up to her room, where the two of them stayed until noon the next day. Popov later discovered that the shadow had been working for Albrecht Kramer, the head of Abwehr counter-intelligence in Lisbon. Kramer claimed that the man had been there for Popov's 'protection', to ensure that the British were not following him. When he had seen Popov give Pinta the questionnaire, he had leapt into action because *she*, unknown to Popov, might have been working for the enemy. Who in Lisbon, after all, could be trusted? Had Kramer and Auenrode seen the additions that Popov had made to the questionnaire for MI5's benefit – as they so nearly had – it would have become quite clear whom *they* could not trust.

When Popov arrived back in England on 4 February the carousel had revolved. He was now under close scrutiny by MI5, which had begun to have doubts about him in his absence. The organization was concerned that it had welcomed him on board too casually, without subjecting him to the usual scrutiny. The man designated to be his case officer, Bill Luke, worried about his ability to lie so convincingly. He had apparently convinced the Germans that he was well connected in England, a country where he barely knew anybody. Was he lying equally convincingly to the other side? It was decided that Luke should accompany Popov on an extensive trip to Scotland. Ostensibly its purpose would be to collect chickenfood for Auenrode. Unknown to Popov, however, it would allow Luke the time to make an informed decision about his bona fides.

Popov travelled to Glasgow, where he met up with Luke and Luke's brother, a linguist who could gauge Popov's self-professed fluency in French, German and Italian. Popov passed his language test and he and Luke went on to spend a number of days sightseeing, spying and drinking. With a Leica camera given to Popov by Auenrode, they visited such attractions as Loch Lomond, Edinburgh Castle, the Firth of Forth and numerous pubs. Popov described to Luke in impassioned terms his hatred for the Nazis and his belief that Germany would lose the war. He explained why he wanted to get his export business started. Not only would a real business serve as better cover for his activities than a notional one, but Yugoslavia desperately needed the goods he could provide from England. In addition, Popov admitted, he wanted an income to supplement his Abwehr wages. His lifestyle, after all, was not a cheap one – and he was not asking for payment from MI5.

A problem arrived on the last day of the trip, after they had booked into the Caledonian Hotel in the centre of Edinburgh. Popov did not have the permission necessary for an alien to stay in the city and two policemen showed up with the intention of interviewing him. Luke tried to intervene, but a whispered word to the police that he was working for MI5 did not help. Finally a telephone call to the Chief Constable of Glasgow resolved the problem. Popov was allowed to stay one night in Edinburgh before his return to London.

By the end of their journey Bill Luke's fears about Popov's loyalties had been dispelled. In an internal memo of 23 February he wrote: 'I have come to the conclusion that he is definitely working for us and not for the Germans.' Popov was 'clever, versatile and firm of purpose' and had 'personality and charm'. Luke praised 'the valuable gratuitous service which he is rendering this country'. But he added a pointed rider. Observing that Popov had been brought up in an atmosphere of comfort and ease, he noted that 'he is inherently lazy and shows absolutely no desire to obtain information for the enemy or to exert himself in connection with his work'. The last comment reads like a school report. In a sense, it was. Popov was B1a's most promising pupil and it was Luke's job, as his tutor, to help him to achieve his potential. But Popov, like a petulant teenager, may have felt that it was not *his* job to gather the information. It was B1a's job. Popov, after all, had the difficult and dangerous job of delivering it to the Abwehr. Why should he have to exert himself to find it?

But if Luke felt that Popov was not pulling his weight, the feeling was soon mutual. In early March, Popov expressed his anger at B1a during a dinner with Luke. The answers to the Germans' latest questionnaire were slow in coming, and those that had arrived were vague and general. This was precisely the weakness that Auenrode had warned him against in Lisbon. Luke tried to calm the Yugoslav by telling him that the Germans would suspect overly detailed answers. Popov disagreed. With his supposed high-level contacts, he felt, he ought to be able to uncover good and precise information.

As time went by, Popov and Luke would ease into their respective roles. B1a did its best to provide Popov (and the other double agents) with good chickenfood and misinformation, and Popov took responsibility for finding more of his own material. Luke often came with Popov on his fact-finding missions to make sure that he was following instructions. But there was another reason for Luke's presence. Popov, like Walter Dicketts, had a photographic memory. He tended to remember everything he saw with vivid clarity, but not everything he saw was suitable to be passed on to Auenrode. So Popov would travel to his espionage objective, absorbing everything along the way. At the destination, however, he would excuse himself while Luke took photographs, which would later be retouched and shown to Popov. In this way he only actually saw what he was meant to see, but still had plenty of colourful detail to pass to Auenrode.

In the meantime Luke and 'Tar' Robertson decided that Popov's cover story should be turned into a real enterprise. The extra money would undoubtedly raise Popov's morale, and if he was unquestionably doing what he said he was doing, the Germans would be less likely to suspect his other activities. The import-export business was set up in an office on Regent Street in London's West End. A plaque outside the building gave the company's name, 'Tarlair Ltd', a cheeky nod to Robertson. But in order for Popov to be able to ship goods to Yugoslavia, British Navy Certificates had to be granted to him. In the ordinary course of things these were very hard to come by, but Popov's special role meant that they were granted without question. This confused the Yugoslav ambassador to Britain, Ivan Subbotic, who was unaware that Popov was a British agent. At lunch one day the ambassador asked Popov whom he was bribing. 'Come now, Subbotic,' said Popov, 'one doesn't bribe the British Admiralty.' A row developed which culminated in Popov telling the ambassador to 'stop being an ass'.

The groundwork was being effectively laid for Popov to become a supremely effective double agent – one who would be sufficiently trusted by the Germans to pass over the strategic deception for which B1a was preparing. But as yet he was a lone wolf without a pack to share his burden. Robertson wanted to develop a network of agents around him. To this end Popov was told to offer candidates to Auenrode at their next meeting. B1a's first nominee was Friedl Gaertner; she was Austrian and her father had been a member of the Nazi Party. The irrepressible Popov was already intimate with her in one sense. He would find it no hardship to formalise their relationship. B1a's other suggested candidate was Dickie Metcalfe, a Foreign Office intelligence officer who had resigned his army commission before the war. Popov was to describe him to Auenrode as a cashiered ex-army officer with a grudge against the military establishment.

With sufficiently detailed answers to Auenrode's questionnaire in place, two sub-agents to offer him, and a real import-export business to run, Popov was ready to return to Lisbon. Many years later he would describe his wartime existence as an 'Alice in Wonderland experience, passing from one world to another, except that in this case both worlds were abnormal'. Popov had always to remember where he was and which part he was playing. His psychological strength allowed him to endure this dangerous and schizophrenic existence. Had Albrecht Kramer seen the notes on his questionnaire, or had Major Müntzinger discovered his links with MI6, he would have fallen again into the hands of the Gestapo. And Johnny Jebsen could not have saved him a second time.

The day before Popov left for Portugal, Robertson had money delivered to the Savoy so that the Yugoslav could pay his hefty bill. Once in Lisbon Popov delivered his latest report and suggested Gaertner and Metcalfe to Auenrode as agents. Both were duly engaged by the Abwehr. As head of a three-strong network, Popov's British codename was changed to *Tricycle*. Metcalfe, a rather stout man, became *Balloon*, and Gaertner became *Gelatine* – a truncated version of 'jolly little thing'. Popov was evidently not alone in recognising her charms.

With the birth of the *Tricycle* network B1a's strength and potential increased. Half of the double agents who were to pass across the Fortitude deception were now in place. But not every spy who came to England was turned into a double agent. Some were executed, others were imprisoned. And then, as we shall see, there was Engelbertus Fukken.

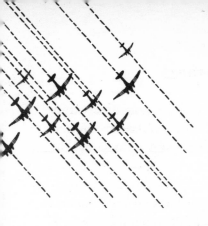

DEALER, SAILOR, DENTIST, SPY

For all MI5's success in catching spies, turning them and running them, the occasional enemy agent eluded their grasp. And the British public could not *always* be relied upon to sniff out the strays.

Between October 1939 and April 1940 Albert Meems, a 52-year-old Dutchman, made four visits to England, staying on each occasion at the Grafton Hotel on Tottenham Court Road. Meems was a dealer in livestock, who spent much of his time in India sourcing exotic animals for European zoos. He was a short, overweight man with facial features reminiscent of a toad. According to an acquaintance, he was a 'clumsy, bluff, half-educated fellow who spoke English, German and Dutch all mixed together' and who could be 'a most amusing and companionable man with an endless fund of tales on the tricks of the trade'. But Meems's trade was not merely in animals. It was also in information. He had been a spy for the Germans during the Great War, and in 1938 he became an agent for Nest Bremen, a one-time outpost of the Hamburg Abwehr.

In April 1940, just after Meems had made his final visit to England, the Metropolitan Police were approached by an English animal dealer whom the Dutchman had contacted during his stay. This dealer, Mr Howard, had known Meems for thirty years and was aware that he had spied for the Germans in the last war. As Britain's international livestock trade had been halted by the present war, Howard suspected that Meems had 'come to this country for the purposes of espionage'.

Howard's suspicions were confirmed after the war. Nest Bremen records captured by the Allies contain evidence of Meems's spying activities in England. But Meems seems not to have been a particularly effective agent. Emil Genue, an American recruited into the Abwehr in 1940, told his Allied captors in 1944 that Meems had been given a mission to report on matters of military interest. But, said Genue, 'he was too little informed on military matters to be able to report anything extraordinary'.

Another spy who escaped capture was Wilhelm Mörz. A sinister-looking individual with a long face and dark hooded eyes, Mörz had been arrested as a German spy in Holland shortly before the German occupation, but had escaped in the ensuing confusion. On the afternoon of 25 May 1940 he was identified climbing into a taxi on Regent Street by an agent of the Czech intelligence service. A search was immediately mounted by Special Branch and a photograph of Mörz was circulated. The picture was recognized by a member of staff at the Cumberland Hotel on Oxford Street. A trail led detectives to nightclub 'hostess' Dawn Karlen, who remembered taking Mörz to her flat. Mörz, it seemed, had been posing as a refugee named Nowak. But the trail went cold despite numerous alleged sightings around the country and a dozen fruitless arrests. On one occasion Dick White, Guy Liddell's deputy in 'B' Division, thought he recognized the spy working as a waiter in a Chinese restaurant on Piccadilly Circus. 'On examination,' wrote White in MI5's case file, 'the waiter did not turn out to be Mörz.' The case was finally closed in August 1941.

The spy who seems to have evaded capture for the longest period was the strikingly named Engelbertus Fukken, a 25-year-old Dutchman who parachuted into Buckinghamshire in the early hours of 3 November 1940. Fukken remained at liberty for almost five months. But on the morning of 1 April 1941 his body was found in a Cambridge air-raid shelter. He was lying dead in a pool of blood with a revolver at his side.

Before going to England, Fukken had been living in Noord-wijt in Holland. Trained as a radio operator, he had been unemployed for some time and twice imprisoned for theft. In July 1940 he told his fiancée that he was leaving Holland for France. She had no idea of the job upon which he was embarking.

On 4 November, Fukken arrived in Cambridge posing as a Dutch refugee named Jan Willem Ter Braak. The Abwehr had furnished him with a British identity card supplied to them by Arthur Owens, and it contained a number of errors marking it out as an obvious forgery. Had Fukken registered with the police, as aliens were obliged to do, he would almost certainly have been identified as an agent. But he never registered. Shortly after his arrival he rented a room from Mr and Mrs Sennitt in Barnabas Road. Mrs Sennitt cleaned his room every day and noticed that he always kept his cupboard locked. There was a good reason for this – it contained an Abwehr wireless set – but the Sennitts had no initial suspicions of their lodger. In fact they seem to have appreciated his company, spending their evenings playing cards and darts together. He said that he was connected with the Dutch Free Forces and expressed a bitter hatred for the Germans. One day a week, he told them, he travelled to London to work for a Dutch-language newspaper.

Early in his stay Fukken handed Mr Sennitt an out-of-date ration book supplied by the Abwehr. Mr Sennitt went to the

Food Office in Cambridge on his lodger's behalf and obtained an emergency card, while Fukken supposedly applied for a new book. When no replacement was forthcoming almost three months later, Mrs Sennitt told him to visit the Food Officer. The suggestion visibly agitated Fukken, but he promised to do as he was told. His anxiety was hardly surprising, for a visit to the Food Office would have alerted the authorities to his existence. The next morning he told the Sennitts that he had been called to London by his employers on the newspaper. But he did not go to London: instead he moved to different lodgings on Montague Road.

Fukken's new landlady, Miss Greenwood, thought him a 'nice young man', but he had only been staying with her for a few days when Mrs Sennitt met him in the town. He told her that he was back in Cambridge for a quick visit, but his former landlady was suspicious. She had already informed the local Aliens' Officer of Fukken's anxiety on being told to visit the Food Office, and she now informed the officer that he had lied about leaving Cambridge. But the officer failed to make enquiries on either occasion.

Fukken might have been safe from the authorities for the time being, but he had another, very pressing problem. His money was running out. He was paying rent, buying clothes, using trains and buses, hiring an office (which he only visited on two occasions), and having lunch almost every day at the Dorothy Café on Bridge Street, where on his first visit he nervously asked the waitress to bring him whatever she would order herself. Clearly Fukken could not apply for a job, so unless the Abwehr provided him with some money he would very soon be destitute.

On the morning of 29 March he had breakfast with his landlady as usual. She went off to the butcher's and while she was gone he packed up his belongings, including the wireless set. Underneath his clothes he put on four woollen vests and two pairs of long woollen pants. When Miss Greenwood returned he was ready to leave. He told her that he was going to the coast to join up with the Dutch Free Forces and gave her his front-door key. He would, he said, return the following weekend. He then went to Cambridge railway station, deposited his cases in a locker, and returned to the town. Nothing is known of his subsequent movements, except that, at some point on 31 March, he shot himself in the head in a newly constructed air-raid shelter at Christ's Pieces.

Engelbertus Fukken might have evaded capture for almost five months, but it is not clear whether he actually made contact with the Germans during this time. Nor is it clear what he did between leaving the railway station and killing himself. In an MI5 document dated 10 September 1941, John Gwyer of B1b (the Enemy Analysis unit) offers answers to these questions. Fukken, he submits, *had* been in wireless contact with the Abwehr from the time of his arrival until the radio set's battery ran down. Once the set was out of action, Fukken had written to the Abwehr in secret ink, asking for a new battery and for money to be sent. Gwyer continues: 'To these requests he received a reply to the effect that another man was landing by parachute in the neighbourhood of Cambridge round about March 29th. [Fukken] endeavoured to keep this rendezvous on the night of the 29th and again on the night of the 30th. Nobody came, and realizing that he had by then not even the price of a meal in his pocket and no means of eating without a Ration Book except at a restaurant, he shot himself early on the morning of the 31st.' Gwyer's hypothesis fits the known facts, but it is ultimately only speculation.

In his history of Camp 020 'Tin Eye' Stephens describes Fukken's death in characteristically sensitive fashion: 'In some access of conscience or fear, [he] finally decided during the month of April spectacularly to announce his presence.' But at least one person *was* genuinely affected by the episode – when she learned of it some years later. In 1947 MI5 was asked by the Dutch government whether an official statement could be made to the effect that Engelbertus Fukken was dead. The government's inquiry was being made on behalf of Miss Eeltje van Roon, Fukken's fiancée. She wanted to know where he was buried and whether he had left any personal belongings. And she also wanted to reclaim the insurance premiums that she had been paying on his behalf since July 1940.

On the same day that Fukken changed lodgings in Cambridge, a new candidate for the Double Cross system parachuted into England. At twenty past eight on the morning of 1 February 1941 Charles Baldock, a smallholder from Warboys in Huntingdonshire, was walking to work with his friend Harry Coulson, when they heard what sounded like revolver shots nearby. They walked in the direction of the noise but saw nothing. They heard another four shots, and then two more, and eventually they came upon a man lying in a field. Baldock approached the man, calling out to him not to shoot. The man put his hands up and threw his revolver into a nearby steel helmet. As Baldock drew nearer he found that the man was lying underneath a camouflaged parachute. Around him were the torn pieces of a cardboard cipher disc. 'What have you been up to?' asked Baldock. 'Solo flying,' said the man. 'Where are you from?' 'Hamburg. I am in no war.' The man pointed to his leg and said, 'Broken.' Coulson went off to get assistance, and three members of the Home Guard, formerly known as the Local Defence Volunteers, arrived. As they moved the man they spotted a fake crocodile-skin attaché case buried in the ground, one of its corners protruding.

The man was Josef Jakobs, a 42-year-old German dentist whose life had taken a series of unpredictable turns. Educated in a Dominican monastery, he served in the Great War, earning an Iron Cross First Class. In 1925 he qualified as a dentist and then practised in Berlin for nine years. In 1934 he was imprisoned in Switzerland for selling adulterated gold for use in dental work. On his release he returned to Germany, where he began procuring false passports for Jews and assisting the removal of Jewish capital from Germany – at significant financial gain to himself. When his activities were discovered he was sent to Oranienburg concentration camp, where he remained for eighteen months. He then joined the meteorological section of the Luftwaffe, before being approached by the Abwehr and agreeing to undertake a spying mission in England.

When he was found by Baldock and Coulson on the morning of 1 February, Jakobs had been lying in the field for over twelve hours. Despite his broken leg, he had gone to great lengths to bury his case, which contained a transmitter. Covered by his parachute, he had passed the night drifting in and out of consciousness. As Baldock and Coulson approached, he had quickly ripped up his disc code, and scattered it around him. The men placed him on a cart and delivered him to the police station at Ramsey. MI5 was quickly alerted to his presence and his possessions were noted: a touring map of England, a dictionary, two identity cards, a ration book, and £497 in £1 notes.

Having been certified fit to travel by a doctor, Jakobs was taken to Cannon Row Police Station, where he was handed over to 'Tar' Robertson, before being sent to Camp 020. At 020 'Tin Eye' Stephens had limited time to interrogate Jakobs, who was in urgent need of medical treatment. But Jakobs told the commandant that his intention in coming to England was to escape to the United States. Stephens noted in his report that 'properly handled, he will prove a more amenable Double Cross agent than others we have handled in the past'. And he seemed willing to do MI5's bidding. 'I obtained an acceptance of my demand,' wrote Stephens, 'that this man should work as the servant of his captors.'

The spying dentist was taken off to hospital, where his condition steadily worsened. He contracted bronchopneumonia, while the splintered bones in his ankle turned septic, necessitating an operation. His doctor's refusal to return him immediately to Camp 020 infuriated Stephens, who felt 'checkmated by the humanitarian motives of the medical profession'. It fell to Dr Dearden, the camp's psychiatrist, to point out that 'to transfer him now might well jeopardize his survival, and thus destroy his usefulness for Intelligence purposes'.

As Stephens itched for Jakobs's return, the story of his capture was becoming alarmingly well known in Huntingdonshire circles. The local MI5 representative wrote to B1a deprecating 'the inability of the Home Guard to keep their mouths shut'. The local commander had been heard telling the tale to guests at a cocktail party at Hinchingbrooke House, the home of the Earl of Sandwich. And a letter written by a local woman to a friend in California was intercepted. 'A German landed by parachute in the Acre Fen,' wrote the woman, 'his ankle was broken (it's a pity it wasn't his neck says I!).' Such publicity jeopardized Jakobs's use as a double agent.

The spy returned on 15 April to 020, where Stephens's breakers were finally able to sink their teeth into their prey. But Jakobs had changed his story. Whereas on 2 February he had expressed his desire to go to America, he now said that he had come to England to assist the fight against the Nazis and to make connections between British Jews and a secret anti-Nazi movement in Germany. He gave the name of a Jewish immigrant, recently arrived in Britain, who could vouch for his anti-Nazi credentials. But when the immigrant, Lily Knips, was interviewed, she gave a rather different impression: she described Jakobs as a man whose motive for helping Jews had been solidly financial.

Why, wondered Stephens, had Jakobs not mentioned his ideological purpose from the beginning? Why had he destroyed his code shortly before his discovery? And why was he, even now, offering information so unwillingly? The reasons, submitted Stephens, 'were obvious'. Jakobs was a 'scrofulous Nazi' who remained unbroken and feared the imminent success of Germany. 'He is telling us just so much of the truth as will keep us content,' wrote the commandant, 'hoping against hope for the success of invasion.' In Stephens's view, 'the last thing he would do would be effectively to assist this country'.

Nevertheless, the interrogation of Jakobs continued, and on 29 April he provided an important piece of information. He was asked about a German spy who was expected to arrive in the country shortly. This spy was described as being tall and blond with blue eyes and a wart over his right eye. Jakobs remembered a man being trained up as an agent who fitted this description. His name, he said, was Richter.

But how did MI5 know so much about this spy? The answer is testament to B1a's growing strength and worth: the Abwehr had sent his physical description and notice of his imminent arrival to Wulf Schmidt, otherwise known as British double agent *Tate*. Schmidt, who shared a case officer, Bill Luke, with Dusko Popov, was steadily earning B1a's trust.

A problem had arisen, however. Arthur Owens, as we have seen, had told Nikolaus Ritter in Lisbon that he had been under British control for several months. During those months Owens had made a number of references to Schmidt in his wireless transmissions. Surely the Germans would conclude that Schmidt was also under British control? And so, in March

1941, it was decided to test the Germans' belief in Schmidt: he would make urgent requests for money, saying that if he received none he would cease his efforts on Germany's behalf. The response to these requests would reveal the Abwehr's level of trust in him.

The Germans' response to the requests was encouraging. They were clearly intent on sending money to Schmidt. He was not going to be abandoned to a Fukken-style fate. On 19 April he received an Abwehr message instructing him to go on certain days to the Regent Palace Hotel in London, where he would be met by a tall, blond, blue-eyed man with a wart. *This* was the information put to Josef Jakobs, eliciting the name Richter. On 14 May, Schmidt received another message telling him that the blue-eyed man had now departed for England and that he would hopefully make the rendezvous as arranged. The spy, Karel Richter, had indeed been dropped by aircraft into a field in Hertfordshire with instructions to deliver a large sum money to Schmidt. But he did not make the rendezvous. Within days he had been arrested and delivered to Stephens at Camp 020.

So far as the Germans were concerned Karel Richter's inexplicable failure to attend the rendezvous meant that Schmidt was still without money. Schmidt reminded the Abwehr of the fact with a characteristic rocket: 'I shit on Germany and its whole fucking secret service.' The substance of Schmidt's messages might come from B1a, but the wording was always Schmidt's own. And so the Germans came up with a new plan to provide him with money, enlisting the assistance of the Japanese embassy in London. Schmidt was instructed to go to the Number 16 bus stop at Victoria Station at 4 p.m. on 29 May. A Japanese man would be waiting at the stop. Both men were to board the bus and alight at Park Lane. They were then to board the next Number 16, and the Japanese man was to hand Schmidt a copy of *The Times* in which money was concealed. The day before the planned transaction, the Abwehr attempted to lift Schmidt's spirits. 'We will help you whatever happens,' he was told.

In the event, the plan almost failed. The Japanese man, Assistant Naval Attaché Mitinori Yosii, got off the first bus at a crossroads on Park Lane, thinking he was at a bus stop. He stood on the pavement as three Number 16s went past. Eventually Yosii realized his mistake and moved to the stop, where the two men boarded the next bus together and sat down. Schmidt asked the naval attaché if he could borrow his newspaper. Yosii said that he could keep it and immediately got off the bus. Inside *The Times* were 200 £1 notes wrapped in paper. It appeared that Schmidt *was* trusted by the Abwehr. That night he wired a message to Hamburg: 'Won't be reporting for a couple of days. I'm getting drunk tonight.'

In the meantime Karel Richter, the man who had been supposed to meet Schmidt at the Regent Palace Hotel, was under intense interrogation at Camp 020. Richter was a 29-year-old merchant seaman from the Sudetenland. In August 1939, deciding that he wanted nothing to do with the imminent war, he deserted his ship in Hamburg and made his way to Sweden, where he was interned and subsequently deported back to Hamburg. Falling into the hands of the Gestapo, he was branded a deserter and imprisoned in Fuhlsbüttel concentration camp. He was later to write that his time in Fuhlsbüttel 'burnt itself into my soul and will always burn there'. While there, he was made to assist with the defusing of delayed-action bombs, and it may have been for this reason that he was called into a room one day and introduced to Hauptmann Bruhns, the man responsible for much of the training of Gösta Caroli and Wulf Schmidt. Bruhns was visiting the camp looking for potential spies. He flattered Richter, telling him that he was young, intelligent and brave, and offered him his freedom in return for the performance of 'especially dangerous work on behalf of Germany'. Richter accepted the offer and signed a form which stipulated that any betrayal of Germany would result in reprisals against his family in the Sudetenland.

Richter was trained by Bruhns – but was ultimately rejected for the proposed mission; his Morse transmission speed was unsatisfactory. He was then taken under the wing of Walter Praetorius, who earmarked him for another mission: the delivery of cash to Wulf Schmidt. The initial plan was to bring Richter to England by boat. On 9 May, setting out from Delfzijl in Holland, a motor launch brought him to within eight miles of the English shore, but the swell was too strong to make a safe landing and the launch returned to Delfzijl. Two days later he was handed over to Karl Gartenfeld, who had already flown Gösta Caroli and Josef Jakobs to England. In the early hours of 12 May the two men took off from Amsterdam. Richter's destination was the outskirts of Cambridge and after a flight of almost two hours Gartenfeld told him that they had arrived. Richter jumped, only narrowly avoiding some rooftops. A last-minute gust of wind blew him into a field. But Gartenfeld's navigation had been out by almost forty miles. Richter was actually near London Colney in Hertfordshire.

After a clean landing Richter hid his parachute, overalls and emergency rations in a hedgerow. He wandered a little way away – carrying his radio set – but for the next three days he was too nervous to move again. During this time he ate only a piece of chocolate and, out of sheer desperation, some damp grass. Eventually he stepped onto a road and was almost immediately stopped and asked directions by a lorry driver. Richter, whose ability to assist the driver was hampered by hunger, exhaustion and a belief that he was near Cambridge, said that he was a foreigner and wanted to go to a hospital. The lorry driver drove on until he found a police officer who could give him directions. As an afterthought, the driver mentioned the confused foreigner he had met further down the road. The officer hurried to catch up with Richter, who repeated his story that he was ill and in need of medical treatment. The officer then asked him for his Aliens' Registration Card. Unaware of the existence of such a thing, Richter produced an Identity Card instead. When the policeman asked where he had come from, he replied, 'Ipswich.' He then said that he had been to Cromer, Norwich, Cambridge and Bury St Edmunds and was now on his way back to Cambridge. The bemused Hertfordshire constable asked Richter to accompany him to the police station in Fleetville. There his Czech passport revealed his real name to be quite different from the name on his Identity Card.

It was not long before Richter was on his way to Camp 020. MI5 might have been tipped off about his arrival, but the spy's capture had more to do with his own ineptitude and the Abwehr's inefficiency than British Secret Service cunning. Even had he managed to make his rendezvous with Schmidt at the Regent Palace Hotel, his chances of survival as an agent would have been slim. The Abwehr had provided him with a wireless set that was unusable without the purchase of further equipment and secret ink that required the addition of a chemical available only to those who had signed the poison book.

At Camp 020 Richter proved to be 'one of the more difficult types in interrogation', according to an internal report. He stubbornly refused to make an admission and informed his interrogators that he would soon be on the other side of the desk. This attitude may have been less a reflection of his loyalty to the Nazis than a genuine fear of what they would do to him and his family if he was found to be collaborating with the British. But the success of such an attitude depended on the imminent arrival of the German invaders – and it certainly failed to endear him to Stephens. During these arrogant and obstinate days Richter's fate was effectively sealed.

His attitude changed, however, after the application of two of Stephens's trademark strategies. The first was the 'cross-ruff'. This involved a series of staged confrontations between Richter and a carefully briefed Josef Jakobs, who undermined him by revealing information about their shared training. The second was being placed into the notorious Cell Fourteen. After these experiences Richter began to reveal the truth about his past and his present mission. Information came slowly but for the most part accurately. He gave a true account of his arrival in England and he agreed to take his captors to the spot where his belongings were hidden. Stephens led a little party to a Hertfordshire field where Richter pointed them towards his equipment. In his history of Camp 020 Stephens recalls that an unconcerned group was having a picnic only yards away. A little girl was overheard asking her mother what the soldiers were doing. 'Never you mind, dearie,' said her mother. 'You never know what the military are up to next.'

Richter's most important revelation related to the purpose of his mission. Not only was he to deliver money to Schmidt, he was also to ascertain whether Schmidt was under British control. He was then to return to Holland to deliver this information personally to Walter Praetorius. Praetorius had told him that Schmidt was the 'pearl' of German agents and that if *he* were false the entire string would be equally false. Praetorius was, of course, correct to be suspicious of Schmidt, but his suspicions had a surprising source. They did not arise out of messages sent by Arthur Owens, but apparently from a single message sent by Schmidt the previous Christmas in which he had offered his greetings to 'the people at the Phoenix Hotel'. The Phoenix was the hotel in Hamburg where Schmidt and Caroli had stayed and received much of their training. Praetorius was adamant, said Richter, that no real German agent would have referred in so many words to such a sensitive location. But the fact that Schmidt was under British control had had no bearing on his choice of words. Wireless candour was simply his style.

By the time Richter made this revelation the decision had been taken to prosecute him under the Treachery Act. 'Richter is quite reconciled to his eventual death by hanging,' states an MI5 résumé of the case three months before his trial had even begun. He was to become somewhat less reconciled as time went along.

From late April onwards, Josef Jakobs had started to cooperate more fully with his interrogators. Stating that he was willing to work loyally for Britain, he had revealed the identity of Karel Richter and agreed to perform the 'cross-ruff'. But pity was not stirred in the heart of 'Tin Eye' Stephens. On 30 April the commandant wrote: 'It may be that [Jakobs] thinks he is building up our confidence, and so long as he remains under that preposterous illusion, we are likely to get further information from him from time to time.' On 24 July the only wartime spy qualified to perform bridgework was formally charged with treachery under the Act. 'I have nothing to fear,' he replied when the charge was read to him. Unlike every other wartime prisoner charged under the Act, Jakobs was not to be tried by a judge and jury. As a member of the German armed forces he would be tried by General Court Martial. The basic form of a court martial was similar to that of a criminal trial. But instead of a judge ruling on matters of law and a jury deciding on matters of fact, the trial would be presided over by a legally trained judge advocate while the defendant's guilt or innocence would be determined by a number of senior military figures, in Jakobs's case four.

Jakobs's trial began on 4 August and lasted for two days. In the course of his evidence he stated that his grandfather was a Jew and that the Nazi Party was the misfortune of Germany. He described the secret anti-Nazi movement which he claimed he became involved with in Oranienburg concentration camp, and he stressed the fact that his intention in coming to England had been to help England against the Nazis and to forge connections between English Jews and the German anti-Nazi movement. He was asked why he had not mentioned this intention either to 'Tar' Robertson at Cannon Row Police Station or during his first interrogation at Camp 020. 'It was too painful for me away from the hospital,' he replied. 'I have had many strong pains.' Why had he buried his transmitter? 'Because I was afraid the men who found me with a wireless would say "There is a Nazi spy" straight away ... I was going to hand it over to the English authorities.' When asked why he had torn up his disc code as the smallholders approached, he replied, 'You must consider I was lying with very, very heavy pains and I do not say what happened.' 'Lost your head, do you mean?' prompted his counsel. 'Yes,' said Jakobs, 'because of cold and pains and my hope that I had to work for you was finished.'

In cross-examination it was put to him that he had been serving his German masters faithfully. 'Never,' he replied. 'If that was so I should have destroyed the wireless apparatus and myself. You never hear from me no more.' Before the court closed to consider its finding, Jakobs was asked whether he had anything more that he wished to add. 'Except when the court find me not guilty I will do all I can to help England,' he replied. 'More I cannot say.'

The court did not find him not guilty. After a very short adjournment Jakobs was convicted of treachery and sentenced to death. Had he been convicted by a criminal court, he would have been hanged, but the penalty imposed by a court martial was shooting. Josef Jakobs faced a firing squad of the Holding Battalion of the Scots Guards on 15 August at the Tower of London. His last words were to tell the soldiers to shoot straight.

When Karel Richter, awaiting his own trial, was told that Jakobs had been executed, he responded despairingly. 'I no longer know what to think,' he wrote to Major Short, Stephens's deputy at Camp 020. 'He [Jakobs] placed himself at your disposal. He had been told that he could save his life if he could give you enough information. You got information from him, and not only that; you also caught me through him … In spite of everything he is now dead.'

But Richter's real purpose in writing four letters to Major Short was to be given the opportunity, as he put it, of earning his freedom. He wrote that he was aware that Wulf Schmidt was under British control. He assumed wrongly that the British had been alerted to Schmidt's existence by his own arrival, but he argued that were he now to be executed or imprisoned, the Germans would no longer trust Schmidt. 'What sacrifice would it be for England,' he pleaded, 'to grant me my life and my freedom, and to trust me a little, if, as a result, *Leonhard* [Schmidt] would continue to exist for [the Abwehr]?'

Richter's words seemed to fall on deaf ears. His prosecution for treachery went ahead as planned. He was convicted at the Old Bailey on 24 October and sentenced to death. But he subsequently lodged an appeal in which he stated that Major Short had informed him during an interrogation that Schmidt was under British control. Robertson wrote to Guy Liddell suggesting that Richter should be immediately reprieved. He gave two reasons: first, were Richter's appeal to proceed, it would alert a potentially large number of people to the existence of the Double Cross system, and secondly, in the event of Richter's execution, a death notice would appear in the press which might alert the Germans to the possibility that Richter had informed the British authorities of Schmidt's existence. This was essentially the point that Richter had been making in his letters to Short.

The matter was hotly debated within the Security Service. Liddell initially subscribed to Robertson's view that a reprieve ought to be granted, pointing out that Schmidt was 'the central figure of our organisation' and that a grave risk was being run 'that the main part of our structure will collapse'. In the end, however, after the intervention of Lord Swinton (whose view reflected that of Churchill that not enough spies were being executed), it was decided to let the case take its normal course. Richter's appeal failed and his execution date was set for 10 December.

In one of his letters to Major Short, Richter wrote: 'You can rely upon it that I shall not be less brave than Jakobs; I too will know how to die, yet not as a Nazi spy on your gallows, but as a man.' This attitude may explain his behaviour on the day of his death. As the executioner, Albert Pierrepoint, entered his cell, Richter glowered like a caged animal, before charging head first at the cell wall. He lay stunned for a moment, then two prison officers dived on top of him. Richter clawed and kicked the officers away, as two more ran to subdue him. Pierrepoint managed to strap his wrists, but the spy broke the leather strap with the last ferocious struggle of his life. With his knee in the small of Richter's back, Pierrepoint applied a new strap and Richter was finally dragged to the scaffold, where his ankles were bound and the cap and noose were adjusted. But before Pierrepoint could pull the lever, Richter seized his own fate and jumped. The noose slipped from around his neck, catching under the bridge of his nose, where it jammed as he fell through the trapdoor. He had very nearly slipped through the noose altogether, but he was pronounced dead, after what Pierrepoint later described as 'my toughest session on the scaffold during all my career'.

It appears that the Abwehr did not question Schmidt's loyalty as a result of Richter's capture. Far from it: Schmidt received a message informing him that he was being awarded the Iron Cross for his services to Germany. So far as the Germans were concerned, they now had two excellent spies in Schmidt and Dusko Popov – and plenty of evidence that any future spies they sent would be caught. They began to see little point in continuing to send agents across the Channel.

The Double Cross system was clearly serving its counter-espionage purpose. But B1a was about to lose one of its stars to the United States of America. While there, he would be sent advanced warning of the Japanese attack on Pearl Harbor. Dusko Popov, lawyer, playboy and *perhaps* 007 prototype, was about to be given the chance to change the course of history.

AMERICA'S WARNING

On 1 August 1941 Wulf Schmidt received the following message from the Abwehr:

> Go at once to the theatre agent Eric Sand, Tea house, Piccadilly House, Piccadilly Circus, name plate is on entrance to teahouse. Introduce yourself as 'Harry' and say 'How do you do, Mr Sand – I am Harry and appreciate very much to meet you.' You will then receive £20,000. Please give acknowledgment of money to us at once, as we have to reimburse at once a similar amount to a friend of Sand. It is better to hide the amount in parts.

Schmidt replied: 'Money troubles are over. Hurried to Piccadilly House. Met Sand as arranged. He appears to be one of the chosen race.' But Schmidt did not really go to Piccadilly House to collect money from the chosen Mr Sand. There was no need. Mr Sand was a participant in Plan Midas, an MI5 sting calculated to enable the Abwehr to pay its agents more easily. B1a, after all, could only operate its double agents if they were being paid by the Germans. If they continued to function without money, the Abwehr would soon realize they were under British control. The added bonus for MI5 was that the Abwehr would effectively be paying the running costs of its Double Cross system.

Plan Midas was the idea of Dusko Popov. Albrecht von Auenrode, his Lisbon spymaster, had given him money to bring to England for his sub-agent Dickie Metcalfe. Popov had agreed to deliver the money, but insisted that another method be found in future. The serial numbers of the notes would be taken down on his entry into Britain, he told Auenrode, and if Metcalfe were caught they would be traced to him. Popov had become adept at thinking like a German spy when he was meant to be one.

On his return to England Popov approached Bill Luke with a simple but ingenious solution to the problem – which would guarantee a large sum of money for B1a. Someone should be found in England who wanted to remove money from the country. That person could notionally pass over a large amount of sterling to a controlled German agent in England, and the Abwehr could transfer an equivalent amount to a foreign bank account in that person's name. MI5 could then collect the money. 'Tar' Robertson liked the idea and it was put into action. A wealthy theatre agent named Eric Glass was approached and he agreed to take part in the ruse, without ever being told its details or true purpose. MI5 offered Popov a 10 per cent commission on the deal, and he went back to Lisbon with the proposal.

In Lisbon, Popov told Auenrode that he had become friendly with a Jewish theatre agent who, believing that Britain was going to lose the war, wanted to transfer his money to New York. He was prevented from doing so by wartime restrictions. Auenrode quickly saw the potential. He recognized in this theatre agent an ideal method of financing Abwehr spies in England, as well as an opportunity to line his own pocket: he would insist on a half-share of Popov's commission. But what Auenrode didn't know was that no money would ever change hands in England, and that the Abwehr money intended for Eric Glass was really destined for British Intelligence.

The plan received the backing of the Abwehr's financial advisor in Berlin, but Popov made a mistake. In giving Eric Glass's name to the Abwehr, he mistakenly called him 'Eric Sand'. He had, he later wrote, 'substituted a part for the whole, sand being an ingredient of glass'. This was a dangerous mistake, as had the Abwehr carried out any checks on English theatrical agents they would have found no one by that name. But they did not check. And so, on 1 August, Wulf Schmidt received his message from the Abwehr and was able to report back that he had picked up the money. This prompted the following message from the Abwehr: 'Heartiest congratulations for good work on no account spend all the money at once on drink for that you can wait until we come. We consider ourselves invited ... Don't rush. For the moment work as before slowly change over. Dress better and go to better class haunts ...'

After this there could be little doubt that Schmidt was trusted by the Abwehr. And now that he could afford to move around Britain freely, and to frequent 'better class haunts', the Germans clearly expected the quality of his reports to improve. B1a, however, did not want his reports to have to improve. There was, as we have seen, a limited amount of chickenfood available for him to pass over. A plan was formed to bring his new-found social and physical mobility to an abrupt end. On 12 September the following message was sent by Schmidt to the Abwehr: 'Was caught in a police raid at Kings Cross Station. Police asked for Identity Cards of all travellers. On being asked whether I had yet registered for military service, I answered the truth – that is 'No' in order not to arouse suspicion by lying … I was told to register at once otherwise I would be prosecuted.'

The Abwehr was very worried for Schmidt. But he was soon to lift his handlers' spirits. He sent a message telling them that a friendly farmer had helped him out. This farmer had written a letter falsely informing the authorities that Schmidt had been working for him for some time and that he had become essential to the running of his farm. Schmidt had taken this letter to the local registration office and had duly been exempted military service. The consequence, however, was that Schmidt must now start work as the farmer's right-hand man. 'This,' Schmidt told his handlers, 'is very inconvenient but is unavoidable and this must be understood by you for better or for worse.' The Abwehr sent back: 'Heartiest congratulations that everything has turned out so well. Nevertheless we recommend you to be on the alert and careful. Break your legs and your neck.'

From the British perspective Schmidt's situation was now ideal. His ability to gather information could be dictated by B1a, and the Abwehr would happily accept the state of affairs.

The Germans might now believe that Eric Glass's money had turned Schmidt into the richest farm hand in Hertford-shire, as well as the administrator for their English spy network, but in reality the Dane had seen none of this money. And nor was Glass to benefit from a healthy American bank balance. The cash intended for Glass had been given by Auenrode to Popov to take to New York, which he did, placing it into an MI5 account. But while the money was still in his hands, Popov had decided to have some fun with it. In the gaming room of the Casino Estoril he placed it down on the baccarat table. This was the money that startled fellow gamers, shamed the little Lithuanian, and perhaps even planted a Bond-shaped seed in the mind of Ian Fleming.

The Abwehr was not simply sending Popov to New York to open a bank account, however. The organization had taken the decision to move him to the United States to allow him to build up a network of agents, just as he had done in England. The Abwehr, aware that America could soon enter the war, had taken stock of its existing American agents and found them wanting. The Federal Bureau of Investigation had detected some, and those who remained were ineffective and closely connected with one another. 'They behave like boy scouts,' Auenrode told Popov. 'I wouldn't be astonished if they soon form an official organization and hand out publicity releases.' The Abwehr wanted an effective new network, with no links to the current set-up. And who better than Popov, who had been so successful in England, to establish it? Unknown to the Abwehr, of course, his 'success' in England had depended on the skill and support of B1a.

If Popov was to become a successful double agent in New York, he would require skilful handling by MI5's American counter-espionage counterpart. Bill Luke initially approached the FBI through the United States embassy in London, and an agreement was reached that the Bureau would take over the running of Popov. B1a was not keen on losing such an integral figure, but he was leaving Dickie Metcalfe and Friedl Gaertner in England to carry on his network, and it was recognized that his contribution to the war effort could be immense in the United States. 'We shall probably ask you to come back in the not too distant future,' 'Tar' Robertson told him before he left. 'For the moment, we can spare you.' And as a young individualist with a passion for money and good living, Popov was looking forward to spending time in a country which promised to suit his temperament.

Popov left London for Lisbon on 28 June 1941, en route to New York. While in Lisbon he met Johnny Jebsen, who had some interesting news for him. Jebsen had recently been sent to Taranto in southern Italy on a fact-finding mission on behalf of the Japanese Foreign Minister. In November 1940 the British aircraft carrier *Illustrious* had launched a surprise attack on the Italian battlefleet anchored off Taranto, putting three of the Italians' six battleships out of action. The remainder of the fleet was forced to retire to Naples. During an otherwise bleak period for Britain Winston Churchill had been able to report positively to the House of Commons: 'It is good news. The Royal Navy has struck a crippling blow on the Italian fleet.' And now, six months later, the Japanese were asking Jebsen to visit Taranto, to report on the episode, on the defences mounted by the Italians, and on the layout of Taranto harbour. Jebsen believed that the Japanese were planning something similar. 'If my calculated opinion interests you,' he told Popov, 'the Japanese will attack the United States.'

With Jebsen's words fresh in his mind, Popov met Auenrode for his final briefing before departing for New York. The spymaster explained that Popov was to do exactly as he had done in England: make contacts, and appoint sub-agents sparingly and only when they were implicitly trusted. Popov was touched by the fact that when Auenrode warned him not to risk his life, his words were loaded with genuine concern. Popov was then shown his new questionnaire. It was in a form that Arthur Owens would have recognized: the microdot. Full-sized photographs reduced to the size of ink dots, microdots had first come to MI5's attention eighteen months earlier, when a batch was handed to Owens by Nikolaus Ritter. Popov was going to need a microscope to study his briefs.

But as he glanced through the questionnaire a more pressing matter seized his attention. A significant section related to questions about the United States naval base at Pearl Harbor. Popov was being asked to report details about the pier installations, workshops, ammunition depots, floating docks and other features. What, asked the questionnaire, were the depths of water and the number of anchorages? These questions were very similar to those the Japanese had recently been asking about Taranto. The connection was immediately clear to Popov: Pearl Harbor must be the Japanese target.

When Popov told Auenrode that Hawaii was 'a bit off my beat', the spymaster emphasized that he must make the trip as soon as possible. 'You'll have to find an excuse for going there,' he said. Auenrode's secretary Elizabeth offered the suggestion that he could combine it with an 'amorous escapade'. Popov's reputation was flourishing on both sides of the wartime divide.

On 10 August, Popov flew to New York. During a stopover in the Azores he enjoyed a dinner of 'beautifully prepared fish fresh from the Atlantic' while the stewards prepared comfortable berths for the next leg of the journey, to Bermuda. Flying was a much more relaxed and alluring business – even in the midst of a war – before the advent of apex fares and self check-in. On arriving in New York Popov took a taxi to the Waldorf Astoria Hotel, before strolling out to receive his first unforgettable impressions of Park Avenue and 42nd Street. He returned within the hour, having bought a red Buick convertible, to find that the suitcases he had put in the wardrobe in his hotel room had been tampered with. Before going out he had faintly outlined their position in pencil and placed a hair across the fastener of one. This was to be his first intimation of the FBI's attitude towards him. But while suspicion on his arrival was understandable, the Bureau's suspicions were to remain until the day he finally left America.

Not long after his arrival Popov was taken to meet Percy Foxworth, the chief of the Special Intelligence Service, a counter-intelligence branch of the FBI. The SIS was located in the Rockefeller Center, its cover provided by a functioning law firm. At this meeting Popov and Foxworth enthusiastically discussed microdots, which the FBI had never encountered before. But on the subject of Pearl Harbor Foxworth was sceptical. 'It all looks too precise, too complete, to be believed,' he said. 'If anything, it sounds like a trap.' Popov tried to convince him that his sources were reliable, but the fact that Johnny Jebsen was a serving Abwehr officer only increased Foxworth's suspicions. Popov was reduced to defending his own credibility. 'With all due modesty,' he said rather desperately, 'the Abwehr considers me its top agent and has absolute faith in me.' The conversation soon turned back to microdots. The form of the questionnaire provoked genuine interest; its substance did not.

On 22 August, Popov's work began. He and his FBI case officer Charles F. Lanman prepared the first secret-ink letter to be sent to Lisbon. Popov told Lanman that he was intending to embark on a trip to Hawaii to gather information about Pearl Harbor. He had planned to follow Elizabeth's advice and take along an English girl he had met, although this may have had less to do with cover than pleasure. 'I'll let you know as soon as I get the go-ahead,' said Lanman. But as Popov was making his preparations, Lanman informed him that the trip was off. And not only that, the FBI was not intending to provide him with any chickenfood on the subject. The decision had come from the Bureau's headquarters in Washington. Popov was stunned. It was as though the FBI had failed to comprehend his reason for being in the United States. And two weeks later this impression was confirmed, during a meeting with its Director, J. Edgar Hoover.

Hoover was a capricious character, who polarized opinion during his lifetime and has continued to do so after his death. To some he was the true and earnest defender of American values. To others he was a malicious hypocrite, relentlessly placing his own ambitions above the welfare of his country. But the fact is that J. Edgar Hoover and the Federal Bureau of Investigation were indistinguishable, and the self-appointed role of both was to preserve the moral health of the United States of America. Ethical cancers included un-American political beliefs, foreign influences, civil liberties, sexual freedoms and unearned wealth. And so it is hard to visualize a figure more perfectly designed to earn Hoover's loathing than an independently wealthy foreign spy with a passion for women, gambling and expensive living.

The meeting between Popov and Hoover was short and unfriendly. It was held in Percy Foxworth's office and it began with the words, 'Sit down, Popov!' Popov sat. Hoover proceeded to berate the Yugoslav for his licentious lifestyle. 'I don't think that a choirboy could perform my job,' said Popov, 'but if I've caused trouble, I pray you forgive me.' Hoover then dismissed Popov from his presence. But Popov did not go. He lit a cigarette and retracted his apology. 'I did not come to this country to break the law or corrupt your organization,' he told Hoover. 'I came here to help with the war effort. I brought a serious warning indicating exactly when, how, and by whom your country is going to be attacked. And I came to help organize an enemy agent system in your country, which would be under your control and your orders.' Hoover was unconcerned. 'I can catch spies without your or anybody else's help,' he said, before complaining that not a single spy had contacted Popov since his arrival.

This comment confirmed for Popov that Hoover – and therefore the FBI – did not understand his intended role. So far as the Director was concerned, Popov was useful only for catching other spies. The idea that he was to set up a living network in order to learn about the enemy's intentions, and to pass over deception, was entirely alien. Undeterred, Popov tried to explain: 'I am not to contact any of their old agents now or in the future, and none of them knows of my existence. I am to build an organization on my own.' He raised his immediate problem: 'To stay on in the job, I must produce results; that means information and new agents. Up to now, I've been permitted to do exactly nothing.' Hoover could not have cared less. 'You're like all double agents,' he said. 'You're begging for information to sell to your German friends so you can make a lot of money and be a playboy.' The meeting came to an end when Hoover interrupted Popov by turning to Foxworth, who had been sitting silently, and said, 'That man is trying to teach me my job.' 'I don't think anybody could teach you anything,' shot back Popov, heading for the door. 'Good riddance!' shouted Hoover.

Popov's American mission was clearly doomed, but the repercussions were greater than one man's failure. On the afternoon of 7 December, while sailing back to New York from a trip to Rio de Janeiro, Popov learned that the Japanese had attacked Pearl Harbor. The Yugoslav, alone among the ship's passengers, was neither surprised nor concerned. With the warning he had delivered, the Americans would have been prepared; the attack must surely have been repulsed. When news filtered through that it had come as a devastating surprise, Popov was astounded.

It appears that the FBI had simply failed to transmit the contents of the questionnaire to the White House. Whether this was because of Hoover's disdain for Popov, poor communication, organizational politics or any other reason is a moot point. The fact is that a warning had been provided. As J. C. Masterman later wrote, it was 'surely a fair deduction that the questionnaire indicated very clearly that in the event of the United States being at war, Pearl Harbor would be the first point to be attacked, and that plans for this attack had reached an advanced stage by August 1941'. In an interview given to the author and journalist Phillip Knightley in 1986, 'Tar' Robertson said, 'The mistake we [British Intelligence] made was not to take the Pearl Harbor information and send it separately to Roosevelt. No one ever dreamed Hoover would be such a bloody fool.' Popov's warning had simply been ignored.

Popov remained in New York until October 1942, gamely urging – and failing – to persuade the FBI to run him effectively as a double agent. His hopes were briefly raised when the Bureau set up a transmitter to send messages to the Abwehr, but the material being sent was never shown to him. In February 1942 Popov was visited by Ewen Montagu of British Naval Intelligence, who reported to the Twenty Committee that the agent was depressed, having been allowed to do nothing since his arrival in the United States. In July, Guy Liddell came to New York and tried to improve matters. He had a meeting with Percy Foxworth and 'impressed upon him that it was impossible to run a man like *Tricycle* the way they were doing'. Liddell's arguments had no effect. 'Having heard that Foxworth was by far and away the ablest and most intelligent representative of the FBI,' Liddell notes wryly, 'I was a little disappointed by the interview.'

In one sense Popov had not assisted his own cause. Aware that the FBI's tone was defined by its chief's stolid Presbyterianism, he took every possible opportunity to flaunt his hedonistic lifestyle. He was startlingly profligate, with his servants, summer houses, skiing trips and expensive presents for Simone Simon, a movie-star girlfriend. Such an existence had initially been necessary, he explained somewhat disingenuously, in order to maintain his cover story, but it later became, he admitted, a form of 'extravagant escapism' given the absence of any real work to do. When, in late July, it seemed that the Germans had finally stopped responding to Popov's purported wireless messages, the FBI decided to hand him back to British Intelligence. The Bureau had no further use for him – and absolutely no interest in his ongoing status with the Abwehr. MI5 still had a great interest, however. Popov was one of its top agents, and if he was blown, so were Dickie Metcalfe and Friedl Gaertner, and quite possibly Wulf Schmidt. If, on the other hand, he could be successfully rehabilitated, he could yet be a central figure in its ambitious plans.

B1a man Ian Wilson was promptly sent to New York to attempt to deal with the mess. B1a knew from ISOS, although Popov did not, that the Abwehr was now deeply mistrustful of him. In March a message from Berlin to Lisbon had been intercepted warning that Popov was probably under American control. The Yugoslav might not be aware of this, but he was well aware that the Germans had left him short of money: an indication that they had lost interest. He was also aware that he had absolutely nothing to report to Auenrode in Lisbon. Not only had he done nothing, but he had no idea of the contents of the wireless messages he had supposedly sent.

Yet, in spite of all these factors, Popov informed 'Tar' Robertson that he wished to continue as a Double Cross agent under British control and that he was willing to return to Lisbon to explain himself to Auenrode. He understood the very significant risk – likelihood even – that he would end up in the Gestapo's unforgiving hands. Ewen Montagu later described his decision to continue as 'the greatest instance of cold-blooded courage that I have ever been in contact with'.

Before Popov could leave New York, Wilson had to attempt to furnish him with *some* material to take to Lisbon and an explanation of what he had been up to for more than a year. Yet the FBI still refused to provide any material, or even any details of the radio messages it had been sending to the Abwehr. In an angry MI5 memo Wilson wrote that the FBI was 'either through incompetence, lack of power, lack of interest or lack of goodwill, of no assistance and let us down badly by [its] failure to provide the traffic on which we were relying'. Eventually, with the aid of MI6 man Walter Wren, and drawing on names provided by Charles Lanman, Wilson drew up a fictional account of Popov's time in the United States which Popov had to memorize before travelling to Lisbon. His wireless set, according to Wilson's story, was built by an anti-British Indian who had studied electrical engineering at the University of Illinois. It was operated by a Croat named Polic whom Popov had met in a bar on 45th Street in New York. He was provided with aviation intelligence by a man at the Aeronautical Chamber of Commerce for whom he had procured a chorus girl. The account was long, detailed and, it was hoped, believable.

Popov arrived in Lisbon on 14 October. Auenrode was not expecting him. From the start Popov chose to stall any awkward questions by going on the attack. He feigned anger, accusing the Abwehr of placing him in trouble by leaving him without money. He had been forced to leave the United States, he said, by the size of his growing debts. It was a clever tactic: Auenrode was caught off guard. He merely blustered, 'Please do not say anything. We have done all we could. It is Berlin's fault ...'

As the interrogation progressed, Auenrode told Popov that the Berlin Abwehr had been unhappy with his work. Berlin, he said, believed that Popov's radio operator had been under American control. It was Popov himself, of course, whom Berlin believed to be under control, but Auenrode held back from making the accusation. Perhaps a fondness for Popov prevented him, perhaps the acute awareness that his own future depended on Popov's bona fides, perhaps a combination of the two. During a subsequent interrogation Otto Kürer, a fellow Lisbon officer, dropped a hint that Auenrode had been doing his best to protect the Yugoslav. '[He] is a very good friend of yours,' Kürer told Popov. 'Therefore please work hard or we shall all have trouble here.'

On 17 October a message from Lisbon to Berlin was intercepted by the British. It plainly stated Auenrode's view that there was now no reason to believe that Popov was under control. Auenrode's personal fears – as well as a genuine sense of loyalty – probably played a part in the Yugoslav's rehabilitation. Similar considerations had kept Arthur Owens and Wulf Schmidt alive as agents – and the scenario would be repeated in future. Four days after this clean bill of health, Popov flew back to Britain to resume the activities he had left off sixteen months earlier. Having received a fright, he was now being given the opportunity to assist with the vital work to come.

His return would be heartily welcomed by B1a. The organization had begun to fulfil its potential, but it still needed to strengthen its hand before it was solid enough to engage in large-scale strategic deception. The arrival of two new double agents was about to give it the Double Cross equivalent of a royal flush.

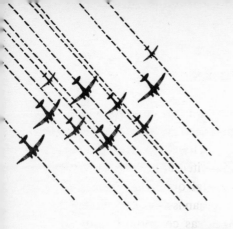

FORTITUDE SPIES

The first of the new men to arrive, on 24 April 1942, was a Spaniard from Catalonia named Juan Pujol García. He was swiftly codenamed *Garbo* by Cyril Mills, the B1a circus proprietor who had a passion for the Swedish actress and an admiration for the little man from Barcelona whose one-man show had been fooling the Abwehr over the past nine months. The Germans believed Pujol to be spying on their behalf in England, but he was not. He was in Lisbon compiling reports using a map of Britain, a tourist guide, a railway timetable and a Portuguese reference book entitled *The British Fleet*.

Pujol was 30 years old when he arrived in Plymouth to begin work for MI5. He was a chicken farmer whose hopes of a quiet life had been wrecked first by the Spanish Civil War and then by the Second World War. Brought up in comfortable surroundings, Pujol was the son of a successful factory owner who instilled in him liberal values. In his memoirs he recalls that his father would quote Leo Tolstoy's words: 'War is so horrendous, so atrocious, that no man, especially one of Christian principles, should feel able to undertake the responsibility of starting it.' According to Pujol, his father's example inspired him to resist 'injustice and iniquity with the only weapons at my disposal'.

Pujol would himself experience enough of war's unjust effects to confirm his father's principles. While performing national service in a cavalry regiment, it became very clear to him that his temperament was not suited to military life. He lacked, he admitted, 'those essential qualities of loyalty, generosity and honour that a cavalryman is meant to possess'. His resistance to army discipline was compounded by a dislike of horse riding: his principal memory of military service was of returning to barracks 'with my buttocks on fire'.

By the outbreak of the Spanish Civil War in 1936, Pujol was managing a chicken farm outside Barcelona. The city was in Republican hands and he was called up for the Republican army. With no intention of serving, Pujol went into hiding at his girlfriend's parents' house. After seventeen fruitless searches of the house he was finally discovered and arrested on the eighteenth occasion. Imprisoned, and fully expecting to be shot as a deserter, he escaped from the prison with forty-eight others, thanks to the intervention of a female detainee who had begun a timely affair with a warder.

Pujol hid in a Barcelona flat for the next year, before obtaining false identity papers, which he used to secure a job managing a poultry farm near the French border. But despite being relatively safe, he now found himself dependent on local Republican councillors who were demanding huge profits from the farm while refusing to invest any funds. Unable to do his job properly, Pujol came up with a plan to cross over to Franco's side, believing that among the Nationalists he 'would be left alone to live my own life'. The best way of crossing the divide, he decided, was to join the Republican army and wait for a chance to desert. But he was determined not to see front-line service and so, falsely claiming to have experience of telegraphy, he volunteered for a posting in the signals corps.

This plan was only partially successful: Pujol was posted to a signals unit – but it was on the front line.

Pujol's job, laying and maintaining telephone cables, may have had an element of danger, but he was now only a short distance from the Nationalists whom he intended to join. He was not alone in this intention. Desertions from the Republican ranks were frequent; Pujol had been with his unit for only a short time when his company barber, who had been caught attempting to cross the divide, was executed in front of the entire battalion. Nevertheless, in what Pujol later described as 'the craziest act I ever did', one evening he slipped out of his trench together with two other men. A patrol spotted their escape, but failed to catch them before they had reached the Nationalist trenches. Pujol's hopes of being sent safely to the rear and building a comfortable new life on the other side were quickly crushed, however. He was intensively interrogated by the Nationalists before being sent to a prison camp at Deusto in Bilbao.

On his release – after the intercession of a priest who had known his father – Pujol had to enlist with Franco's army. And he was soon in trouble again, this time after being spotted wearing a monarchist cap at a political rally. He was humiliated by his commander who slapped him twice in the face, tore the stripes from his uniform and sent him to another prison camp. He was released from the camp shortly before the end of the war.

Whatever Pujol's feelings had been before the civil war, by its end he was set against ideology and militarism, for which he blamed the oppressive attitudes he had consistently encountered. He had – perhaps out of principle, perhaps out of fear – done his utmost to avoid front-line action, yet even in his peripheral activities he had been humiliated. His flowering as a British double agent would owe a great deal to his experiences at the hands of bullies and ideologues on both sides of the Spanish divide. As Europe fell to the Nazis in the first year of the war, Pujol came to see Britain as the lonely defender of his own values, resisting the pitiless advance of the bullies.

But while Pujol was keen to help the British, they were not so keen to receive his help. In January 1941 Pujol's wife, Aracelli, approached the British embassy in Madrid on behalf of her husband. She told the consular officials that she knew of a man who wanted to work as a spy in Germany or Italy. Nobody at the embassy was interested. 'I decided,' Pujol writes in his memoirs, 'to prepare the ground more carefully before I approached them again.' His plan was to force the British hand. If he could first be accepted as a German agent, he figured, he would have access to such a quantity of valuable information that the British would not resist his next approach. So began a chicken farmer's marathon struggle to be taken seriously by the British authorities in the Iberian peninsula.

The plan began with a visit to the German embassy in Madrid, with the story that Pujol was willing to spy for Germany, either in Lisbon or in England. He met Gustav Leisner, the chief of the Madrid Abwehr. Leisner was not interested in the Lisbon option, he made perfectly clear, but if Pujol could find his own method of getting to England, he *might* be willing to take him on. Pujol's response to this challenge was to invent an intricate scheme involving Spain's Security Police and a currency-exchange deal, which Leisner duly dismissed as an absurd proposition. His persistence was noted, however, and he was given a small amount of money and told to travel to Lisbon to apply for press accreditation and a British visa.

In Lisbon, Pujol had a false Spanish diplomatic passport printed in his name, and on his return to Madrid, in the absence of his usual contact, he met two other members of the Madrid Abwehr: Friedrich Knappe-Ratey and the higher-ranking Karl-Erich Kühlenthal. Neither of these Abwehr men was initially impressed by Pujol; he was told that his visit was inconvenient and that he should go and not bother to return. By now he was accustomed to this kind of treatment from both sides, and he was not about to give up. As he was leaving he lied to the Abwehr men that the British consulate in Lisbon was willing to grant him a visa. This had the desired effect: Knappe-Ratey made contact again the following day.

Pujol's chance had come. He restated his complicated foreign-exchange proposition, but this time he added that the Spanish Security Police were attempting to send him to the Spanish embassy in London as an honorary attaché. Knappe-Ratey told him that if this story was genuine, the Abwehr would certainly be interested. In order to convince his potential spymaster, Pujol thickened the plot. He telephoned a Spaniard, Fernández, whom he had met in Lisbon, saying that he wanted to return to Lisbon but that his wife believed him to have a lover there. Would Fernández send him a telegram urgently summoning him to Lisbon, which he could show Aracelli? Fernández did as he was asked and Pujol took the telegram to Knappe-Ratey, claiming it was from a contact in the Lisbon office of the Spanish Security Police. He then brought out the fake diplomatic passport, explaining that it had just been issued by the Spanish authorities. The way was now clear for him to travel to England, he told Knappe-Ratey, but his story must be kept quiet, or else his cover in England would be blown.

This was a complicated and extremely risky ruse – but it worked. Knappe-Ratey asked him to delay his departure for England by a few days while he sought instructions from Berlin. Pujol was given training in secret writing, and a number of questionnaires reduced to microdots. The Abwehr man reassured him that during his mission in England he was merely to act as an observer and would not be carrying out any 'dangerous exploits'. Kühlenthal gave him some final instructions, telling him to recruit sub-agents in England who could continue his work when he returned to Spain. He also gave him a Madrid cover address to which to send his secret-ink correspondence and promised him that Aracelli would receive an allowance while he was away. On 12 July, Pujol travelled to Lisbon with his wife and son, from where – so the Abwehr believed – he was to travel to England. But he was not going to England – unless he could persuade the British embassy officials in Lisbon to take him there. And he knew from past experience how difficult that could prove.

Pujol's fears were confirmed when he failed to receive even an interview at the British embassy in Lisbon. 'Why,' he writes, 'was the enemy proving to be so helpful while those whom I wanted to be friends were being so immovable?' But he was now committed to pretending that he was in England, and he came up with a story for fooling the Germans. On 19 July he posted a letter in Lisbon to the cover address in Madrid. In it he wrote that he had arrived in England and had met a pilot who flew the Lisbon–Bristol route. For $1 per letter the pilot was willing to bring Pujol's letters from England to Lisbon and then post them on to Madrid. In this manner the English censor would be avoided. The pilot would also pick up any post from a designated cover address in Lisbon and bring it to England. For this cover address Pujol provided the Abwehr with the real address of his friend Fernández, but Fernández did not know why he was being used. Pujol simply told him that he needed a false address so that a lover in Madrid could send him letters without Aracelli discovering them.

Pujol intended this complicated arrangement to be only a short-term solution. As soon as he had received a reply from Madrid – demonstrating that the Abwehr truly believed him to be in England – he took it, his secret ink and his questionnaire directly to the British embassy. He was convinced that an official would now hear his story, consider his evidence and engage him as an agent. But he was wrong on the second two counts. He received a hearing, but the embassy officials were no more interested than they had been on the previous occasion.

Clearly Pujol was stuck in Lisbon for the foreseeable future, and so he had to press on with his charade. Using his map of Britain, his tourist guide, his copy of *The British Fleet* and a dictionary – as well as newspapers and whatever else he could find in the city's public library – he began sending the Abwehr the kinds of reports he imagined a spy would send. He concocted details of munitions factories from pre-war information about British industry found in the library. He placed military camps and training centres in likely spots described in the tourist guide. *The British Fleet* provided the names and descriptions of vessels seen passing in and out of British ports, although Pujol was careful about giving too many names of ships in case they had already been sunk by the Germans.

Sometimes Pujol became a little carried away. In one report he described manoeuvres on Lake Windermere involving huge amphibious tanks capable of carrying twenty men, and partly submerged transport ships towed by armed landing craft. These vessels existed only in Pujol's fertile but thoroughly inexpert imagination. One major problem was his lack of understanding of the workings of pounds, shillings and pence, so that on one occasion his claimed expenses for train fares between Glasgow and London amounted to £0 87s 10d. Aware that he might be digging a hole for himself, he wisely

GOT 21/90/00/429/Ops A

F10000
BOX00015
5

SE2027
SCHEDULE C   WO205/173

MOST
SECRET

PERMANENT PRESERV
CITED IN OFFICIAL

Fortitude

DECEPTION

PLAN.

Historical Section
Offices of the Cabinet

HS/21Ay/13/00015/5

1944 APR
MAY.

PERMANENT PRESERVATION.
CITED IN OFFICIAL HISTORY

CLOSED
UNTIL
1972

PERMANENT PRESERVATION
CITED IN OFFICIAL HISTORY

TO BE KEPT UNDER
LOCK AND KEY

It is requested that special care may be taken
to ensure the secrecy of this document.

Field Marshal Erwin Rommel during a visit to the Atlantic Wall.

Dudley Clarke, Madrid, October 1941. 'Why he wore this disguise, nobody quite knows...'

The breaker and his prison. Colonel 'Tin Eye' Stephens would rub his hands with glee on hearing that a new spy was on his way to Camp 020.

Wulf Schmidt and his transmitter; together they dropped into a Cambridgeshire field. Schmidt was the longest serving of BIa's double agents.

Engelbertus Fukken; a quiet Dutchman who escaped detection for almost five months.

Josef Jakobs; 'Shoot straight.'

Dusko Popov. Agent, double agent, playboy, gambler, lawyer, profligate, lover, show-off and a very brave man.

Johnny Jebsen; a German Intelligence Officer with a hatred of Nazis.

Johann JEBSEN

FBI Director, J Edgar Hoover; Dusko Popov brought him a warning about Pearl Harbor months before the Japanese attacked. He ignored it.

Karel Richter tries to remember where he left his parachute.

Wulf Schmidt and Assistant Naval Attaché Mitinori Yosii. Possibly the most conspicuous men in London.

TOP SECRET

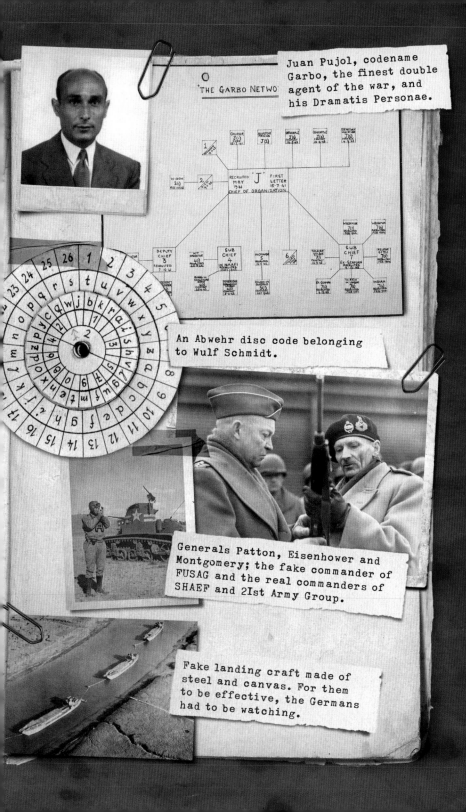

THE GARBO NETWORK

Juan Pujol, codename Garbo, the finest double agent of the war, and his Dramatis Personae.

An Abwehr disc code belonging to Wulf Schmidt.

Generals Patton, Eisenhower and Montgomery; the fake commander of FUSAG and the real commanders of SHAEF and 2Ist Army Group.

Fake landing craft made of steel and canvas. For them to be effective, the Germans had to be watching.

OPERATION - TITANIC   PART II DIVERSIONARY PLANS
APPX 'B'

TOP SECRET
BIGOT

Planning maps for Operations
Bigrium, Taxable, Glimmer and
Titanic.

A map showing Allied units where German Intelligence believed them to be on 15 May 1944.

A Mulberry Harbour; designed, built and floated in just seven months — all in the utmost secrecy.

American airmen watch landing craft heading for Normandy on D-Day and a De Havilland Mosquito in D-Day Markings.

GARBO

Friday 9th June, 1944.

Message sent 0149 hours GMT.

SPANISH

Gr. 65

TENGO RAZONES DE PESO QUE JUSTIFICAN MIS ASEVERACIONES X ASI PUES EL HECHO QUE ESTAS CONCENTRACIONES QUE ESTA EN EL SURESTE Y ESTE DE LA ISLA ESTEN EN LA ACTUALIDAD INACTIVAS DEBEN TENER LAS RESERVADAS PARA REALIZAR CON EL LAS OTRAS OPERACIONES DE ENVERGADURA X LOS CONSTANT BOMBARDEOS QUE SUFRE LA AREA DEL X PAS DE CALAIS X Y I SITUACION ESTRATEGICA DE ESTAS FUERZAS HACEN XX

English translation.

I have strong reasons to justify my assurances. Th fact that these concentrations which are in the east south east of the Island are now inactive means that must be held in reserve to be employed in the other l scale operations. The constant aerial bombardment the area of the Pas de Calais has suffered and the s disposition of these forces.....

GARBO

Friday 9th June, 1944.

Message sent 0155 hours GMT.

SPANISH

Gr. 51

QUE SOSPECHE DE ATAQUE A AQUELLA REGION FRANCESA RUTA A LA PAR MAS CORTA PARA SU ILUSIONADO OBJETIVO FINAL O SEA BERLIN FACILITADO ESTE AVANCE POR UN CONSTANTE MARTILLEO DE AVIACION POR TENER LAS BASES MAS CERCA DEL CAMPO BATALLA Y CAYENDO ADEMAS DETRAS DE NUESTRAS FUERZAS QUE ESTAN LUCHANDO EN LA ACTUALIDAD CON EL ENEMIGO DESEMBARCADO EN OESTE FRANCIA

English translation.

...give reason to suspect an attack in that region of Franc which at the same time offers the shortest route for the final objective of their illusions, which is to say, Berlin. Which advance could be covered by a constant hammering from the air since the bases would be near the field of battle they would come in behind our forces which are fighting at the present moment with the enemy disembarked in the west of France.

The key moment of Fortitude; the message sent by Juan Pujol in the early morning of 9 June 1944 which proved that the German General Staff would move a division on an agent's report alone.

stopped quoting English currency and began claiming his expenses in US dollars. Other rather obvious inaccuracies were his claim that foreign embassies would decamp to Brighton for the summer to escape the oppressive heat of London and his belief that drunken orgies regularly took place in Liverpool's notorious 'amusement centres'. But Pujol's most notable error was his assertion that Glasgow men would do anything for a litre of wine. This was even less true in 1941 than it is today, but it did not seem to alert the Abwehr to a problem.

Pujol followed Kühlenthal's advice and began appointing sub-agents. They were, of course, imaginary, but their recruitment served a purpose other than Kühlenthal's. Aware of the possibility of mistakes, Pujol could attribute any errors to a particular sub-agent's unreliability. The sub-agent could be censured – or perhaps relieved of his role – and Pujol would avoid suspicion. These sub-agents were supposedly cultivated on Pujol's travels around Britain, during which he seemed to meet a remarkable number of German sympathizers. His first sub-agent (other than the airline pilot) was a Portuguese man named Carvalho, living in Newport, south Wales. Next came a Swiss national named William Gerbers, from Bootle near Liverpool. Third on the roster was a wealthy Venezuelan studying at the University of Glasgow. These early sub-agents all lived near important ports, allowing Pujol to send detailed reports on the shipping movements which were of such interest to the Abwehr.

Throughout this period Pujol continued trying to interest the British in his services. Towards the end of October, while in Madrid, he once again contacted the British embassy, and spoke to a consular official named David Thompson. But despite producing his microdots, he failed to convince Thompson of his loyalty. His desperation was growing. He could not continue his deception indefinitely; *The British Fleet* could only yield so much information. In November he made a visa application for himself, his wife and his child to emigrate to Brazil. But by now Aracelli had decided to step into the breach. Unknown to Pujol, she visited the United States embassy in Lisbon, where she met the Assistant Naval Attaché, Theodore Rousseau Jr. She told Rousseau that she knew of a German agent in possession of documents relating to military affairs, and in her melodramatic fashion she offered to sell him the information for $200,000.

Having startled Rousseau with her price, Aracelli somewhat undermined her position by providing him with the information – a letter written in Pujol's secret ink – for free. A subsequent meeting was arranged between Aracelli, Rousseau and a Lisbon MI6 man. Now that the United States had entered the war, such cooperation was possible. Unfortunately the MI6 man adopted such a patronizing tone towards Aracelli that she left the meeting in a fit of temper without producing the material she had brought with her: a microdot, a bottle of secret ink and a letter from Knappe-Ratey to Pujol. As she got up to leave, the MI6 man tossed a twenty-escudo note onto the table as a parting token of his condescension. Luckily the American persevered: Rousseau met Aracelli again and apologized for the MI6 man's behaviour. This time Aracelli admitted to Rousseau that the spy in question was her husband, and a meeting was arranged between Pujol and Rousseau for mid-January 1942.

Pujol finally had the opportunity to tell his whole story to somebody willing and able to help. And Rousseau in turn encouraged MI6 to become involved. Rousseau's timing was good, because MI6 was just beginning to develop its own interest in Pujol. Its counter-espionage section – Section V – had become aware of ISOS messages passing between Madrid and Berlin indicating that Madrid had an agent in Britain who was sending back detailed information. Section V had come to the conclusion that this agent – known to the Germans as *Arabel* – might not be in England at all. His reports were so inaccurate as to seem invented. Section V made the link between the apparently invented reports and the Lisbon agent who was claiming to invent reports for the Abwehr. It appeared distinctly possible that *Arabel* and Juan Pujol were the same man.

MI5, in the meantime, was both concerned and confused by the *Arabel* intercepts. Concerned because the reports suggested the existence of a spy and three sub-agents in Britain. Confused because they invariably proved inaccurate. But MI5 was not able to make the link between *Arabel* and Juan Pujol – because nobody at MI5 was told about Pujol. Section V was not sharing its information. Nor – unknown to MI5 – was it sharing much of its ISOS material: MI5 was not being shown some of the *Arabel* intercepts, nor was it seeing many of the intercepts relating to Dusko Popov in the United States.

This was because the chief of Section V, Felix Cowgill, guarded his organization's information very closely. He had, according to Ewen Montagu, 'a pathological inability to inform anyone of anything that he can possibly avoid'. But this posed a danger to British interests as a whole, because the remits of Section V and MI5 partially overlapped. In broad outline MI5 was responsible for counter-espionage within the United Kingdom and the British Empire, while counter-espionage outside of these borders was the responsibility of Section V. But many cases did not allow for such a tidy demarcation. Pujol might have been physically outside of the United Kingdom, but notionally he was on MI5's patch.

Clearly Section V ought to have informed MI5 of Pujol's existence. But no communication took place until 22

February. On that day Ralph Jarvis, the head of Section V in Lisbon, was in London, where he happened to ask 'Tar' Robertson whether any of B1a's double agents corresponded with a particular Abwehr cover address in Madrid. This was the address used by Pujol, and Robertson immediately recognized it in relation to Dusko Popov. Jarvis then telephoned Felix Cowgill to ask whether he could tell Robertson about Pujol. Permission was granted and so, almost by accident, B1a was tipped off to the existence of a man who had spent months virtually begging to be employed as a British double agent.

It did not take long for MI5 to make the link between Pujol and *Arabel*. In his diary for the following day Guy Liddell writes, 'It seems not unlikely that this accounts for the very wild messages on the ISOS about our shipping.' He also recorded that the Abwehr had just asked Dickie Metcalfe, Popov's sub-agent, to confirm some of Pujol's messages. MI5 had been about to discredit them, which might well have resulted in the blowing of Pujol. It was just as well for the future of B1a – and that of Pujol – that Jarvis had bumped into Robertson.

A week later Liddell wrote to Section V demanding a full report on Pujol. On the basis that the Catalan was ostensibly working in England, Liddell argued that his case ought to be closely coordinated with those of the other English-based double agents, all of whom were under MI5 control. It was, he felt, in everybody's interests that Pujol be brought to England to be run by B1a. Section V, however, was jealous of its recent discovery. Cowgill proceeded to make Liddell an offer. He would agree to bring Pujol to England to be interrogated, so long as he was returned to Lisbon to be run by Section V. Liddell would not agree to this. In his diary for 26 March he makes his views plain:

Felix was evidently suffering from professional jealousy. He had found this agent through the good offices of the American Naval Attaché and he did not wish to give him up or to allow us to have access to him even though in all our interests it might be better that he should remain here. Fundamentally his attitude is 'I do not see why I should get agents and have them pinched by you.' The whole thing is so narrow and petty that it really makes me quite furious.

While two branches of British Intelligence fought over him, the oblivious Pujol went on sending his fictitious reports. On 26 March he reported the sailing of a convoy of fifteen ships from Liverpool bound for Malta. This convoy – had it been real – would have been the first sent directly from the United Kingdom to relieve the beleaguered island. On 3 April the report was forwarded from Madrid to Berlin, resulting in a large operation being mounted by the Kriegsmarine and the Luftwaffe to ambush the non-existent convoy. Pujol was trusted and valued by the Germans. His potential as a British double agent was immense, but while he was in Lisbon he remained at constant risk of being blown, either by a mistake of his own or by an Abwehr investigation. It was imperative that he be brought under proper control in England as soon as possible.

In the end Section V accepted the logic of Liddell's arguments. A Section V man in Lisbon, Eugene Risso-Gill, tracked Pujol down and arranged to smuggle him on board a ship leaving Lisbon for Gibraltar. The operation had to be carried out in great secrecy. Departures from Lisbon were carefully monitored by the Abwehr; Pujol could not simply climb aboard the BOAC scheduled flight to Bristol. He later recalled that his legs were shaking as he walked up the gangplank of a ship. Twenty-four hours later he arrived in Gibraltar, before boarding a military aircraft which landed in Plymouth late on the afternoon of 24 April. He was met by two MI5 officers, Cyril Mills, who would codename him *Garbo*, and Tomás Harris, who would turn him into the finest double agent of the war.

Pujol, like Popov before him, was not subjected to Camp 020's interrogation process. Having been processed at the London Reception Centre in Wandsworth, he was debriefed by Tomás Harris and Desmond Bristow, a Spanish-speaking Section V officer. They were soon convinced by his story, and excited by his potential. Some members of the Twenty Committee initially questioned him, believing his story too fantastic to be true. It was decided, therefore, to alert all members of the Twenty Committee to the existence of Ultra – which showed him to be genuine. Pujol was now a British double agent: at last he could send the Abwehr letters from the country in which he had pretended to be for the last nine months. He asked that his family be brought to London, and so Aracelli and their young child were smuggled out of Lisbon. The Pujols set up home in a large MI5 safe house at 15 Crespigny Road, a short walk from Hendon Central Underground Station.

Initially it had been decided that Cyril Mills would be Pujol's case officer, but his lack of Spanish proved too great a handicap. The job was instead taken by Tomás Harris. Harris, a man of creative sensitivity as well as formidable intellect, was perfect for the role. While keen to encourage Pujol's audacity, he possessed sufficient judgement to know when to restrain him. Of all the brilliant and unusual characters in B1a, J. C. Masterman considered Harris to be 'in some ways the most remarkable'.

A 34-year-old artist with a Catholic Spanish mother and a Jewish English father, Harris had been educated in Spain before winning a scholarship to the Slade School of Fine Art at the prodigious age of 15. He opened his own London gallery seven years later, before joining his father as a director of the Spanish Art Gallery in Mayfair. His entry into the intelligence world came in 1940, when his friend Guy Burgess recommended him for a position at Brickendonbury Hall, the first Special Operations Executive training school. From there he moved to B1g, the Iberian Section of MI5's B Division, on the recommendation of another friend – and B Division officer – Anthony Blunt. Harris and his wife Hilda were to earn a reputation for hospitality, and the Harris family home in Mayfair became a social hub for the more gregarious MI5 and MI6 officers, where they would come into contact with members of the art world and the occasional politician. One of the regulars at these gatherings was Kim Philby of MI6. According to Philby's memoirs, Harris approached him in June 1941 and asked whether Philby would be interested in a position with Section V that required special knowledge of Spain. Philby took the job and subsequently succeeded Felix Cowgill as head of Section V.

Harris's close ties to Burgess, Blunt and Philby have led to the inevitable suggestions that he was a Soviet spy. But Harris was a sociable man to whom people instinctively warmed; he had ties just as close to numerous individuals with no links to the Soviet Union. It has also been alleged that Harris's death in a car crash in Majorca in January 1964 may have been a KGB 'hit' to prevent him from revealing Blunt's role as a Soviet agent. But Hilda Harris's account of the crash, in which she was injured, strongly suggests that it was caused by her husband's own negligence. The fact is that no evidence has come to light – despite recent opening of the relevant Soviet archives – to indicate that Tomás Harris was a Soviet spy.

Study of the MI5 archive, however, reveals that he was instrumental in turning Juan Pujol from a double agent with potential into B1a's finest weapon of the war. Having considered Pujol's style and methods closely, Harris had as his first job to ensure that his correspondence under British control achieved the correct tone. The Germans must not be alerted to the actual change in Pujol's circumstances. And they must be prevented from reappraising his older messages – where a number of glaring but undiscovered errors lurked. Therefore the standard of his information had to improve, but not, in the first instance, too dramatically.

In order to explain the improvement, two courses of action were decided upon. First, Pujol was given a notional job, doing freelance propaganda work for the BBC and for the Ministry of Information. Secondly, his network of imaginary sub-agents would start to increase. In mid-May he notified the Germans that he had met a senior official in the Spanish Department of the Ministry of Information. This man, who was said to believe that Pujol was anti-German, was supposedly very indiscreet in Pujol's presence. His high office granted him access to valuable information, and he would eventually prove, according to Harris, 'to be the most important of all *Garbo*'s contacts'. A second new sub-agent was a Gibraltarian waiter whose anti-British attitudes resulted from the forced evacuation of civilians from Gibraltar in 1940. He was known as Agent No. 4 and sometimes as 'Fred' by the Germans. During a visit to the Labour Exchange, he was directed to take work in Chislehurst Caves on the south-east edge of London, digging tunnels for a vast underground arms depot. He would prove to be a key sub-agent during Operation Fortitude.

Soon Pujol was collecting sub-agents like cigarette cards. By the end of the war he had created twenty-seven notional contacts. This would keep Pujol and Harris (and other members of the expanding *Garbo* team) very busy coordinating the agents' activities and keeping the Germans up to date

with them, but it also allowed for a tremendous level of crea-
tivity. Characters, scenarios and plotlines had to be invented
and moved forward. The task might have taxed a team of
scriptwriters, let alone a chicken farmer and an art dealer. As
the numbers of sub-agents mounted, the odd one had to be
dropped, either because the Germans were not responding
well to their material, or because they were located in an area
from which it was unsafe to pass information. But the principal benefit of having so many sub-agents was that the Germans
concluded that no further agents were needed in Britain.
Pujol's network became the perfect counter-espionage
measure.

Pujol's output was prodigious. By the end of the war he had
written 315 letters to the Abwehr in secret ink, some as long as
8,000 words – as well as the innocuous but equally long letters
over which they written. And not only was his correspondence
long, it was also long-winded. Starting with his very first letter
to the Germans, his writing had a distinctly wordy quality. The
following sentence (from a letter to MI5) gives a vivid taste:
'My conscience has always disliked the difficulties and imbro-
glios which are the pestilential result of angry excuses and
argumentative battles, for there is no greater calamity nor
more contagious plague than is to be found in trouble makers
who love discussions of motives, and the more they stir them
around the deeper they become involved.'

Pujol's style was the antithesis of Wulf Schmidt's terse and
abrupt manner, but it served a practical purpose. It allowed
him to send long letters without having to include much actual
information. And Harris noted that Pujol's verbosity began to
influence the style of the Germans in their own letters back to
him. 'From their first telegraphic message in secret writing
consisting of a few lines,' he wrote, 'they were worked up to
the climax of sending us no less than 24 foolscap pages of

secret text in one letter.' And the more the Germans wrote, the more they revealed of their own intentions. But Pujol was going to have to start moderating his style to a degree. Verbosity was a useful tactic when there was little of interest to send, but he would now have a decent amount of chickenfood to communicate from a large number of sub-agents, and he would soon be the vehicle for strategic deception, with a great deal of important misinformation to put across.

Pujol's letters took over a week to reach Lisbon. They were carried in the British diplomatic bag to the Lisbon embassy and posted from the city to the cover address in Madrid. As Pujol's network increased, and strategic deception drew nearer, it became important to improve on this system. The solution was wireless transmission. The Germans were duly told that the Gibraltarian waiter had a wireless mechanic friend who knew of a transmitter for sale. The friend, who would become Agent 4(1), was supposedly a Spanish Republican willing to operate the transmitter in the belief that it would be used to communicate with anti-Franco resistance forces in Madrid.

At first the Abwehr did not rise to the bait, but in March 1943 it provided Pujol with a code and transmissions began. The transmitter – in reality operated by an English radio ham named Charles Haines – quickly became Pujol's primary means of communication. And the codes proved to be 'the highest grade cipher ever used by the Abwehr', according to the Government Code and Cipher School at Bletchley Park. The code was duly broken, and Pujol had fulfilled one of the key roles of the Double Cross system, as envisaged by J. C. Masterman in December 1940.

But for all his Double Cross success, Juan Pujol's personal life was not flourishing. Each morning he was travelling from the family home in north-west London to an office in Jermyn

Street where he and Tomás Harris worked long hours. In that respect he was typical of many thousands of commuters who returned each evening to their wives in the suburbs. But in every other respect he was unique. Aracelli, in the meantime, was unhappy in England. She was not supposed to mix with other Spaniards, she spoke no English, she missed her mother, and her husband was devoting all of his time and energy to his work. She begged to be allowed to return to Spain, even for a week, but MI5, while never actually denying her request, would not agree to it either. Harris was concerned that if she was given a straight 'no' to her request, she would react badly. She was, he wrote, 'a hysterical, spoilt and selfish woman'.

In June 1943, frustrated by MI5's inability to focus on her request, and by Pujol's refusal to allow her to attend a party at the Spanish embassy, Aracelli telephoned Harris, saying that she did not want to live in England for a minute longer. If she was not allowed to leave the country immediately, she said, she would go to the Spanish embassy, where she would reveal the truth about her husband. A crisis loomed – but Pujol came up with a plan to defuse the situation. It was a plan so riddled with melodrama that it came close to surpassing Aracelli's own histrionics.

First a note was delivered to Aracelli by the CID. It was written by Pujol, claiming that he had been arrested and that she should hand his pyjamas and toiletries to the officers. As Pujol guessed she would, Aracelli telephoned Harris in tears to protest at her husband's arrest. Harris proceeded to play his part in the drama: he told Aracelli that MI5 was willing for her to return to Spain but that Pujol would have to go with her. When, continued Harris, this had been put to Pujol, he had lost his temper, declaring that MI5 could not force him to give up his work. He had become so angry, said the case officer, that he had had to be arrested on disciplinary grounds. At first

Aracelli defended her husband, stressing how much his work meant to him. But a few minutes later she telephoned Harris again, in a much angrier mood. She was going to run away with her children, she told him. A little later she telephoned Pujol's wireless operator and asked him to come immediately to the house.

When Haines arrived he found Aracelli sitting slumped in the kitchen. She was incoherent and all the gas taps had been turned on. Haines turned them off. Aracelli revived, but later that night she again tried to kill herself. According to Harris, there was 'a 90 per cent chance that she was play acting'. All the same, it was decided that somebody should stay with her through that night.

The following morning Aracelli's attitude seemed to have changed. She was interviewed, at her own request, and promised that if her husband was pardoned she would never interfere or ask to return to Spain again. She spent the day in tears, but by now Pujol's plan was in full swing. Aracelli was driven blindfold to Camp 020, where Pujol was supposedly being held. He was brought in to see her, unshaven and in prison clothes. He asked her whether she had been to the Spanish embassy. She swore that she hadn't, had never intended to go, and that if he was released she would give him all her support in the future. Pujol told her that the following day he was due to come before a disciplinary tribunal which would decide his fate. Aracelli was still crying as she left the camp.

She was informed the next morning that the tribunal had recommended that Pujol be allowed to continue as a double agent. And she was given a warning about her future behaviour. Pujol returned home that evening. His plan had succeeded, and Aracelli was to give MI5 no further trouble. According to Harris, the incident further boosted B1a's trust in Pujol: 'It showed us the degree to which he was prepared to co-operate in order to ensure that his work should continue uninterrupted.' Given that she well understood the importance of the work her husband was doing, it was certainly irresponsible of Aracelli to behave as she did. But it should be remembered that *she* had approached both the British and American embassies in Lisbon on his behalf; had she not made the second approach, Pujol might never have arrived in Britain. Despite her histrionics, it is hard not to feel sympathy for a woman floundering in a strange country, whose husband was lost to events beyond her control. And it is hard to know what to make of a man capable of imagining and carrying out such an elaborate – and cruel – deceit on his own wife.

As for Pujol, he was enjoying his life in London, and the fact that he was appreciated by his British handlers. The extent of this appreciation is clear from the words of J. C. Masterman: 'Connoisseurs of double cross have always regarded the *Garbo* case as the most highly developed example of their art.' Masterman, a cricket devotee, went on to make an analogy between the finest batsmen of their respective eras, and their B1a counterparts: 'If in the double cross world *Snow* was the W. G. Grace of the early period, then *Garbo* was certainly the Bradman of the later years.'

Masterman might have been referring to their impact as agents, but there are other parallels to be drawn between Arthur Owens and Juan Pujol. Owens, as we have seen, was a sociopathic liar, the central figure in his own frenzied melodrama. It never seemed to matter to Owens whom he was serving – all that mattered was his own sense of importance. It certainly mattered to Pujol whom he was serving. His liberal background and his experiences during the Spanish Civil War had set him squarely against the extreme ideologies of the day. But he had a similar drive for power and purpose, a similar need to exist on his own terms, and a similar desire to be at the centre of his own invented narrative. He was not as chaotic a figure as Owens, but his melodramatic instincts were almost as pronounced. It was around these two fantasists – one treacherous and capricious, the other loyal and dependable – that the Double Cross system was constructed.

With Pujol on board, B1a was invigorated. And its strength would be further consolidated on 2 October 1942 with the arrival in England of Roman Czerniawski, a 32-year-old Polish Air Force officer and resistance fighter. Czerniawski would prove an unusual double agent, so busy with his own military activities and political intrigues that B1a had often to work around his busy schedule. He was described by his first case officer, Christopher Harmer, as 'intensely dramatic and egotistical'. These traits, which he shared with plenty of other double agents, were attributed by Harmer to the Pole's remarkable recent experiences.

Czerniawski, one of his country's finest fighter pilots, had served as an intelligence officer in Paris after the German invasion of Poland. When France fell he went to Toulouse, where he set up and ran the Interallié network, the first large-scale resistance organization in occupied France, with well over 100 members. The Interallié ran a clandestine sea and air courier service to England, as well as four wireless transmitters which provided Allied Intelligence with the German Order of Battle. Czerniawski was the first agent to leave occupied France by air, flying to England in October 1941, where the exiled General Sikorski presented him with the Virtuti Militari, the Polish equivalent of the Victoria Cross. After his return to France he was betrayed by a female member of the organization and arrested in November 1941, along with many of his agents.

Fully expecting torture and death at the hands of the Gestapo, Czerniawski prepared to take his own life. But the brutality never came. The Germans had been impressed both by the Pole's personal daring and the manner in which he had organized the Interallié. Instead of torturing him, they put a proposition to him. They would allow him to 'escape' from his prison near Paris, if he agreed to work as an agent in England, sending back military intelligence and helping to set up a Polish Fifth Column. In order to persuade him, a colonel of the General Staff came to the prison to deliver a discourse on the benefits of collaboration. Similar, in its way, to Rommel's justification of the German occupation of France (quoted in Chapter One), the colonel's lecture offers a frightening glimpse of the Nazis' sense of destiny. He began with an explanation of the Germans' behaviour in Poland:

> I admit that the methods of treating the Poles have been more than harsh. The Poles, however, are an obstacle to our great conception of a unified Europe. No large plan or conception can be realized without sacrifice. The German nation has already made many sacrifices – other nations too will have to sacrifice certain things. In particular, the Polish nation – a young and dynamic nation – refuses to grasp this. It is a pity that this dynamic power is not being exploited in collaboration on realizing our programme.

Czerniawski asked the colonel why the German government felt entitled to impose its will on other nations. The colonel offered a bold analogy:

> Once upon a time, Rome succeeded in organizing Europe and advancing the development of her civilization by several centuries. At present, the German nation, aware of its dynamic propensities and of the advantage of possessing a man of Hitler's stature, has undertaken to realize a

programme which appeared impracticable. Under planned leadership, the economic, social and cultural issues of Europe will be normalized shortly. The realization of this programme would have taken many centuries.

Having delivered his paean to progressive Nazism, the colonel returned to the subject of Czerniawski's own people:

Do the Poles realize that they are jeopardizing this programme and their own position? It cannot be doubted that all the nationalist problems will be sorted out after the war, and that all nations will form separate states within the framework of 'Future Europe'. We do not deny the rights of the Polish nation, but we ask its co-operation. Now, instead of rising to the opportunity, and joining your dynamic power with our efforts at realizing our programme, you have tied yourselves on the one hand with Capitalist-Jewish England, and on the other with Communist-Bolshevik Russia. Neither one nor the other will do anything for you as far as full sovereignty is concerned. By joining us, you will contribute to the realization of our programme to advance Europe by several centuries in one leap.

Such stirring words did not have the desired effect on Czerniawski, but he had the sense to appear impressed. At the same time, he knew not to feign a sudden ideological conversion. He reflected on the matter for a while, before putting down in writing his apparently wholehearted acceptance of the fact that the future of Poland lay in collaboration with Germany.

So far as the Germans were concerned, Czerniawski promised to be a fine agent in England, where the Polish government-in-exile was located and a large number of Free Polish troops and airmen were based. Not only had he a great deal of spying experience, but he already possessed excellent contacts in influential Polish circles. He was perfectly placed to gather both information and recruits for a Fifth Column. He was told to concentrate his reports on the production of aircraft and tanks, and on troop movements and the Allied Order of Battle. Given that the Fortitude deception would be carried out primarily through misinformation on the latter, he was to prove a great asset to the Allied deceivers.

On 29 July 1942 Czerniawski was visited in prison by two NCOs, who drove him to a flat in Paris. They got lost on the way and the Pole, still technically a prisoner, had to stop a gendarme to ask for directions. When they eventually arrived at the flat they were met by the colonel who had delivered the Nazi sermon. He informed Czerniawski that he was now free. Like other agents before him, Czerniawski was given a document to sign which stated that he was undertaking his mission voluntarily and that if he failed in his duty the Germans would be entitled to take reprisals. Czerniawski was well aware that his captured Interallié colleagues, his mother in Poland and his brother in a German prisoner-of-war camp were all at the mercy of the Nazis.

After making his way through France and Spain, Czerniawski reached England from Gibraltar in early October. Courtesy of the Germans, he brought with him French currency, crystals and ciphers for wireless transmissions, the codename *Hubert*, and a story to give the British authorities explaining his escape from German custody. He was interrogated by both British and Polish Intelligence, but during these interrogations he made no mention of the rather crucial fact that he had been recruited by the Germans as an agent. Instead he gave the story invented for him by the Germans that he had escaped from a car while under escort by the secret police. This manufactured story was considered extraordinary by his interrogators, but it was accepted as the truth.

Czerniawski did not divulge his true story because he did not trust the Polish interrogating officers: he believed that some of them could be German agents. He only confessed the truth a month later to Colonel Gano, the Chief of the Polish Intelligence Service, whom he trusted. At the same time, Czerniawski produced a document entitled *Le Grand Jeu*, in which he told his full story and declared that he now intended to work as a double agent. 'It is a difficult game,' he wrote in the unpublished document, 'but it must yield enormous advantages, especially during decisive moments which are drawing nigh.' And as though to demonstrate his readiness for the difficulties of the 'Great Game', he produced both the wireless crystals (which had been concealed in the heels of his shoes) and the ciphers.

This change of story caused a storm among the Polish intelligence officers who had initially believed him; they had been made to look extremely foolish. And now that he was putting himself forward as a double agent, there was a great deal of hard thinking to be done by 'Tar' Robertson and his team. Czerniawski claimed now to be telling the truth, but he had already lied convincingly once. The possibilities were examined. Perhaps Czerniawski was still lying and the Germans had told him to act as a double agent under Allied control. Or perhaps he was telling the truth, but unknown to him the Germans had not really believed his conversion to their cause and had guessed that he would work as a double agent in England. If either of these scenarios was accurate, then the Germans would know that Czerniawski was working for the Allies, and they could discover a great deal simply by reading his wireless messages in reverse.

This would have disastrous consequences in the event of a strategic deception campaign. If, for example, Czerniawski were to send a false message to the Germans that the Allies intended to invade Norway, the Germans could read this message in reverse to conclude that no invasion of Norway was really planned. And, by a process of elimination, they could ascertain the genuine Allied strategic plan.

After much consideration, however, MI5 concluded – correctly – that Czerniawski was not a triple agent. There was no real danger of the Germans reading his messages in reverse. On 12 December Guy Liddell wrote, 'His whole story has been carefully examined and in the main we believe it to be true … It has been decided to let him operate a transmitter under close supervision.' Eight days later Czerniawski made wireless contact with the Germans. He was now a fully fledged double agent. His first B1a case officer was Christopher Harmer, a Birmingham solicitor in peacetime, whose initial task was to allocate him a codename. He chose *Brutus*, giving his exquisite reasoning years later:

> Roman Czerniawski had been turned by the Germans, and then re-turned by us, so I thought 'Et tu, Brute?' And, of course, he had carried out a very brave mission in Paris during the first year of the Occupation when most people thought Germany would win the war, so I thought of *Brutus*'s final speech from Julius Caesar which begins 'He was the noblest Roman of them all'.

Only two weeks after Czerniawski made his first wireless contact, the question of whether he should be allowed to continue as a Double Cross agent was examined by the W Board. But the thorny issue was no longer his relationship with the Germans. It was now his relationship with the Poles. As a

serving Polish officer, Czerniawski was under a military duty
to his commanding officer, Colonel Gano of Polish Intelligence, not to withhold any information from him. And while
the Poles might have been allies of the British, the fear that
Czerniawski might provide them with details of other double
agents, as well as sensitive operational information, caused the
W Board considerable concern. It decided that Czerniawski
should be run separately from other agents and used as little
as possible for strategic deception – although he could be used
to pass across a false Order of Battle.

But the biggest risk to Czerniawski's future as a double
agent came not from sensitive information, nor from his
history with the Germans. It came from his own personality,
described by Christopher Harmer as 'vain and conceited', and
from his incorrigible political intriguing. Harmer was about to
find his work severely compromised by the Pole's enthusiastic
extracurricular activities.

Shortly after his arrival in England, Czerniawski had been
given a job in the Polish Intelligence Service, and he was soon
at odds with his fellow officers. At first this was because he had
fooled them with his story. But his arrogance quickly aggra-
vated the problem. He had been a brilliant agent in the field
and an inspiring chief of the Interallié network, and he was
continually keen to remind his desk-bound colleagues of the
facts. But he was not merely alienating fellow members of the
Intelligence Service. In early 1943 he published and circulated
a document criticizing the Inspector General of the Polish Air
Force, Major General Stanislaw Ujejski.

Ujejski had attended a reception in December 1942 at the
Soviet embassy in London, held in honour of the twenty-fifth
anniversary of the Red Army. Like many Poles at the time,
Czerniawski was virulently anti-Soviet, and he published and
circulated a document severely criticizing the inspector

general's attendance. In June he was arrested by the Polish Air Force police and held in custody for six weeks, before being released pending court martial. During his time in prison Czerniawski wrote self-justifying letters which, according to Harmer, demonstrated 'a desire to dramatise himself and his life, and a capacity for exhibitionism which almost suggests the first signs of delusions of grandeur'.

Harmer had good reason to form such a harsh view. B1a had taken on a skilled double agent whom it trusted to collect much of his own information and to operate his own transmitter. But this agent was now jeopardizing his own case through hot-headed actions. An angry Harmer was allowed to visit Czerniawski in prison and together they composed a message to send to the Germans. This gave an essentially accurate account of Czerniawski's difficulties but concluded with a warning that he was likely to be arrested and was therefore going to hide his wireless set and all compromising documents. The message was then sent by an operator imitating the agent's style.

No messages were sent until late July, when Czerniawski was released pending court martial. He duly sent the Abwehr a message which described his arrest, detention and release. He reported that he was awaiting trial, which was true, and warned that it would be far too dangerous to transmit for the time being. He asked instead for a means of secret writing and an Abwehr cover address. The Germans provided the cover address, but no advice as to secret writing. Intercepted ISOS messages began to reveal that his German handlers were growing suspicious of Czerniawski.

Fortunately, however, the situation began to improve. At his court martial Czerniawski was sentenced to two months' imprisonment, but he had already served six weeks and the remainder of the sentence was suspended until the end of the war. He was a free man again, but B1a was taking no further chances with its mercurial agent. Czerniawski would no longer be allowed to transmit the majority of his own messages, and an operator was found to take the job. The Germans were told that Czerniawski had discovered a recently retired Polish Air Force officer living near Reading who was keen to operate the transmitter for ideological reasons, his family having been murdered by the Russians. The wireless operator was code-named *Chopin* by Christopher Harmer, who had an evident talent for names. According to Hugh Astor (who would succeed Harmer as case officer in the months before Operation Fortitude), 'Radio operators are always known as "pianists", so *Brutus*'s radio operator was given a codename which seemed appropriate for a Polish pianist …'

As time passed, ISOS messages confirmed that the Germans were regaining trust in Czerniawski. His rehabilitation seemed complete when a message was received shortly before Christmas 1943, expressing the Abwehr's great appreciation of his work. As a result, felt B1a, the time had now come to overturn the verdict of the W Board restricting Czerniawski's use in relation to strategic deception. And the Board had no hesitation in setting aside their previous decision. Fears that the Poles might be alerted to matters confidential to Britain had subsided. It was now time for the Allies to work together towards shared goals with every weapon at their united disposal. And one of those weapons was strategic deception.

In a memorandum to the W Board in July 1942, 'Tar' Robertson had announced that B1a now felt ready to play its part in large-scale strategic deception. It had, he said, become clear that B1a's network of German spies was the *only* network of spies in England. A close watch was being kept on wireless signals, written correspondence, and of course ISOS messages, and these channels were failing to reveal the existence of genuine agents who were not already under B1a control.

Robertson therefore felt confident enough to propose that 'the combined General Staff in this country have in MI5 double agents a powerful means of exercising influence over the [German High Command]'. B1a was ready to play its part in Dudley Clarke's vision of strategic deception. It was the enemy commander, Clarke had observed, whose actions had to be influenced, into whose mind the deceivers must place themselves. And the Double Cross system would surely prove the most effective means of getting there.

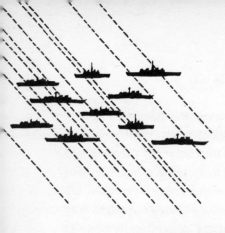

BODYGUARD OF LIES

In January 1943 Winston Churchill, Franklin D. Roosevelt and their respective advisers met in Casablanca to decide on forthcoming Allied policy. In the build-up to the conference there had been strong disagreement between the British and the Americans. The American Chiefs of Staff were impatient to mount an all-out attack on occupied France. It should, they felt, be launched as soon as possible, before coastal defences were too heavily fortified, and to relieve pressure on the beleaguered Russians.

Churchill and the British strategists were more cautious. Any operation to dislodge the Germans from north-west Europe, they believed, would require greater strength than the Allies currently possessed. The past two and a half years had consistently demonstrated the awesome fighting capabilities of the German army, and the recent failure of the British and Canadian raid on Dieppe had provided a warning against sending another inadequate force across the Channel. Should the Germans resist a premature attack on 'Fortress Europe', it might prove impossible to mount another for years to come.

In the event, Churchill persuaded Roosevelt that the coming year's operations should focus on the Mediterranean. An invasion of Sicily would be launched, which, if successful, would lead to an assault on Italy. The air offensive against Germany would be intensified. But for the American Chiefs of Staff these were only ever side issues. A pressured Churchill agreed that an assault on France would be mounted in the spring of 1944.

In April 1943 Lieutenant General Frederick Morgan was designated Chief of Staff to the Supreme Allied Commander (COSSAC). Morgan and his staff were charged with developing a workable plan for Operation Overlord. And while the operational plan was clearly COSSAC's priority, it was also given a deception section, known as Ops (B) and headed by Lieutenant Colonel J. A. Jervis-Read, working alongside an intelligence officer, Major Roger Hesketh. And Ops (B)'s function, according to COSSAC's formal directive, was to create a deception scheme for Overlord. Such an important role for strategic deception would have been impossible only a short while earlier. Something had clearly happened to alter official thinking in the year since the Controlling Officer, Colonel Oliver Stanley, and his assistant, the thriller-writer Dennis Wheatley, had mounted Operation Hardboiled, their notional attack on Stavanger in Norway, which was discussed in Chapter Two.

Although amateurish in its execution, Hardboiled had at least launched strategic deception in the United Kingdom and given the Controlling Officer and his tiny staff something to do. Of itself it did little to convince the Chiefs of Staff that deception had a major role to play in future operations. But in its wake two events occurred which were to enhance the status of both strategic deception and the controlling body.

First, Sir Archibald Wavell, the commander who had appointed Dudley Clarke to his staff in the Middle East, wrote a letter to Churchill on 21 May 1942 urging him to take strategic deception seriously. He wrote: 'May I suggest for your personal consideration that a policy of bold imaginative deception worked between London, Washington and the commanders in the field by only officers with special qualifications might show a good dividend?'

Churchill was no great admirer of Wavell, but the concept of strategic deception appealed to his unorthodox instincts and he circulated the letter among his Chiefs of Staff. They in turn forwarded it to the Joint Planning Staff. And, on the same day that Wavell sent his letter, British strategic deception received a more enduring boost. Lieutenant Colonel John Bevan was posted to work under Stanley. But as Stanley wished to return to political life, Johnny Bevan was almost immediately appointed Controlling Officer in his place.

Bevan, 46, was a peacetime stockbroker with sad eyes and more than a passing resemblance to Bing Crosby. In 1918, as a 25-year-old major, he had come to Churchill's attention while serving in France as liaison officer to the Supreme War Council. Following the signing of the Treaty of Brest-Litovsk, he had been told to present an assessment of the Germans' Order of Battle to an audience in Paris which included Churchill, Lloyd George, Clemenceau, Foch, Haig, Pershing and various French and British army commanders. His presentation was impressive – and accurate – and Churchill spent the next two evenings probing him for his view of enemy intentions. Churchill would retain a positive memory of the insightful young man, a fact which would do no harm to the future of British strategic deception.

Johnny Bevan was a charming and self-effacing man. 'When things were looking pretty bad for his side at cricket,' an Eton contemporary told Dennis Wheatley, 'he would shuffle in, about sixth wicket down, knock up a hundred, and shuffle out again looking rather ashamed of himself.' What truer gauge of a man's character than his demeanour on the square? But

Bevan was also prone to fits of bad temper. 'All of us who worked under him,' remembers Wheatley, 'ignored his occasional downright rudeness.' Above all, though, Bevan was a dynamic and hard-working enthusiast who would breathe life and direction into the London Controlling Section, as the controlling section was renamed shortly after his arrival. One of his first undertakings was to move the LCS from its elegant but remote offices on the third floor of a Whitehall building into the cramped and airless Cabinet War Rooms, where it would share space with the Joint Planning Staff. Bevan was determined to place strategic deception at the heart of proceedings.

Bevan's most striking declaration of intent was initially to confuse Wheatley. In June 1942, a few weeks into his appointment, Bevan took him aside in exasperation. 'Dennis,' he said, 'we are never going to get anywhere like this. We might just as well both be on leave for all the good we are doing. Nobody tells us anything or gives us any orders.' Bevan was experiencing the same impotence that had frustrated Oliver Stanley before him. But he had a solution. 'We have got to have a directive,' he said, 'and as no one else seems prepared to give us one, we must write it ourselves.' 'Yes, sir,' replied Wheatley, who had no idea what a directive was.

He soon discovered that it was a military charter, setting out a body's function. Bevan's directive announced the function of the London Controlling Section to be the preparation of deception plans on a worldwide basis, the coordination of other deception plans prepared by military commands, and the responsibility for ensuring that all these plans were executed properly. And so Bevan created formal guidelines for strategic deception, while ensuring that its overall control rested with the LCS. The Chiefs of Staff approved his directive, and it paved the way for the acceptance of strategic deception as a genuine weapon of war. 'From that point,' as Wheatley recalled in his memoirs, 'Johnny Bevan and I went to work.'

A surprising amount of this work involved eating and drinking with senior officers; deception was still a new creed, after all, and it paid to spread the word convivially among those whose cooperation might prove useful. Much of the social burden was bravely shouldered by Wheatley, who despite his junior rank was admired as a novelist and known as a cordial host. He later recalled: 'Not a week passed but Admirals, Generals and Air Marshals dined or lunched with me, or I with them; so I was able to introduce Johnny on the "old boy" level to all these people.' The 'old boy' network would prove a valuable expedient for the fledgling deceivers.

The determined rise of the London Controlling Section coincided with 'Tar' Robertson's July 1942 memorandum to the W Board, expressing B1a's readiness to use its double agents for strategic deception. The Double Cross system and strategic deception were coming of age together. As J. C. Masterman put it, 'we [B1a] had ready an instrument which had been tried and tested and which we could offer to the Controlling Officer for use in his deception plans'. But Bevan still had no knowledge of the existence of the Double Cross system. And so the W Board decided that there should be immediate coordination between the two branches: Bevan should be brought into the Double Cross picture immediately.

In addition it was suggested that Bevan should be made chairman of the Twenty Committee and that the Double Cross system should be turned into an arm of his deception body. But this suggestion was quickly dismissed: Double Cross was best left to be run by the experts on existing lines, as an independent channel through which Bevan's deceptions could be passed. Strategic deception, after all, was only one of its recognized purposes. And so Bevan became a full member of the Twenty Committee, while he and his staff in the Cabinet War Rooms began working closely with Robertson's men in St James's Street.

It would not take long for their combined efforts to bear fruit. One afternoon in late July 1942 Bevan returned to the LCS offices from a meeting with the Chiefs of Staff with news of the proposed Allied invasion of French North Africa, codenamed Operation Torch. LCS was to be responsible for a cover plan, or rather a series of cover plans as there were to be three sets of landings, around Casablanca, Algiers and Oran. These would be carried out by three task forces, one sailing from the United States and the other two from Britain. The LCS's basic intentions were to make the Germans keep their troops away from North Africa, to prevent them from discovering the existence of the task forces for as long as possible, and once they had discovered them, to make them think that they were heading for destinations other than North Africa.

To these ends a multitude of cover plans were produced in a very short time. Operation Overthrow suggested that the task forces were heading to France, Operation Solo I to Norway, Operation Solo II to Dakar in West Africa, Operation Kennecott to Sicily, and Operation Townsman suggested that they were intending to relieve Malta. LCS drew up a timetable, running from August through to the actual landings in November, for measures to be put across to suggest the various feints. And double agents – Wulf Schmidt, Friedl Gaertner, and most notably Juan Pujol – were to pass across much of the deception.

In September, Pujol set the scene for a possible invasion of France with a letter warning the Germans that 'rumours which are circulating that the English cannot invade for lack of tonnage are put out with the intention of confusing you'. Shortly afterwards he reported that Scottish and Canadian troops were training on the west coast of Scotland, as though in preparation for action in mountainous country. In the same area, he wrote, ski troops and supplies of anti-freeze and snow-chains had been spotted. All of this pointed towards a forthcoming attack on Norway.

One of Pujol's notional sub-agents, the Swiss national Gerbers, presented a problem. He was supposedly based in Bootle, reporting on shipping activity. But had he really been observing the Mersey docks, he would have spotted a great deal of fevered preparation for the genuine landings. And so Pujol first reported to the Germans that he had heard nothing from his agent, before 'discovering' that Gerbers had actually died following an illness. As evidence, Pujol sent the Abwehr an obituary notice from the *Liverpool Daily Post* which had been placed by B1a. In reply the Germans sent a message of condolence to Gerbers's widow, to be passed to her by Pujol.

In order to suggest that Gibraltar was to be a base for the relief of Malta, Major David Strangeways of the Duke of Wellington's Regiment was dispatched to Gibraltar, armed with a copy of Wheatley's latest novel. Inside this was a letter from Wheatley to a Foreign Office official explaining that landing craft being assembled on Gibraltar were to be used to assist Malta. While on Gibraltar, Strangeways left the book and letter in his hotel room, where it was almost certain to be examined and copied by Spanish hotel staff in the pay of the Germans. This would not be the major's final contribution to British deception.

These are just a small sample of the measures taken in support of the various Torch cover plans. And the Germans were certainly unclear about where any possible landings were coming. An intercepted message from Hitler to his operational

staff on 5 October ordered that the Channel coast be put on a
state of alert 'on the basis of numerous reports from agents'.
The situation reports of the Commander-in-Chief West, Field
Marshal Gerd von Rundstedt, were being intercepted weekly,
and they consistently demonstrated his belief in an imminent
assault on the Channel coast. The Germans also accepted the
threat to Norway. On 2 November central and northern
Norway was put on a state of full alert. In the event, the task
forces were not detected until 6 November once they were
already inside the Mediterranean, and even then they were
believed to be on their way to Sicily or Malta. 'When the Afri-
can landings were made, they were a complete surprise,' the
former Chief of Operations Staff at Wehrmacht High
Command, General Alfred Jodl, told Allied interrogators after
the war.

The question of how much of this confusion was thanks to
LCS's cover plans is open to question. It is quite possible that
the Germans had actually deceived themselves. Hitler was
forever paranoid about the possibility of an attack on his 'zone
of destiny' Norway; Rundstedt, who was responsible for
defending the Channel coast, was always sensitive to any hint
of a threat; and the general atmosphere of uncertainty encouraged rumours, some of which reflected the cover plans, others
of which bore no relation to Allied disinformation. As Sir
Michael Howard has written, 'Even if the LCS and the Twenty
Committee had not existed the enemy might have blinded
himself with his own fears. But then again he might not.'

In the end, whether due to its own efforts or not, the LCS's
goals had been achieved: the Germans had kept their troops
away from North Africa, they had been very slow in discovering the Allied task forces, and even then their ultimate destination had remained undiscovered. And it is worth noting that
the deceptions had obeyed Dudley Clarke's hard-earned rules

of strategic deception: they were put over by numerous small details, they incorporated sufficient verifiable facts to make them feasible, they were formulated with knowledge of the operational plans, they played where possible on the enemy's existing fears, and most importantly of all, each was conceived with a clear idea of how the LCS wanted the enemy to *act*.

Operation Torch was a defining period for the LCS, but it also represented a turning point for B1a. Close liaison with Johnny Bevan's men had allowed its agents to be used as successful vehicles for strategic deception: its expressed goal since J. C. Masterman's memo of December 1940. And one of those agents – Juan Pujol – had come to occupy an exalted position in the eyes of the Germans. A week before the invasion Pujol had written two letters to the Abwehr. The first passed on information from his Venezuelan sub-agent in Glasgow that a large convoy had left the Clyde. The second reported that the Venezuelan was now observing troop ships and battleships sailing out of port in Mediterranean colours, and more importantly, that Pujol had seen a top secret document at the Ministry of Information suggesting that an invasion of French Morocco and/or Algeria was imminent.

The first letter, dated 29 October, was forwarded to MI6 in Lisbon, with instructions that it should only be sent on to Madrid once the Germans had spotted the task forces. The second letter was postmarked in England on 2 November, but not posted until the 7th. Both letters therefore reached the Abwehr *after* the invasion, but gave the impression of having been sent well in advance. 'Your last reports are all magnificent, but we are sorry they arrived late,' replied the Abwehr, who truly believed that Pujol had tried to warn them in good time. His reliability confirmed, he was sent ciphers in March 1943. With his Spanish Republican acquaintance acting as operator, Pujol was now a wireless agent. So far as the Abwehr was concerned, its top agent's intelligence need never be delayed again.

And so by April 1943, when COSSAC received its orders to start planning Operation Overlord, three factors – the determination of Johnny Bevan, the recent liaison between LCS and B1a, and the success of Torch – had combined to turn strategic deception into a respected weapon, endorsed by the Chiefs of Staff. This explains how COSSAC came to be given a two-man deception section and instructions to create a deception plan. And as the Allies would be concentrating their efforts on the Mediterranean for the remainder of 1943, COSSAC's first deception task was to prepare a plan to keep enemy forces away from the Mediterranean until the end of the year.

The resulting plans – Operations Starkey, Wadham and Tindall – were known collectively as Operation Cockade. Starkey was to feign an attack on the Pas de Calais on 8 September. A mock invasion fleet was actually to set sail for France before turning back, and this was intended to bring the Luftwaffe up to battle. Wadham was to feign an American invasion of Brittany two weeks later and Tindall was to give the impression that Norway was continuously threatened. In effect these plans were extensions of Operations Overthrow and Solo I, which had covered the invasion of North Africa.

Operation Cockade was formulated by COSSAC with a great deal of input from Johnny Bevan and the London Controlling Section. Its most enduring achievement was to begin the implementation of an inflated Order of Battle. The enemy had to be convinced that sufficient troops were present in Britain to mount the various invasions, and so the planners turned to the idea previously used so successfully by Dudley Clarke in the Middle East. Clarke had expended a great deal of time and effort on his 'standing dish', and now the Allies were to recreate his efforts in Britain, using double agents to suggest the existence of imaginary units. These included the US 46th and 55th Infantry Divisions and the British Fourth Army, the last two created to intensify the threat to Norway.

As was the case during Torch, double agents played a leading role in Cockade. Dusko Popov travelled to Lisbon on 16 July with a mass of information intended as clues to Allied intentions. His doctor had informed him that the military was insisting on hospital beds being reserved for its use in the near future. His tailor was telling him that a large number of senior officers were requesting new battledress. Somebody else had told him that Southampton was preparing for heavy air attacks owing to its forthcoming role as a supply base. He had even seen barges being transported southwards by lorry on the road out of Oxford. An invasion of France seemed possible.

Juan Pujol took up the theme. He reported that assault barges were moving along the south coast, that camps were being built around Southampton, and that his first sub-agent, Carvalho, who was based in Southampton, was advising that an attack on France appeared inevitable.

Wulf Schmidt, meanwhile, was reporting significant troop movements in Deal and Dover, and this was confirmed by Pujol's Agent 7, a Welsh seaman currently in Kent. A large number of motor torpedo boats had arrived in Dover, said the sub-agent, and embarkation runways had been cleared of obstacles. On 7 September, Carvalho told Pujol that the 54th Infantry Division and two Canadian divisions had arrived in Southampton, and two days later the Venezuelan sub-agent in Glasgow informed Pujol that that a reliable source had tipped him off that an operation would take place at dawn the next morning.

This patchwork of information reveals how the double agents were used to put across an integrated story. But Double

Cross was not the only vehicle for the deception. Landing craft – both real and dummy – had congregated at Southampton and in the Thames Estuary. There was a genuine build-up of troops in the south of England, many of whom were actually to set sail for France. Commando units were carrying out raids on the French coast. Minesweepers were clearing the Channel. On D-Day itself the weather was poor and the 'invasion' had to be postponed by twenty-four hours. But, early on the morning of 9 September, it was launched.

The genuine convoys set out from Kent and Hampshire towards the French coast. It was expected that the Luftwaffe would be lured into the sky to attack them, so aircraft of both Bomber Command and Fighter Command flew over the ships ready to engage in battle. Ten miles from Boulogne the convoys halted, as planned.

But the Germans did not react. The Luftwaffe was not scrambled and the shore batteries stayed quiet. The Germans were aware that something was happening, but whatever it was did not seem to merit much concern. In his memoirs Sir Frederick Morgan writes that a German artillery officer was 'overheard calling his captain on the radio to ask if anybody knew what this fuss was all about'. The simulated invasion of northwest Europe failed to create any interest in those about to be invaded. So the convoys turned round and sailed for home.

That afternoon the BBC broadcast an announcement that large-scale invasion exercises had been carried out in the Channel, and that the Germans had failed to take any action. Pujol and Tomás Harris were concerned that, should this be believed by the Abwehr, it would question Pujol's reliability. They acted quickly by informing the Abwehr that the story put out by the BBC had been untrue, that the troops had been surprised and disappointed that the operation had been suspended, and that rumours were circulating that it had been called off because of the current political situation: Italy had signed an armistice several days previously and there were those in power, suggested Pujol, who hoped that Germany might now do the same.

Pujol's Madrid handler, Karl-Erich Kühlenthal, seems to have been relieved by this analysis. He quickly sent it on to Berlin, with his own touch of hyperbole: he related that the suspension of the operation had 'caused disgust among the troops'. Several days later Pujol and Harris were themselves relieved to discover that the incident had not harmed the Catalan in Abwehr eyes. They received a message from Kühlenthal saying that Berlin was very satisfied with Pujol's reports and telling him to keep watching for troop movements as the threat from the south coast of England still existed. In the end none of B1a's double agents were compromised by passing over Cockade material. Indeed Dusko Popov's role helped to rehabilitate him following his near-disastrous sojourn in the United States.

Once Operation Starkey was cancelled, Wadham – the notional attack on Brittany – was also called off. Tindall, the threat to Norway, was a little more successful. The threat was maintained until the end of the year, during which time twelve German divisions were held in Norway. But such was Hitler's vigilance concerning Scandinavia, they might have been held there even in the absence of Tindall.

Overall, Cockade was a failure. Far from tying German troops down in north-west Europe, ten divisions had been removed from Rundstedt's control by September. Wehrmacht High Command had correctly gauged that the Allies would be concentrating their efforts on the Mediterranean in 1943. On one view, the best that can be said of Cockade is that it did no harm.

And yet Cockade actually served a number of vital functions. It gave the deceivers and Double Cross men badly needed practice. It underlined the trust that the Germans had in their British controlled agents: Harris, for one, came to realize that 'providing we did not arouse suspicion prior to the carrying out of Overlord, we had established a channel for deception that was capable of rendering a valuable service'. It gave the planners of Starkey the opportunity to consider the logistics of a cross-Channel operation in advance of Overlord. And it established an inflated Order of Battle – which was to be fully accepted by the enemy thanks to the sheer determination of Lieutenant Colonel Alexis von Roenne to stress the existence of every apparent Allied unit in the west. All of these factors would prove very important for the year ahead.

Of course, while COSSAC, with the help of the London Controlling Section, had been planning Cockade, it was also developing the plan for Operation Overlord, the invasion of north-west Europe scheduled for the spring of 1944. In practice, the lack of a Supreme Allied Commander until December 1943 was compromising General Morgan's ability to work effectively. His plans for the scale of the invasion were constrained by restrictions imposed by the Chiefs of Staff and by the limited availability of landing craft. The final Overlord plan would be far more ambitious in its scope than anything Morgan had envisaged. But his most lasting contribution to Overlord would be its most fundamental element: the site of the invasion.

Morgan considered the options; since the invasion was to be mounted from Britain, the Pas de Calais was the obvious choice. It was the closest point to England, offering the shortest sea crossing and the most comprehensive air cover. It also offered the reasonably sized ports of Calais and Boulogne, a number of beaches over which the invasion could be maintained, and the quickest direct route to Paris and on to Berlin. But precisely because it was the obvious site, the Pas de Calais suffered a serious disadvantage: it was very heavily defended. So heavily, in fact, that it could be eliminated as an option. Another possibility was Brittany, but as it lay beyond effective air cover, it too was dismissed. The Cotentin was deemed too dangerous as the Allies might become trapped inside the peninsula. And so on 15 July 1943 Morgan wrote to the Chiefs of Staff: 'We may be assured of a reasonable chance of success only if we concentrate our efforts on an assault across the Norman beaches about Bayeux.'

Normandy offered good air cover, open beaches with shallow gradients, and a relatively short sea crossing. It offered only one sizeable port, Cherbourg, but this handicap would be overcome by the use of artificial floating harbours, codenamed Mulberry Harbours, through which the invasion could be supplied and maintained. Normandy was less well defended than the Pas de Calais, and troops coming ashore would not be restricted by waterways, which would allow them to spread relatively quickly over a substantial area.

Once an embryonic operational plan existed it was possible to start considering a deception plan. So while Cockade was still unfolding around them, Johnny Bevan and his London Controlling Section issued their 'First Thoughts' on the cover plan for Overlord. Their nascent proposal was to convince the Germans that no invasion was to take place until preparations for the real invasion became so obvious that it could no longer be denied. At this point the Germans should be led to believe that the invasion was not to be aimed at Normandy.

The first difficulty with this idea was that it represented a sudden reversal of the Cockade plan: the Germans had just been told that an invasion of western Europe was coming and now they were to be told that it wasn't. But the problem could be overcome, believed the LCS, if the enemy was led to believe that the invasion had been cancelled, and that the Allies had decided to rely instead on a bombing offensive to crush Germany, supported by attacks on Scandinavia and southern Europe.

Morgan expressed pessimism about these 'First Thoughts'. Would it not be better, he suggested to Johnny Bevan, to create such an exaggerated Order of Battle that the Germans would feel compelled to abandon the defence of France? The simple answer was 'no'. Operation Camilla had taught Dudley Clarke that the deceiver cannot simply lead an enemy commander to expect an attack: he must be clear as to what he wants the commander *to do* as a result. If the Order of Battle was exaggerated too greatly, Bevan told Morgan, the Germans 'might reinforce France to such an extent that Overlord would prove an impossible proposition'. And clearly that was not the desired result.

In August 1943 Churchill and Roosevelt met at the Quebec Conference, where they approved the outline Overlord plan. It was now possible for Bevan and his team to begin work on a more comprehensive deception plan, still largely based on their 'First Thoughts'. The result was Plan Jael, named for the biblical heroine who lulled a tired Canaanite general to sleep, only to drove a stake between his eyes as he slept. The plan's purpose was not dissimilar: to make the enemy believe that no threat of invasion existed, and therefore to lull him into weakening his strength in north-west Europe. Once he was aware that an invasion was inevitable, he would be led to expect it in the Pas de Calais and Belgium. After that the metaphorical stake would be driven between his eyes.

It is clear that Jael would rely on the Germans being prevented – for a considerable length of time – from discovering that an invasion was being prepared. But COSSAC's deception team, Jervis-Read and Hesketh, was concerned that this fact could not be concealed. The Germans were expected to rely for their intelligence information on three sources: wireless intercept, aerial reconnaissance and agents' reports. Wireless intercept was considered a particularly effective source. The Germans held the entire coastline of western Europe, and it was believed that they could tap into Allied wireless traffic with ease. It was also believed that German aerial reconnaissance was very effective. So far as agents' reports were concerned, the army representative on the Twenty Committee expressed the view generally held outside B1a: 'The German General Staff will not move a single division on an agent's report alone, it must be supported by other evidence.'

And so COSSAC's worry, in the summer of 1943, was not that Bevan's Plan Jael could not be prepared, nor that it could not be passed to the enemy, but that it could not be executed effectively. The Germans would be bombarded with real information about the movements of troops and ships. And it would simply not be possible to convince them that no threat of invasion existed.

In place of Plan Jael, COSSAC drew up its own plan in September, officially codenamed Torrent but known as Appendix Y. Assuming that the Germans would have a basic knowledge that an invasion was coming, the plan was intended to keep them in doubt as to the date and time of the invasion, and to make them falsely believe that both the main assault and the follow-up were coming in the Pas de Calais. And once the invasion had actually taken place, the plan was intended to contain German forces in the Pas de Calais for at least fourteen days.

For the plan to work the Germans would have to be convinced that the Allies possessed sufficient forces to mount an invasion of the Pas de Calais *after* the Normandy landings. Dummy barges, fake radio traffic and double agents were all to be used to give this impression. A camouflage policy of total concealment in south-west England (where the real invasion forces would be based) and discreet display in the south-east (where the fake forces would be based) was to be employed. Dummy aircraft would be displayed in the south-east and notional divisions were to be situated around the Thames Estuary. And because the Allies expected the Germans to be watching and listening closely, real troops would be needed to simulate the movements of these divisions. 'All the preparations we wanted the Germans to believe in,' writes Roger Hesketh in his study of Operation Fortitude written at the end of the war, 'would have to be physically represented, so that they might be believable from the air (to deceive reconnaissance) and from the ground (to deceive the spies).'

When it was circulated, Appendix Y drew a great deal of criticism. The American commanding general in England, Lieutenant Jacob L. Devers, was unwilling to commit to it, and Dudley Clarke, still running 'A' Force from Cairo and shortly to be made a brigadier, noted that it did not observe his golden rule. It laid down what the Germans were to think, but not what they were to do. But Appendix Y did, at least, introduce the idea of portraying the real invasion as a feint, which would induce the Germans to keep their reinforcements from Normandy.

At the Teheran Conference, held between 28 November and 1 December 1943, Stalin, Churchill and Roosevelt took the final decision to launch Operation Overlord in May. It was also agreed that a landing in the south of France (Operation Anvil) and a Soviet summer offensive would both take place at around the same time. On the last afternoon of the conference Churchill – aware of Russian concerns that he would suspend Overlord – decided to reassure Stalin by outlining the current deception proposals for Overlord. He went on to stress that strategic deception could function properly only if the Allies worked together. Stalin in turn spoke of Red Army deception tactics and agreed to cooperate. 'In wartime,' said a relieved Churchill, 'truth is so precious that she should always be accompanied by a bodyguard of lies.'

Churchill might have been quoting the deceivers' motto, so well did his words encapsulate the distorted integrity of their enterprise. And when, on 6 December, Bevan was asked to produce the definitive cover plan for Overlord, it was duly codenamed Operation Bodyguard. In his memoirs Dennis Wheatley recalls Bevan 'haggard from sleeplessness', struggling with rewrite after rewrite. The finished plan, delivered on 21 December, contained elements of both Jael and Appendix Y. It set down deception policy worldwide for 1944, with the overall intention of preventing German forces from interfering with the forthcoming operations: Overlord, Anvil and the Russian summer offensive.

The enemy was to be persuaded that the bombing of Germany – Operation Pointblank – would be prioritized to bring about Germany's collapse. The Germans would be led to expect a cross-Channel invasion in late summer, with at least fifty divisions available to take part, twelve of which would be involved in the initial assault. Numerous other threats were to be posed, for example, to Norway, to the north-west coast of Italy and to the Balkans, and these deceptions would be implemented by the theatre commanders concerned. It was also to be suggested that approaches would be made to Turkey to join the Allies, and to Sweden to allow its airfields to be used by Allied aircraft. These were just some of the measures which would, Bevan hoped, induce the Germans to keep their forces away from the real operations.

Reaction to Bodyguard was mixed. The British Chiefs of Staff accepted it almost unreservedly, but the American reception was cooler. The Joint War Plans Committee ultimately concluded that it 'can do no harm and may do considerable good by misleading the enemy for several months as to our intentions'.

So far as German expectations were concerned, on 3 November 1943 Hitler issued his Führer Directive No. 51. It read:

> I can no longer take responsibility for further weakening the West, in favour of other theatres of war. I have therefore decided to reinforce its defences, particularly those places from which the long-range bombardment of England will begin. For it is here that the enemy must and will attack, and it is here – unless all indications are misleading – that the decisive battle against the landing forces will be fought.

The 'weakening' Hitler refers to was the removal of ten divisions from Rundstedt's command while the LCS was implementing Cockade. But no such weakening could now be expected. Hitler had decided – correctly – that the main thrust of Allied strategy for 1944 would be against 'Fortress Europe'. On the face of it, this was bad news for both the Allied operation planners and the deceivers, but Hitler's directive reveals the opportunity that now existed for the Allies. Their invasion, Hitler believed, would be focused on 'those places from which the long-range bombardment of England will begin': the Pas de Calais. The real attack was coming in Normandy, and so long as the deceivers could reinforce Hitler's belief (and so long as the capricious Hitler maintained his belief), the possibility of catching the Germans by surprise was there. Dudley Clarke had, after all, stressed the importance of playing on an enemy commander's existing fears. The deceivers could now put theory into practice in Europe.

In December 1943 Roosevelt informed General Dwight D. Eisenhower that he was to be Supreme Allied Commander and head of SHAEF (Supreme Headquarters Allied Expeditionary Force). SHAEF duly relieved COSSAC of its Overlord planning role. General Sir Bernard Montgomery, was placed in command of the 21st Army Group, which initially controlled all Overlord ground forces. And as soon as Montgomery arrived in England at the beginning of January he began stamping his mark on Overlord. He replaced the existing staff of the 21st Army Group with his own men and tore into COSSAC's operational plan. The invasion front was too narrow, he insisted, and the number of proposed assault troops too modest. Five divisions were needed and the resources would simply have to be found. Eisenhower agreed with him and a revised date of 5 June was set for Operation Neptune.

The changeover from COSSAC to SHAEF meant that COSSAC's deception section, Ops (B), came under the control of SHAEF. The role of head was initially offered to Dudley Clarke, but he turned it down. The post was instead taken by Noel Wild, Clarke's taciturn 'A' Force deputy. J. A. Jervis-Read, the former head, was placed in charge of physical deception, and Roger Hesketh led the Intelligence subsection. Since an important part of Hesketh's job would involve the use of double agents (or 'special means', as Double Cross was coyly known), Christopher Harmer, Czerniawski's case officer, was seconded from B1a to act as liaison. And just as Bevan had been let in on the Double Cross secret in 1942, so Wild was alerted to B1a's odd little cast of characters, and he too became a member of the Twenty Committee.

While SHAEF Ops (B) was now in charge of Overlord deception operations, Bevan's LCS was still responsible for coordinating the implementation of European cover plans, and it was not always clear who was actually responsible for the Overlord cover plans. In practice, however, Ops (B) and the LCS worked as one. The men in charge of the various relevant organizations, Wild and Hesketh at Ops (B), Bevan and Ronald Wingate at the LCS, and Robertson and Masterman at B1a, were all similar enough types, able to work together beyond official structures and responsibilities. They would visit one another and lunch together. Bevan was even given a desk in the Ops (B) offices. The smooth running of the system clearly owed much to the fact that they were all on Wheatley's 'old boy level'.

And so Wild at Ops (B) began work on a cover plan for the Normandy landings. The plan came to be known as Fortitude. It had originally been codenamed Mespot, but the name failed to appeal to Churchill and as a result was changed. Fortitude was split into two halves: the Fortitude North half was the deception intended to pin German troops in Norway, while the Fortitude South half was the deception on which Wild was currently working. And as the implementation of each cover plan was the responsibility of the relevant commander, Fortitude South would be implemented by the commander of the 21st Army Group, General Montgomery. The head of Montgomery's deception section, known as G(R), was Colonel David Strangeways, a man very much in Monty's own mould.

David Strangeways is the officer we last met being dispatched to Gibraltar with a copy of Dennis Wheatley's latest novel. Since then he had been working for Tactical HQ 'A' Force in North Africa and Italy, where he had made a considerable name for himself – and not just for his deception planning. Strangeways was awarded the DSO for his conduct during the fall of Tunis in May 1943, when he had darted into the German HQ to seize documents and cipher machines before they could be destroyed.

Montgomery was notoriously particular in his choice of staff officers, and Strangeways' blend of intelligence, courage and arrogance was likely to appeal to him. Wheatley met Strangeways in the run-up to Torch, and remembered him as 'a small good-looking man, with a brisk, efficient manner, and a very quick mind' but noted that 'he had not the least fear of expressing his own opinions with the utmost frankness'. Expanding on this theme, Christopher Harmer, who arrived at SHAEF as Strangeways was taking up his role with the 21st Army Group, recalls the impression that Strangeways made on the cosy establishment: 'Strangeways had a lot of Monty's arrogance and contempt for everyone who fell outside his particular ken. And just as Monty was behaving as though he was commander-in-chief rather than Eisenhower, so Strangeways rode roughshod over the established deception organization – and in no time established the reputation of an impossible and insufferable enfant terrible.'

Noel Wild was currently drafting the Fortitude South plan which Strangeways would be responsible for implementing. It would be helpful, therefore, for the two men to strike up a good working relationship. But according to Harmer: 'Strangeways' relationship with Noel Wild was as bad as it could have been. They were diametrically opposite. Wild was from an ultra smart cavalry regiment, well connected and well heeled, laid back, a member of the right clubs. Strangeways was an infantryman from the Duke of Wellington's Regiment, very pushy and aggressive, apeing Monty's attitudes and behaviour.'

The initial Fortitude South plan drawn up by Wild accepted that the Germans would notice the preparations for the real invasion. But through a combination of physical deception in south-east England, radio traffic and Double Cross they would be persuaded that this activity was really in preparation for an invasion of the Pas de Calais intended for the middle of July involving fifty divisions. And so when the real invasion came in Normandy, in June, they would be unprepared. And in order to continue suggesting a threat to the Pas de Calais after the invasion, Wild continued with the Appendix Y idea that six divisions should be maintained in the south-east.

Strangeways found much fault with this plan. At a series of deceivers' meetings he proceeded to air his objections with, to recall Wheatley's words, 'the utmost frankness'. On 25 January, Major General Sir Francis ('Freddie') de Guingand, Montgomery's chief of staff and therefore a higher authority than Strangeways, wrote to SHAEF, proposing a number of improvements. One stands out above the others: far more emphasis should be placed on deceiving the Germans *after* the real invasion. In fact, from D-Day onwards the Germans should be led to believe that the *principal attack* was still to come in the Pas de Calais. In this way German reserves might be held up in the Pas de Calais, rather than being sent to reinforce Normandy.

The final draft of Wild's plan took account of some of Strangeways' complaints. The plan was now divided into two. The first part, Story A, focused on the period before the actual invasion. At this time the Germans would be persuaded that an assault was to be carried out in mid-July on the Pas de Calais. It would involve fifty divisions and enough landing craft to transport twelve divisions at once. All of this was as before, although it was now suggested that, should the Germans work out that the mid-July date was a ruse, then the threat to the Pas de Calais would be fully developed.

But Story B, focused on the period after the real invasion, took notice of Strangeways' suggestions. The Germans would be led to believe that the Normandy landings had been a feint intended to draw their reserves away from the Pas de Calais, and that sufficient landing craft for two assault divisions were ready in the south-east of England, as well as another four held in readiness in the Portsmouth area.

But Strangeways was still not satisfied. For one thing, the suggestion that fifty divisions were available for the invasion was fantastic. The exaggerated Order of Battle activated during Cockade was not suggesting this many notional troops. However generous Roenne's projections were, this number would surely be questioned by the Germans. For another thing, it must seem unlikely that two separate invasions – first of Normandy and then of the Pas de Calais – could be under the control of Montgomery. And for a third thing, the plan placed a great deal of emphasis on physical deception. Harmer remembers: 'I worked on this plan during my first week with Hesketh [at SHAEF] and I remember that it depended heavily on dummy landing craft and tanks assembled north and south of the Thames. Which it was hoped would be seen by aerial reconnaissance.'

The plan also depended on the movements of real troops and different kinds of elaborate display. All of which, Strangeways realized, would be very heavy on resources – and quite unnecessary. The enemy was carrying out very little aerial reconnaissance: Allied control of the skies was all but blinding the Germans. As a result Strangeways took the decision to abandon the use of real troop movements and to limit physical display to dummy landing craft. SHAEF attempted to overrule him, but failed. The antagonism between SHAEF and Strangeways intensified, until a confrontation was inevitable. Harmer recalls:

We were all electrified by reports of a meeting which had taken place between representatives of the two Intelligence Services, SHAEF and the 21st Army Group, to discuss

implementation of the cover plan. At this meeting, Strangeways had stated that the plan was useless and publicly tore
it up in front of everybody, announcing that he proposed to
rewrite it, and had Monty's authority. It gave maximum
offence! What was said about Strangeways hardly bears
repeating!

I remember Roger Hesketh saying sarcastically, 'His new
plan will be just a rewrite of the previous one with a few
new ideas thrown in.' Well, it wasn't, of course. I remember
it being delivered by a special messenger to our room in
Norfolk House [SHAEF Headquarters in St James's] and
Roger sitting down to read it. After a long time, in total
silence, he handed it to me without comment and asked my
views. I read it, and asked, 'Could we possibly get away with
simulating an entirely fictitious army group?'

Strangeways' idea was to create a new fictional army group,
FUSAG (the First United States Army Group), concentrated
in south-east England, which was intended to threaten the Pas
de Calais. FUSAG was, in reality, a skeleton unit which the
Germans had discovered through a radio intercept. It had
been a planning formation, and was not currently in use. But
brought to apparent life, and made up of genuine units notionally attached to it, its existence could make the threat to the
Pas de Calais appear more credible. References to fifty divisions from previous versions of the plan could be dispensed
with, as could the suggestion that two distinct invasions came
under a single command. From now on – in German eyes –
SHAEF would consist of the 21st Army Group and FUSAG.

Strangeways' rewritten version of Fortitude South included
an implementing plan, Plan Quicksilver, divided into six
sections. The first section was the most important. It underlined that before D-Day the Germans should simply be told

that SHAEF consisted of the 21st Army Group and FUSAG, and that FUSAG was located in the south and south-east of England and consisted of the First Canadian Army (II Canadian Corps and VIII United States Corps) and the United States Third Army (XX Corps and XII Corps) supported by the US Ninth Air Force. In other words, it should not yet be suggested that FUSAG was threatening the Pas de Calais. But after D-Day the Germans should be told that FUSAG would attack the Pas de Calais once the 21st Army Group had lured sufficient German reserves to Normandy.

Quicksilver's second section dealt with the need for dummy radio traffic reflecting the notional moves of FUSAG units to their new locations in south-east England. These moves were expected to be confirmed by double agents' reports. But what Strangeways did not know when he drafted Quicksilver was that not only were the Germans not watching Britain from the air, they were probably not listening very closely to wireless traffic either. Roger Hesketh's account of Fortitude suggests two reasons why the Germans were not intercepting the messages painstakingly broadcast in order to deceive them: first, because the bulk of German intercept apparatus was concentrated on the battle fronts, and secondly, because Britain was producing such an overwhelming amount of radio traffic that comprehensive interception was practically impossible.

Once Christopher Harmer had read Strangeways' version of Fortitude South, he noticed a problem which threatened to blow the entire FUSAG story shortly after D-Day. General Omar Bradley had been written in as FUSAG commander, but he was due to be landing in Normandy with the assaulting divisions. Harmer mentioned the fact to Hesketh, who passed it on. Within a short time Bradley's name had been replaced by that of Lieutenant General George S. Patton, who was not due to arrive in Normandy for several weeks.

But apart from his own – crucial – contribution to the Fortitude South plan, Harmer's prevailing memory of the time is of the very reluctant admiration felt by other deceivers for a man unwilling to engage on the 'old boy level':

> I certainly remember the intense antagonism at the time on the part of the Intelligence establishment about Strangeways' behaviour, and the complete astonishment of everyone I spoke to at the audacity of his FUSAG concept. After the initial shock, I think everyone was a bit shamefaced that they hadn't thought of it themselves. In any case, they all just had to accept it. For my part, I swallowed it hook, line and sinker.

David Strangeways was to leave the army in 1957 on conscientious grounds after being asked to command a task force carrying out nuclear testing on Christmas Island. Two years later he was ordained as a Church of England deacon. After his death in 1998 an obituary described his sermons as 'direct and to the point', which could equally describe his dealings with colleagues in 1944 and also his blunt memories of Fortitude South, given to the Imperial War Museum in a 1996 interview:

> I rewrote it entirely. It was too complicated, and the people who made it had not ever done it before. Now they did their best – but it didn't suit the operation which Monty was considering. So I rewrote the thing entirely ... You see so much depended upon the success of the deception plan. Because if we hadn't got away from that deception plan – goodness knows what would have happened.

We shall shortly discover what did happen. In the meantime it is worth noting that Fortitude South, which was originally expected to be put across by physical deception, wireless transmission and Double Cross, would not, in fact, be put across by two of these. The Germans had lost their ability to see into Britain and did not seem to be listening either. For the sake of Operation Overlord it was to be hoped that the army representative on the Twenty Committee was wrong when he said, 'The German General Staff will not move a single division on an agent's report alone, it must be supported by other evidence,' because it is difficult to see where that other evidence would come from. Germany's spies in Britain were about to take on a very great significance – for both sides.

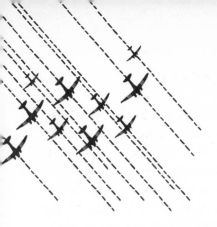

FORTITUDE NORTH

There was very good reason for Operation Bodyguard to include threats to Norway and the Balkans as part of its overall deception policy for 1944. From these edges of occupied Europe, Hitler would be able to call on a large number of divisions to rebuff the invasion of western Europe. And Fortitude North, the operation intended to present this threat to Norway, was actually the latest in a series of deceptions with the same objective. Operations Hardboiled, Solo I and Tindall had all previously sought to take advantage of Hitler's preoccupation with Scandinavia. In a post-war interrogation Nikolaus von Falkenhorst, the general who had planned and executed Hitler's invasion of Norway in 1940, explained that 'giving up Norway would have seemed to [Hitler] an acknowledgement before the whole world that on 9 April 1940 he had made a mistake'. The 1940 offensive had been Hitler's own campaign, carried out primarily to preserve German access to nickel from Finland and iron ore from Sweden. And in 1944 Norway was still the staging post for the supply of these materials. It was perhaps not surprising that Hitler considered the region to be his 'Zone of Destiny', and one that he was willing to defend vigorously.

Churchill seems to have shared Hitler's Scandinavian obsession. To some extent this reflected his belief in attacking

'Fortress Europe' at its peripheries. But as First Sea Lord he had been deeply involved in the Norway campaign of 1940 (for which he had avoided much of the subsequent blame), and he had endorsed the Commando operations at Lofoten and Vågsøy, before actively pressing for a landing in northern Norway in 1942.

And so a range of factors, from pride to pragmatism, were combining to ensure that Norway was extremely well defended in early 1944. And now the deceivers would attempt to keep those defences in place – and, if possible, to augment them – by leading the Germans to expect an Allied invasion.

Operation Fortitude North proposed a combination of physical measures, radio signals and Double Cross activity to achieve its aim. Its most fundamental element was an inflated Order of Battle designed to make the Germans believe that an imminent invasion was credible. A fictional British Fourth Army, based in Scotland, was to be responsible for the attack. It was to be commanded by Lieutenant General Sir Andrew 'Bulgy' Thorne. Thorne had been a pre-war military attaché in Berlin, in whom Hitler had taken a particular interest upon discovering that they had shared a sector of the Western Front in 1914. Hitler came to rate Thorne highly, and his appointment was calculated to attract the Führer's attention to the threat. It almost certainly succeeded. An article written by Thorne was found in Hitler's bunker after his death in 1945.

Thorne chose Colonel Roderick Macleod, the former Military Assistant to the Chief of the Imperial General Staff, to orchestrate the deception. Macleod was appointed on 4 March, just thirteen days before the plan was to be put into action. In his initial briefing he was told his task was to represent an army about to invade Norway, with the intention of pinning down its Germans divisions. Two distinct notional attacks would be aimed at Narvik and Stavanger, suggested mainly by wireless traffic which would be intercepted by the Germans in Norway and France. The imaginary army would consist of Army HQ and three corps, each corps made up of three divisions. One corps – the American XV Corps in Northern Ireland – would be genuine, while the two imaginary corps based in Scotland – the British VII and II Corps – would each contain one genuine division, the British 52nd and 58th Divisions respectively. All the rest of the units would be notional, and represented by wireless. These would be the US 55th Division and the US 7th, 9th and 10th Ranger Battalions, all based in Iceland. The overall picture would, Macleod was assured, be strengthened by the use of agents, and he would also be able to ask for the assistance of the RAF and Royal Navy. In total, twenty-eight officers and 334 other ranks under Macleod's command would have to simulate the activity of over 100,000 men.

Little reliance was to be placed on physical deception; Scotland was considered to be outside the range of effective German air reconnaissance. Nevertheless, a limited amount was planned. The Royal Navy was to fill the Firth of Forth with available shipping, and a naval reconnaissance, Operation Veritas, was to be launched on 26 April. The RAF was to set up displays of real and dummy aircraft around Peterhead, Glasgow and Edinburgh, and would intensify aerial reconnaissance over Norwegian targets, mainly airfields. Bombing raids would be launched, starting on 14 April. And members of the genuine divisions were to prepare seriously for what they believed were real operations. One member of the British 52nd Division who received specialized training recalls, 'We were issued with shoulder flashes which said "Mountain". They were quite obvious. We all sewed those on and that was added to our divisional sign, so that we were a pukka Mountain Division.'

Macleod's particular responsibility was Operation Skye, a comprehensive wireless net intended to mimic the traffic produced by a real army. Each of Macleod's units had its own cover story, worked out to fit the overall plan, and its signals would be divided into three categories: operational, training and routine. The operational signals would be sent in cipher, while training messages would be sent by radio. Care was to be taken that the officers taking the parts of commanders and staff officers remained in their roles, in case the Germans came to recognize their voices. 'A man could not,' realized Macleod, 'be a corps commander one day, and a brigade major the next.'

Operation Skye was launched on 26 March with frenetic activity. Macleod remembers the grand opening: 'Operational and routine messages flew down and up the W/T sets from army to corps, from corps to divisions and brigades, from brigades and divisions to corps and army. In 52nd and 58th Divisions brigade exercises were held. We had artillery exercises and even an artillery practice camp with shooting on a range, all by wireless.'

In effect all the activities of a real army, down to deliberations about new weapons and upcoming courts martial, were discussed and reported on the web. Macleod also began inserting 'calculated indiscretions' into messages to give the Germans the impression that his units were bound for Norway. References were made, for instance, to a mountain battery, and a demand was issued 'for a return of skiers'. And in addition to Macleod's ground forces, other services played their wireless part. The RAF created four fictional light-bomber squadrons, and the Navy created two phoney forces: Force 'V' for Narvik and Force 'W' for Stavanger.

Although SHAEF Intelligence reported to Macleod that references to his broadcasts were appearing in intercepted

German messages, it appears that the Germans were not listening as closely as had been hoped. And so it became vitally important that double agents be able to put the deception across effectively.

Fortitude was the major test for which B1a had been preparing for a very long time. And Fortitude North represented the first part of that test. The synchronization of the agents into the overall deception plan was a complicated business, made simpler by the fact that the individuals responsible worked well together. Roger Hesketh and Christopher Harmer were based at SHAEF headquarters in St James's Square, while 'Tar' Robertson, J. C. Masterman, Tomás Harris and Hugh Astor were around the corner in St James's Street. They could wander back and forth to discuss the approach to be taken, the agents to be used and the messages to be sent. By early 1944 B1a could call, in total, on fifteen active double agents. But only those who could send and receive messages quickly – the wireless agents – were considered suitable for an operation of the magnitude and immediacy of Fortitude. And of these the most trusted in early 1944 were Juan Pujol, Dusko Popov, Roman Czerniawski and Wulf Schmidt.

In early 1944 the W Board had overturned its restriction on Czerniawski's use for strategic deception. The Pole was clear to be used in Fortitude and in April he was notionally sent to Scotland to play his part in Fortitude North. The majority of Polish troops were currently based in Scotland and, as a trained military observer, he could offer precise and detailed information to the Germans. Czerniawski was a clever choice to put across the Scottish Order of Battle.

Pujol's Venezuelan sub-agent was based in Glasgow and so was well placed to report on naval exercises on the River Clyde. But B1a realized that the workload in Scotland might appear too great for just one man, and so Pujol was given a second imaginary sub-agent north of the border. Agent 3(3), as he was memorably known, was said to be a Greek seaman who had served on a British merchant ship before deserting. The Germans were told that he met the Venezuelan, who decided that he would make a good agent for Pujol. Unfortunately 3(3) turned out to be a committed communist, but the Venezuelan overcame the problem by pretending that he was a communist too. Therefore 3(3) was engaged in the belief that he would be reporting to the Soviets. And so the make-believe Greek seaman was sent to the coast of Fife to report on shipping.

Since returning from the United States, Dusko Popov had collected a number of sub-agents to add to Dickie Metcalfe and Friedl Gaertner. They were all Yugoslavs who had escaped to England as a result of a wonderfully complicated plan cooked up by Popov.

The way the plan worked was this: Popov's brother Ivo, an agent in Yugoslavia, would select the individuals who were to come to England. These individuals would pretend they were willing to work for the Nazis and Ivo would hand them on to Popov's old friend Johnny Jebsen, who was still working for the Abwehr despite his anti-Nazi convictions. Jebsen would then escort them to Berlin to be trained as Abwehr agents. After that, they would then make their own way to Britain, to begin work – so the Germans believed – for the Abwehr. In reality they would be greeted by Dusko Popov and Robertson on arrival, before starting work as B1a double agents. The first man to arrive in England in this way was Eugen Sostaric, a Croat naval pilot, whom the British codenamed *Meteor*.

A man who came down Popov's escape route after Sostaric was the Marquis Frano de Bona. A childhood friend of Popov, the marquis was trained by the Abwehr to be a radio operator. On his way to England he spent four days in a

Madrid brothel where, despite having a wonderful time, he picked up crabs. On arriving in London he moved in with Popov, becoming his wireless operator. Unfortunately he also became rather well known on the London dinner-party circuit as the hairy marquis with crabs and was duly given the codename *Freak*.

As well as acting as Popov's radio operator, the marquis was a double agent in his own right, and it was decided that he would play an integral part in the Fortitude North deception. Indeed two days before Colonel Roderick Macleod opened up his wireless net, the marquis sent the message which got Fortitude North under way. He radioed to the Germans that British II Corps had appeared near Stirling in Scotland, having arrived from Yorkshire. Six days later Pujol informed the Germans that his Venezuelan sub-agent had noticed the 52nd Division in Dundee, as well as an unidentified formation whose sign was a shell on a dark background. 'This insignia is completely unknown to me,' Pujol told his handler.

Two days after that, the marquis supposedly met an American XV Corps liaison officer in London, who told him that the corps, made up of the American 2nd, 5th and 8th Infantry Divisions, was now in Northern Ireland, as was the British 55th Infantry Division. The officer also told the marquis that he had been posted to General Thorne's staff in Edinburgh, as XV Corps was now under the control of Thorne's Fourth Army. The marquis sent all of this information to the Germans, who were duly grateful: 'Your latest wires are very satisfactory. Please continue. Congratulations.'

And so, piece by piece, the false Order of Battle was fed to the Germans. By cross-referencing the agents' information, they could begin to piece together a detailed picture. And there was more to come. In a letter due to reach the Germans on or about 6 April, Friedl Gaertner reported that the husband of a friend was working for General Thorne, who 'had been given command of some new army or other they are forming'. The husband's deputy was apparently going to be an American.

On 12 April, Czerniawski returned to London from Scotland and wasted no time in sending the Germans his observations. The Fourth Army, he said, was made up of British II Corps with headquarters in Stirling and British VII Corps with headquarters in Dundee. The latter's insignia, he said, was a seashell on a blue rectangle. This ought to have cleared up any mystery in German minds concerning the insignia spotted by Pujol's Venezuelan friend. Czerniawski also said that he had located the British 58th Division near Stirling and 52nd Division in the Dundee area. The Pole's series of messages finished with his own appreciation: an attack on Norway was to be expected at the beginning of May.

No attack came, but on 14 May Pujol sent the Germans the Venezuelan's account of a naval exercise in Loch Fyne, which the sub-agent apparently believed was being carried out in preparation for an assault on Norway. Pujol called the Venezuelan down to London, leaving 3(3) to cover Scotland. In London the sub-agent reiterated his firm belief that the first attack of the European invasion would be on Norway. Pujol forwarded this view to the Germans with a qualification that he did not himself agree. 'Nevertheless,' he wired, 'I take notice of this opinion since [the Venezuelan] is in a better position than I am to assess this question.' The benefit to Pujol of having sub-agents is clear: he could suggest an imminent invasion of Norway, but blame the sub-agent when the suggestion turned out to be wrong.

All of these reports taken together gave the Germans enough information, not only to conclude that a threat to Norway existed, but to be able to piece together almost all of the Fourth Army's constituent parts and their locations. But apart from physical deception, wireless traffic and double agents' reports, other deceptive measures were taken in relation to Fortitude North. In May, General Thorne paid a visit to Belfast, where he ostentatiously inspected the troops of the American XV Corps as though he was their genuine army commander. This was done for the benefit of the many German spies thought to be in Eire, moving freely back and forth across the border with Northern Ireland. These spies would now be able to confirm that XV Corps was indeed a part of the Fourth Army. Macleod records that Thorne greatly enjoyed his time in Northern Ireland, 'and on his return said that the troops were as good as the Guards, a high compliment from one who was himself a Guardsman'.

Other measures taken included the declaration that the Firth of Forth was a 'Protected Area', meaning that nobody was allowed within ten miles without a special pass. This was intended to emphasize that something highly covert was about to take place there – an invasion of Norway, for example. Speeches were made by both Eisenhower and Haakon VII, the Norwegian king in exile in England, calling on the Norwegian resistance not to take action too soon, the implication being that their patience would presently be rewarded. And in May the Soviet Union began a build-up of troops and shipping in Kola Fjord, near its border with Norway, suggesting an imminent attack. Churchill's conversation with Stalin at the Teheran conference, and the subsequent visit of Johnny Bevan to Moscow to explain the purpose of Bodyguard, had borne fruit.

One other major plan was carried out in aid of Fortitude North, and it was a diplomatic deception plan. It was intended to suggest that the Allies were trying to persuade Sweden to take part in a coming attack and it was codenamed Operation

Graffham. In March 1944 the British were making genuine demands on Sweden through diplomatic channels – for example to prevent the export of ball bearings from Sweden to Germany. Graffham grew out of the realization that further extreme demands could persuade the Germans that Sweden was being urged to abandon its neutrality.

On a visit to London in March the British ambassador to Sweden, Sir Victor Mallet, explained to Bevan that much of the Swedish army was pro-German and it was unlikely that Sweden could actually be persuaded to join the Allies. Nevertheless, he approved the idea of a deception plan. Bevan suggested that Mallet make a number of demands to the Swedish government on his return to Stockholm. These included allowing aircraft to refuel at Swedish airfields, permitting reconnaissance units to fly over the country, and granting facilities for Norwegians attempting to leave Sweden. Mallet did as he was asked.

To underline these overtures, Wulf Schmidt sent a message to his handlers on 25 March which read, 'Mallet, British Ambassador in Stockholm, is in London for special conferences, according to a friend who knows him well. After intensive interviews he is going back there very soon. Said to be taking extra staff. Friend believes that important negotiations with Sweden are being started.' And the Germans noticed Mallet's efforts. An intelligence report, which was seen by Hitler, noted:

From a reliable diplomatic source (Stockholm) 11 April 1944: 'The English Ambassador, Mallet, who was in England for some time, gave on his return a talk to the Embassy staff, which according to an agent's statement contained the following passage ... We have always had good relations with our Swedish friends and hope that these will remain so. We must, however, reckon with the possibility that this good relationship will be put to the test. We can no longer calmly look on while neutral countries deliver goods to our enemies, which do us harm.'

While speaking to Bevan, Mallet particularly liked Bevan's idea that someone of importance should be sent to Stockholm to speak to the pro-Allied Commander-in-Chief of the Swedish Air Force, Bengt Nordenskiöld. Mallet suggested that the emissary should be Air Commodore Thornton, an old friend of Nordenskiöld who had served as British Air Attaché to Sweden before the war. Thornton was sent to Stockholm on 1 April, receiving a sudden and very unofficial promotion to Air Vice Marshal for the purposes of the trip. He arrived in Sweden in civilian clothes and was hurried from the airport to the British embassy in a car with the blinds down. He was ushered in and out of Nordenskiöld's headquarters through a back door. In short, his movements were so flagrantly secretive that the Germans could not help but take an interest. And it was the Allied hope that every move Thornton made would be photographed and every word recorded.

Thornton's actual conversation with Nordenskiöld revolved around the possible repercussions of an Allied invasion of Norway. Were this to take place, noted Thornton, the Germans would likely murder the Norwegians currently in internment camps and destroy Norwegian facilities as they departed. Would the Swedes be willing, therefore, to send their army in to act as a police force to prevent such slaughter and mayhem? This proposal certainly raised the possibility in the Swede's mind that the Allies were seriously considering an invasion.

In his memoirs Dennis Wheatley claims that the room in which this meeting took place was bugged by the pro-German Swedish Chief of Police, who had a transcript of the conversation sent to Berlin, where it was placed before Hitler. To add credibility to this story, Wheatley alleges that it was told to him by Bevan. But Sir Ronald Wingate, in his official LCS record of Fortitude, writes: 'We received reliable evidence at the time that the Germans believed that the Air Vice Marshal had visited Sweden to attempt to organize an Allied landing of paratroops in south Sweden, and that if they obtained definite confirmation that this was intended for the purpose of a further attack, they were determined to forestall it with lightning action against Sweden.'

Whatever the truth of the assertions of Wheatley and Wingate, there can be no doubt that, on 28 May, Alexis von Roenne's FHW delivered the following report of Thornton's visit:

Credibly sounding reported overtures by an English Air Force officer in Sweden, which were apparently aimed at obtaining air bases in Sweden for invasion purposes, may be interpreted as a hint of a minor landing operation being planned in south Norway or Denmark. The likelihood of a more powerful group landing in those parts as part of the larger operational strategy is still considered to be slight.

There is actually much truth to this account. Thornton *was* an English Air Force officer who *did* approach the Swedes about access to their air bases. There is no truth in the suggestion that a 'minor landing' was planned – but it did reflect the story of Operation Graffham.

Another effect of Graffham was the trouble it caused Thornton on his return to Britain. He may have been only an air commodore, but he travelled to Stockholm posing as an air vice marshal, and not unreasonably he claimed his expenses at the senior officer's rate. His request was initially refused – until a wise head on the air staff reversed the decision. In the Alice in Wonderland world of deception, where black could be white, why shouldn't a man be rewarded for being something he wasn't?

Macleod gives a glimpse into this upside-down world. During the implementation of Fortitude North he and other officers would escape occasionally to the golf course, or to shoot on a friendly farmer's land. He writes:

> I think this kept us sane in the atmosphere of make-believe in which we lived which was apt to engender a strange mental attitude. As time went on we found it hard to separate the real from the imaginary. The feeling that the Fourth Army really existed and the fact that it was holding German troops immobilized made one almost believe in its reality.

Some double agents found it difficult to separate the real from the imaginary at the best of times. It is interesting to discover that one of the level-headed deceivers was similarly affected.

So what can ultimately be said about the effects of Fortitude North? Before a conclusion is drawn, it is worth noting an FHW situation report from early March – before the start of the operation – which states that German Intelligence was already accepting the possibility of an assault on Scandinavia, if only to tie down German forces on subsidiary fronts and divert them from 'the decisive Atlantic Front'.

In April, however, thanks to the work of the double agents, particularly Czerniawski, the Germans were aware of a more detailed threat. The FHW situation report for 23 April reads: 'An Abwehr source which has hitherto reported accurately has been able to provide a clarification of the distribution of forces in Scotland.' The report went on to list most of the Fourth

Army's parts, including II Corp, VII Corps, 52nd Division and 58th Division. 'The Seventh English Army Corps, whose location was hitherto unknown, is in the Dundee area,' says the report. It is hardly surprising that VII Corps' location was hitherto unknown: the deceivers had only recently invented it.

The fake Order of Battle was thus accepted, although the Marquis de Bona's information relating to XV Corps and its divisions in Northern Ireland seems to have been mislaid or disregarded by German Intelligence. This seems surprising, given that the marquis had been congratulated on his messages. Nevertheless, the double-agent system was managing successfully to conjure up a fake army.

Physical and wireless deception, on the other hand, seem to have had very little effect. For all Colonel Macleod's valiant and extensive efforts, there is almost no evidence that the Germans were listening to his radio transmissions. And while the odd aerial reconnaissance flight was carried out by the Luftwaffe, an FHW situation report in March complained that 'these single results do not give a clear picture of the shipping situation in Northern English ports'. Essentially the Germans were not watching.

So far as other measures were concerned, Operation Graffham can be considered a success in that it led to speculation that the Allies were attempting to enlist Sweden's help in mounting an assault. This assault was not, however, expected to be anything more than a 'small operation'.

During the life of the operation, intercepted German sources gave periodic suggestions that it was working. On 6 May an intercepted message indicated the 'strong possibility of a diversionary operation in Norway'. Ten days later the Japanese ambassador to Berlin wired a very similar message to Tokyo. But on 25 May the FHW situation report stated that 'the extraordinarily small number of ships in the east Scottish harbours is remarkable and confirms that no noticeable movement from these areas to Norway is planned'.

This is not to say that an assault could not be launched from the *west* coast, but the truth is that Fortitude North did not ultimately convince the Germans that a sizeable attack was to be mounted on Norway, nor was the enemy ever persuaded to reinforce the area with further divisions.

The B1a case officers were taught a lesson. They had been accustomed – for the most part – to limiting their agents' reports to concrete facts from which the Germans could make their own suppositions. This reflected Dudley Clarke's rule that a cover story should be put across in small chunks which the enemy could piece together to arrive at his own conclusions. Yet during Fortitude North B1a had successfully put across the Order of Battle, and the Germans had *still* not made the necessary deduction that a significant assault was coming. Perhaps the enemy needed to be spoon fed with the agents' own personal belief in addition to the facts. Tomás Harris, Pujol's case officer, certainly thought so. From now on he determined to 'supply every form of ammunition, for the arguments of those Germans inclined to believe in our cover plan'. This approach would come to play a decisive role in Fortitude South.

Roger Hesketh of SHAEF Ops (B) would later write: 'Fortitude North, though successful as a deceptive operation, had no influence upon the course of the war.' Perhaps not, but the Germans had displayed repeated concerns about the possibility of a minor diversionary attack and at no point did they weaken their forces in the 'Zone of Destiny'. Since 1940 Norway had been defended by an average of around 250,000 German troops. Only 100,000 of these had been necessary to maintain control, as Jodl explained to his captors in 1945. The other 150,000 were insurance against Allied attack.

Throughout the life of Fortitude North, these insurance troops remained where they were.

Johnny Bevan's original section in the Bodyguard plan relating to Scandinavia reads: 'A threatened attack against Scandinavia should help to contain some first-quality divisions and limited naval and air forces. Such a deception plan would be assisted if the Germans were induced to believe that Sweden was prepared to co-operate with the Allies and if the Russians mounted a threat against enemy occupied territory in the Arctic.'

If this is the standard by which Fortitude North should be judged, then the deception might even be considered a modest success. The divisions were contained, the Germans believed that Sweden was prepared to cooperate with the Allies, and even the Russians were convinced to mount a threat against the enemy in the Arctic.

But a much bigger task was still to come – in the genuine Zone of Destiny. This task would be to convince German Intelligence, and ultimately Hitler, that the war's decisive attack was coming not in Normandy but in the Pas de Calais. Fortitude South was to be a far more ambitious, vital and dangerous undertaking.

FORTITUDE SOUTH

By the end of February 1944 David Strangeways had rewritten Fortitude South and inserted his own implementing plan: Quicksilver. He was now to be responsible for putting Fortitude South into action. And the most important aspect was the fake Order of Battle. To recap, this consisted of the First United States Army Group (FUSAG), which was to pose the threat to the Pas de Calais. It was to be made up of genuine units, all known to the Germans, which would bolster the credibility of the deception. They were as follows:

First Canadian Army (Leatherhead)
II Canadian Corps (Dover)
2nd Canadian Infantry Division (Dover)
4th Canadian Armoured Division (East Grinstead)
VIII United States Corps (Folkestone)
79th US Infantry Division (Heathfield)
28th US Infantry Division (Tenterden)
83rd US Infantry Division (Eltham)
Third United States Army (Chelmsford)
XX Corps (Chelmsford)
4th US Armoured Division (Bury St Edmunds)
5th US Armoured Division (East Dereham)

6th US Armoured Division (Woodbridge)
XII Corps (Chelmsford)
80th US Infantry Division (Hadleigh)
35th US Infantry Division (Brentford)
7th US Armoured Division (Chelmsford)

The units which made up FUSAG may have been genuine, but their locations were not – nor were their proposed roles. It was decided that the First Canadian Army would be depicted as making the initial assault, while the Third US Army would follow it up. We have seen that Christopher Harmer suggested that General George Patton should be portrayed as FUSAG's commander, since the actual commander, General Omar Bradley, would be coming ashore shortly after D-Day. This made good sense: the appearance of the commander of FUSAG on the Normandy beaches would almost certainly end the threat to the Pas de Calais. Much better to place Patton – who as the genuine commander of Third US Army would only be coming ashore much later – in charge of FUSAG.

But it was a clever choice for other reasons: German High Command had a great admiration for Patton and his unorthodox dynamism; Hitler once described him as the Allies' best commander. The Germans would expect him to take a leading role in the most decisive operation of the war. And he was known to have a rivalry with Montgomery, making it logical that he and Monty be placed in charge of the two army groups launching separate attacks on the French coast.

Patton – the emotional tough guy with the high, squeaky voice – had run into recent difficulties which had almost ended his career. In Sicily in August 1943, on visits to evacuation hospitals, he had had two lively encounters with patients. First, on 3 August he came across Private Charles Kuhl, who was lying in bed with a temperature, suffering from dysentery and malaria. Spotting that Kuhl was unwounded, Patton flew into a rage, calling him a coward and slapping his face with a glove. He then grabbed him by the shirt collar, lifted him from the bed and threw him out of the tent, helping him on his way with a kick.

A week later Patton repeated the performance. He saw another patient, Private Paul Bennett, unmarked and without bandages or plaster casts. Bennett, who had served four years in the infantry, was suffering from what is now known as post-traumatic shock. According to his commanding officer, he was a 'brave and dedicated man' who had begged to remain with his unit but had been ordered to hospital by his battery surgeon.

But Patton was not about to offer the soldier counselling. He asked Bennett what was wrong with him. 'It's my nerves,' he replied. 'What's this man talking about?' Patton barked at the orderly. 'What's wrong with him, if anything?' Then, before waiting for an answer, he began screaming, 'You dirty no good son-of-a-bitch! You cowardly bastard! You ought to be lined up against a wall and shot, although that's too good for you! In fact, I ought to shoot you myself, right now, God damn you!' Patton pulled out his pistol and struck Bennett in the face. 'I want you to get that man out of here right away,' he said to the orderly. 'I won't have these other brave men seeing such a bastard babied!' With tears rolling down Bennett's face, Patton hit him harder, knocking his helmet out of the tent. As the general stormed off in fury, he loudly articulated his theory: 'There's no such thing as shell shock! It's an invention of the Jews!'

Unfortunately for Patton, the second incident was witnessed by two journalists, one from the International News Service, the other from Britain's *Daily Mail*. Both men were persuaded not to report the story, but Eisenhower was furious when he heard of it. However, rather than court-martial Patton, who was expected to play an important part in forth-coming operations, he ordered him to apologize to the individuals and their units. In a letter to Patton, Eisenhower wrote: 'Firm and drastic measures are at times necessary, but this does not excuse brutality, abuse of the sick, nor exhibitions of uncontrolled temper in front of subordinates.' For his part, Patton wrote in his diary: 'My motive was correct as I was trying to restore the men's souls by making them mad with me. I shall make what amends I can. I regret the incident as I hate to make Ike mad when it is my earnest study to please him. I am very low.'

The story did, in fact, come to public attention when the Washington columnist Drew Pearson repeated it on his syndicated radio programme. And towards the end of the year Patton was devastated to discover that he was not to be given the overall command of US ground forces for the imminent invasion of Europe. He was instead given the command of the Third Army under Montgomery. That slight was to be only notionally redressed by giving him the fictional command of FUSAG.

It is interesting to note the enemy's reaction to Patton's difficulties. So far as German High Command was concerned, his actions amounted to little more than an effort to maintain discipline. Alfred Jodl believed that the publicity concerning his actions was an Allied attempt to deceive the Germans into thinking that Patton was finished. And so when indications began to filter through (from double agents initially) that Patton was in command of FUSAG, the Germans were very willing to believe the news.

Patton's actual job as FUSAG's notional commander consisted mainly of travelling around south-east England (where the FUSAG units were supposedly based), publicly saying the right things and keeping the pretence going. Describing himself as 'a goddamned natural born ham' who enjoyed 'playing Sarah Bernhardt', he wrote in a letter to a friend: 'I had some very interesting trips while I was working as a decoy for the German divisions, and I believe that my appearances had a considerable effect.' Whether or not he was really enjoying himself in a non-existent job, he tried to keep to the FUSAG script. When he met Brigadier General James Gavin in the lobby of Claridge's Hotel in London, he stopped for a chat. As they parted, he turned and called back loud enough for the entire lobby to hear, 'See you in the Pas de Calais, Gavin!'

But while SHAEF was keen for Patton to draw attention to himself in his FUSAG role, it wanted to avoid attention being drawn to his real job as commander of the Third Army, with its units based far from their notional FUSAG locations. For this reason he was forced to qualify the speech he gave time and again to the men of the Third Army:

> Don't forget. You don't know I'm here at all. No word of the facts is to be mentioned in any letter. The world is not supposed to know what the hell they did to me. I'm not supposed to be commanding this army – I'm not supposed to be in England. Let the first bastards to find out be the goddamn Germans. Some day I want them to raise up on their hind legs and howl, 'Jesus Christ! It's the goddam Third Army and that son-of-a-bitch Patton again!'

Patton would remind his men of what it meant to be American:

The Americans love a winner and cannot tolerate a loser. Americans despise cowards. Americans play to win – all the time. I wouldn't give a hoot for a man who lost and laughed. That's why Americans have never lost and will never lose a war, for the very thought of losing is hateful to an American … The army lives, sleeps, eats, fights as a team. This individual heroic stuff is a lot of crap. The bilious bastards who wrote that kind of stuff for the *Saturday Evening Post* don't know any more about real battle than they do about fucking.

Patton understood his audience, ending his speech with a homespun crack:

There is one thing you will be able to say when you go home. You may all thank God for it. Thank God that at least thirty years from now, when you are sitting around the fireside with your brat on your knee, and he asks you what you did in the great World War Two, you won't have to say that you shovelled shit in Louisiana!

Despite his protests that he derived satisfaction from his FUSAG role, the inactivity and pretence seem actually to have worn Patton down. In a letter to his wife he wrote, 'This damned secrecy thing is rather annoying particularly as I doubt if it fools anyone. Every time I make a speech I have to say "Now remember you have not seen me" – a voice crying in the wilderness.'

In April, Patton's voice was to return from the wilderness. Although Eisenhower had warned him not to speak in public without permission, he agreed to make a brief speech to the 'Welcome Club' for American servicemen at Knutsford, near the Third Army's genuine headquarters in Cheshire. In the speech he said that 'it is the evident destiny of the British and Americans, and of course the Russians, to rule the world'. These words were reported in newspapers worldwide, but Patton's reference to the Russians was omitted, making it seem as though he had slighted the Soviet allies. A public-relations storm developed – out of a speech that Patton had not been authorized to make in the first place. He was in trouble again.

For a second time Eisenhower had to consider whether to dispense with his general's services. Witnesses at the Welcome Club were able to confirm that Patton *had* mentioned the Russians, and while the lack of permission remained an issue, Eisenhower again concluded that Patton was too valuable to sack. But he wrote him another censorious letter: 'I am thoroughly weary of your failure to control your tongue and have begun to doubt your all-round judgment, so essential in high military position.'

For his part, Patton could not understand how the story had emerged. He had been aware of the presence at the Welcome Club of an official from the British Ministry of Information, but he had been assured that no reporters were there. In his reply to Eisenhower he wrote, 'my last alleged escapade smells strongly of having been a frame-up'. Had LCS and Ops (B) considered this episode an opportunity to bring Patton's presence in England to a wide – and therefore a German – audience? Had the Ministry of Information man leaked the speech?

Patton thought so. But the controversy caused by his reported words, particularly in the United States, very nearly forced Eisenhower to send him home. That can hardly have been the deceivers' intention. And while at this point in late April the deception plan had the Third Army's HQ located near Knutsford, there was surely a risk that Patton's presence would suggest to the Germans that he was in command of the

Third Army rather than FUSAG. It might not be surprising that Patton considered the episode a 'frame-up', but there is little evidence that he was right.

And so with the FUSAG Order of Battle worked out, and a loose-cannon commander in place, Strangeways and the deceivers had now to implement Fortitude South. As with Fortitude North, it was to be done through a variety of means: physical deception, wireless operations, and most significantly B1a's double agents.

Physical deception was the element of the deception on which least emphasis was placed. In older versions of the plan this had not been so. The movement of real troops and the building of fake camps had been envisaged on a sizeable scale, along with widespread displays of dummy tanks and aeroplanes. Strangeways had stripped his plan of most of these elements. Partly this reflected a lack of resources, for if the work had to be compromised, or if the preparation necessary was too elaborate, the deception risked being revealed. An example of this had occurred earlier in the war in Holland when the Germans built a full-scale replica of an airfield out of wood. It proved so painstaking to put together that Allied intelligence was able to observe its construction and note its completion. The next day a British aircraft flew overhead and dropped a single wooden bomb onto it. But Strangeways' primary reason for eschewing physical deception was that the Luftwaffe was simply not carrying out enough reconnaissance to make the effort worthwhile.

Strangeways did, however, make use of physical deception on the coast, where there was still a chance that displays of fake landing craft would be noticed by the Germans. Dummy assault landing craft were known as wetbobs, while dummy tank landing craft were known as bigbobs. The fact that 'wetbob' is an Etonian term for a rower (a 'drybob' being a cricketer) offers a clue as to the background of the average deceiver. Two hundred and fifty-five of these dummies were built and displayed on the south and east coasts.

In March, Lieutenant Hugh Clark and his company of the Worcester Regiment were sent for intensive training in the building and maintenance of bigbobs. One hundred and seventy feet long and thirty feet wide, weighing five and a half tons, they were made from steel tubes floated on buoyant steel drums, covered by heavy canvas. It took thirty men over six hours to assemble each craft from over a thousand separate components. In May the components were delivered to Clark's company in Folkestone, where they were fitted together in great secrecy. Folkestone Harbour was sealed off to civilians and tarpaulins were hung across the streets while Clark's men built seventeen dummies on the beach. 'Quite often,' remembers Clark, 'we would be working half the night in water up to our waists.' Once the bigbobs had been floated, the Royal Navy moored them in position in the harbour. Clark and his men would then have to maintain their condition each day, mending joints, tightening canvas and reattaching flotation drums. The level of secrecy surrounding the dummies is apparent from an incident that occurred on the River Orwell in Suffolk. Dummies moored on the river did not have lights and one night a sailing barge ran into a wetbob. The skipper and crew of the sailing barge were promptly take into police custody – and not released until after D-Day.

When Strangeways took over responsibility for physical deception, he noticed a problem. While provision had been made for the landing craft, nobody had given any thought as to how the notional troops were meant to board them. 'They'd forgotten,' Strangeways says, 'to make any hards along the coast.' 'Hards' were embarkation slipways. 'Once I got going,' he continues, 'I said, "Oi, where are the hards?" And you daren't make dummy hards, because if they are dummy, and spotted as dummy, better no hards at all. So they were made. Everything was organized.'

Although Strangeways had cut heavily back on the amount of physical display to be used, his 'R' Force nevertheless proceeded to construct a few fake troop camps in the southeast of England. And a fake dock facility and oil storage complex was built near Dover. This was the work of set builders from Shepperton Studios, following designs by the architect Basil Spence, and its completion was marked by an inspection from King George VI and General Montgomery. Even the monarch had a role to play in Operation Fortitude.

As FUSAG's notional assault would require a great deal of air support, dummy airfields began appearing in south-east England. Fake aircraft, made of wood and canvas, were dispersed on the fields, and landing strips were marked out by lights. At night car headlamps were pulled backwards and forwards at intervals to simulate the movement of aircraft. Responsible for this lighting was Colonel John Turner, whose department, based at Shepperton, had excelled in the building and lighting of decoys during the Blitz. Turner was also placed in charge of lighting the bigbobs, wetbobs and hards on the coast. This was no easy task. In the south-east the lighting had to be designed to attract attention to the dummies; in the south-west it had subtly to draw attention away from the real invasion force. And Turner's job was made no easier by his frequent clashes with Strangeways, whom he described in a letter to the Air Staff as a man 'embedded in his own worth'.

And so physical display was to play *some* part in Fortitude South, even if it was a far less significant part than had been anticipated by LCS and Ops (B) when drafting Jael and Appendix Y. A more significant part would be played by the Royal Air Force, whose attention in the weeks leading up to

Operation Neptune was focused on the Pas de Calais. 'The dear old Air Force really played jolly good ball,' remembers Strangeways. 'For every reconnaissance in the actual operational area, I had two reconnaissances flown in the dummy area.' And the same ratio was applied to the bombing of coastal defences, radar installations and airfields: for every ton of bombs dropped on Normandy, two were dropped on the Pas de Calais. And during this period attacks on railway junctions were focused entirely on the area north-west of the Seine – near the Pas de Calais. These targets had not been chosen by the deceivers, however, but by Allied railway experts as the best means of bringing the French rail network to a standstill. The targets just happened to suit the deceivers' preference.

Another piece of deception carried out by the RAF concerned fighter bases in England. The majority of fighter aircraft intended to support the invasion flew out of bases in Hampshire. To prevent the Germans from drawing conclusions from this, in late May an operation against the Pas de Calais was mounted in which fighters took off from airfields in Kent, Sussex and Surrey. The idea was to suggest that these airfields in the south-east would be employed as 'advanced bases' during the forthcoming invasion of the Pas de Calais. And just in case the Germans had failed to spot what was happening, three agents – Wulf Schmidt, Roman Czerniawski and Juan Pujol's Sub-agent 7(2) – were conveniently on hand to report it.

In fact, the incident demonstrated a dangerous lack of coordination within B1a – because not only did all three agents happen to witness the episode, but they all went on to give the same explanation for the use of advanced bases. As Roger Hesketh writes: 'That this very singular item of operational intelligence should simultaneously have reached the ears of a Polish staff officer, a Welshman resident in Dover and a

German prisoner-of-war resident in Kent, all of them enemy agents, was indeed straining German credulity.'

Fortunately, however, the German handlers in their various locations cannot have been comparing notes. Had they been, *Brutus*, *Garbo* and *Tate* would surely have all been blown – all but bringing down the Double Cross system with them. This incident amounted to another narrow escape.

An important element of Fortitude South was wireless deception. Just as Colonel MacLeod was simulating the Fourth Army in Scotland, so two units – the British No. 5 Wireless Group and the American 3103rd Signals Service Battalion – began mimicking the movement of FUSAG formations from their staging posts to their concentration areas in south-east England.

The two units employed different methods. No. 5 Wireless Group, attached to Strangeways' 'R' Force, used mobile radio trucks, each simulating the traffic of a division and its brigades, to mimic the activity of an entire corps. A monitoring section would study the genuine traffic of the units it was meant to be recreating, and a team of writers (signals, artillery and infantry officers) would prepare scripts tailored to Fortitude South. These scripts, often referring to the specialized training the units were supposedly receiving, were then recorded by the wireless operators and officers, to be transmitted by the mobile trucks from a particular location at a particular time.

The 3103rd Signals Service Battalion was larger and more conventional in its methods than No. 5 Wireless Group. It was a static operation, composed of seventeen radio teams in thirteen different locations in south-east England, all of whom worked together to mimic the activities of a corps. Its communications were delivered in real time and created the impression that large numbers of American units were forming up in the region and undergoing final training before the invasion.

Between them No. 5 Wireless Group and 3103rd Signals put across a vivid and false picture of Allied activity. A directive to signallers warned: 'You must realize that the enemy is probably listening to every message you pass on the air and is well aware that there is a possibility that he is being bluffed. It is therefore vitally important that your security is perfect.'

There were two problems with this well-meant warning. The first concerned the enemy's ability to track the location of transmissions. Much of their effect, after all, relied on their being traced to south-east England. But direction finding was a haphazard technology. Guy Liddell, in his diary on 29 May, records that the British Radio Security Service had just passed him two bearings for a German wireless agent; the first placed the agent in Scotland, the second in Austria. 'So much for RSS's powers of direction finding,' he writes. The Germans would have faced similar difficulties. But the second problem was more fundamental. As we have seen, the Germans were not listening very closely to the Allies' wireless traffic. Whether because they were overwhelmed by its sheer volume, or because they were focused on the battle fronts, they proved immune to the material so conscientiously provided for their benefit.

As was the case with Fortitude North, therefore, for the deceivers' message to reach its audience it would have to be delivered by the Double Cross system. It was a challenge relished by 'Tar' Robertson and his colleagues at B1a. At the meeting of the W Board on 21 January, Robertson declared that 'the critical period' for the Double Cross system had arrived. Operation Fortitude was the event for which the system had been building since the early days of Arthur Owens. This was what the endless scrabbling for chickenfood had been in aid of. Robertson told the board members that he was '98 per cent certain that the Germans trusted the majority of agents' and gave them an update on B1a's most important figures.

Czerniawski was now cleared for strategic deception, and promised a great deal. Pujol's situation seemed straightforward. He was trusted implicitly by the Germans, and with his notional network of sub-agents was ready to contribute fully to Fortitude. Schmidt's position was more uncertain, mainly due to an incident that had only recently come to light. Gösta Caroli, erstwhile parachute spy, double agent and Schmidt's close friend, was being held in Camp WX on the Isle of Man. Next door to this was an internment camp for Nazis. It was discovered that the two camps had been in communication, with notes being attached to bricks and hurled between them. The result was that Caroli's presence *may* have become known to internees in the Nazi camp, one of whom had been allowed to return to Germany on an exchange basis. So it was possible that Schmidt was now blown. On consideration, however, the risk was thought to be slight, and Robertson told the W Board that Schmidt would still be used, although with care. And Dusko Popov, reported Robertson, had just returned from an extremely successful visit to Lisbon. There could be no doubt that Popov was thoroughly trusted by the Germans.

But the situations of Popov and Pujol were not as secure as Robertson made out. A serious problem was arising – caused by Johnny Jebsen, Popov's great friend, and the man who had recruited him into the Abwehr.

Jebsen led a dual life. On the one hand, he was an Abwehr officer. On the other, he was immersed in shady financial dealings, many on behalf of influential Nazis whom he hoped would protect him from retribution. In August 1943, during a meeting with Popov in Lisbon, Jebsen expressed his fears that his dealings had exposed him to danger from the Gestapo. Popov assured his friend that, if the danger became too great, he would do his best to bring him to safety in England. As the two men chatted on, Jebsen started revealing some highly confidential information. He spoke of a recent conversation with Admiral Canaris, the chief of the Abwehr, who had told him that he didn't care if every German agent in Britain was under control, so long as he could tell German High Command that he had agents in Britain reporting regularly. The men conversed as amiably as ever, and as usual neither of them openly acknowledged that Popov was a double agent. But Jebsen knew it and Popov knew that he knew it. Popov was confident enough of the fact to be able to suggest to Robertson, on his return to England, that Jebsen also be engaged as a double agent.

But before Jebsen could be approached, he made contact himself. In fear that he was about to be arrested by the Gestapo, he walked into the British embassy in Madrid and asked to be evacuated to Britain. He soon calmed down, but MI5 (through MI6 in Madrid) pursued him and persuaded him to work for the British. Almost at once Jebsen doubted his decision. For one thing, he told his new handlers, he felt like a traitor. For another, he was placing himself in grave danger. On reflection, however, he was already at risk, and the British might be able to evacuate him to safety when the time came. And so under the codename *Artist* Jebsen began working as an agent under MI6 control.

The information provided by Jebsen turned out to be good. *Far too good*. In December he gave the British enough material to have Pujol arrested as a German spy. This placed B1a in a difficult position on the eve of the Fortitude deception. If Pujol was not arrested, Jebsen would realize that he was a double agent. The British were confident that he would not willingly compromise Pujol and Popov. But the danger to Jebsen from the Gestapo was growing. There was a real risk that under

Gestapo interrogation he would reveal the truth about B1a's most valued double agents.

B1a and the Twenty Committee searched for a solution. Bringing Jebsen to Britain was suggested – but that would mean blowing Popov and Pujol. The Twenty Committee was so short of ideas that it briefly considered assassinating Jebsen. Ultimately it was decided to do nothing and hope for the best. But Tomás Harris, Pujol's case officer, was not reassured. At the end of February he recommended that Pujol should not be used for the Fortitude deception. He was persuaded to remove his objection, but the risk remained: if Jebsen were to compromise Popov and Pujol in the midst of Fortitude, the Germans would know that the information they were receiving was the opposite of the truth. And as it was apparent that the Allies would be landing in either Normandy or the Pas de Calais, the enemy would receive an immediate answer to its most pressing question.

This danger had an important – and very fortunate – consequence for Fortitude South. It was now considered too dangerous to allow the agents to reveal the Pas de Calais as the Overlord objective before D-Day. It was decided instead that they would concentrate on building up the Order of Battle so as to merely suggest the Pas de Calais as an objective. This was a sensible decision. Because even if Popov and Pujol were not blown by Jebsen, they would not now be giving information so misleading that the Germans could doubt their reliability when the landings came in Normandy. After D-Day, however, they could go all out to suggest that a second assault on the Pas de Calais was imminent.

And so the first major piece of Fortitude South misinformation was passed by Popov to the Germans in Lisbon in early March. It consisted of page after page of detailed observations, mainly concerned with the Order of Battle, but also relating to factories, aerodromes and ports. And there was no familiar face to greet Popov in Lisbon on this occasion. His handler was no longer Albrecht von Auenrode. In February, Admiral Canaris had been dismissed as chief of the Abwehr and many of its personnel had been dismissed along with him. The Abwehr had been gaining a reputation for both incompetence and disloyalty; it had failed to predict the invasions of North Africa and Sicily, and its non-Nazi personnel were not trusted by hardliners. If Canaris's recent admission to Jebsen was to be believed – that he did not mind his agents being under enemy control so long as he could inform High Command that they were sending regular reports – then his organization was unquestionably failing to serve its function. The Abwehr was duly merged with Ernst Kaltenbrunner's Sicherheitsdienst (SD), the Nazi Party's own intelligence service.

On arrival in Lisbon, therefore, Popov found himself reporting to an SD officer, Alois Schreiber. Popov found Schreiber cold and unfriendly compared with his old friend Auenrode. And the debriefing, which lasted through the night, was gruelling. But the SD man subsequently reported to Berlin that he had no suspicions, and once Berlin had tele-graphed its comments back, Schreiber's attitude to Popov became distinctly warmer.

The reason for the warmth was simple: Berlin had conveyed its total satisfaction with Popov's report. Despite Auenrode's repeated assurances, Berlin had, in the past, held doubts about the Yugoslav's loyalty. But with this latest report – the first piece of Fortitude South deception – all such fears were banished. It was a good start for the deceivers. The informa-tion that Popov passed across fixed the locations of a large number of Fortitude South units, many of which were yet to move to their notional positions in south-east England. Popov was setting the scene so that the units' eventual moves would attract attention. The report was mentioned in FHW's situation report of 9 March: 'A V-man [agent] message which reached the Abteilung on 7 March 1944 brought particularly valuable information about the British formations in Great Britain. The reliability of the report could be checked. It contains information about thee armies, three army corps and twenty-three divisions, among which the displacement of only one formation must be regarded as questionable.'

And so, until D-Day, the deceivers' job was to build up the Order of Battle, and they set to it with gusto. Whenever a double agent was supposedly on the move in the FUSAG area, the case officer was to check through a card index prepared and updated by Christopher Harmer, giving detailed information about which units were notionally in which area. The case officers could then, according to Harmer, 'bring into their messages as much, or as little, as they considered appropriate'.

Pujol was to be the linchpin of the false Order of Battle. His sub-agents were put in place around England's south coast – which was where both the British and the Germans wanted them. The Gibraltarian waiter was sent to Southampton, supposedly because he had started working in the NAAFI in Chislehurst Caves, and was now being transferred. A retired Welsh seaman, Agent 7(2), was covering Dover. 'Rags', the Indian poet, was in Brighton. A Welsh commercial traveller, Sub-agent 7(5), was in Devon. The treasurer of a wonderfully imagined group of Fascist Welshmen – the Brothers in the Aryan World Order – was in Harwich. These sub-agents, by establishing themselves in their areas, could become familiar with the insignias of local units and, by making friends, could discover their names and locations.

Pujol was also able to call on the assistance of his influential friend in the Ministry of Information, and on a secretary in the

War Ministry with whom he was apparently having an affair, for more official information, and on an American NCO in the US Army Service of Supply for specific details about FUSAG's formation. With all of these informants, a relentless stream of information seemed to be coming Pujol's way, and he was forced to rein in his verbose style of corresponding as the sheer mass of facts to be transmitted to the Germans did not allow for babble. He began sending up to six wireless messages a day and, as Tomás Harris points out, it was doubtful whether one man could really have done all the work he was purporting to do. But despite receiving over 500 messages and the odd secret-ink letter between January 1944 and D-Day, the Germans gave every impression of trusting their precious and very possibly superhuman Catalan.

Roman Czerniawski was also highly trusted by the Germans. An Intelligence report of 25 January confirms that 'he is very well regarded and up till now has produced much accurate information on south-east England'. In order to take advantage of this level of trust, it was decided that he should be notionally posted to FUSAG, where he would be privy to good information on the Order of Battle. A B1a memo makes the limited intention clear:

> The appointment should be such as to give him access to such information as we require him to pass on and no more. It should also remove him physically from Chopin and the transmitting set so that we can limit the number of messages sent to suit our purpose. For these reasons it is considered that he should not work at the main FUSAG headquarters at Wentworth on the one hand, nor in London on the other.

Instead Czerniawski was to be sent to a new and entirely notional FUSAG section based in Staines, formed to recruit Poles in occupied France and Belgium who might assist the Allies when the advance began. The section would be headed by an American colonel, and Czerniawski would be required to visit various FUSAG units before they embarked on their assault. In this way he would learn a manageable amount about the Order of Battle. And the section's very existence ought subtly to reinforce the enemy's belief that FUSAG was to invade in the Pas de Calais, as a great number of the Poles in France (the men to be recruited by the section) were working in the Lille coalfields – in the Pas de Calais.

It is worth noting that for all Czerniawski's importance to Fortitudes North and South, it was only through the strenuous efforts of his first case officer, Christopher Harmer, that he was still a double agent at all. For some time after Czerniawski's arrival in England there were those in B1a who had considered him to be too much of a risk to be persevered with. Harmer recalls that J. C. Masterman 'intrigued behind my back to destroy *Brutus* as an agent when I was building him up'. Aware of the Pole's potential for the strategic deception ahead, Harmer had fought hard to preserve him. There is, of course, a thin line between confident belief and reluctance to doubt. Harmer's convictions were about to be put to the test.

There was more uncertainty in 1944 concerning Wulf Schmidt, B1a's longest-serving double agent. Not only had B1a received a recent scare over the Camp WX incident, but it was also finding it difficult to gauge the Germans' level of trust in Schmidt. Pujol, Popov and Czerniawski were controlled by Madrid, Lisbon and Paris respectively, all of whom communicated with Berlin by wireless. These communications could be decrypted and read as ISOS messages. Schmidt, however, was controlled by Hamburg, which communicated with Berlin by landline – which could not be intercepted. Nevertheless, the Germans had recently provided Schmidt with a more secure cipher: a sign that his handlers *were* placing trust in him. They were also sending him detailed questionnaires and frequently reassured him that he was highly valued.

And so it was ultimately decided that Schmidt would play a full part in the Fortitude South deception. In 1944 he was still notionally on the farm in Hertfordshire where he had started work in September 1941 to avoid having to register for military service. He was now to be sent to work on a farm near Ashford in Kent. The story was that Schmidt's employer in Hertfordshire had learned that a friend, a Kentish farmer, was having to devote practically all of his time to his Home Guard duties. So he had agreed to lend Schmidt to his friend for the foreseeable future. Schmidt duly reported to the SD that he had found lodgings in nearby Wye, which were 'ideal for radio purposes'. In reality he did not go to Ashford at all. A transmitter was erected in a field in Kent, from which his transmissions were broadcast by remote control.

On the eve of Fortitude, B1a had gained another double agent who was communicating with the Germans by wireless and who was therefore a candidate for Fortitude South. The agent's name was Lily Sergueiev, codenamed *Treasure*. Her path to B1a's door stretched back to 1937, when a German journalist had tried to recruit her into the Abwehr. The Franco-Russian Sergueiev had rejected his approach. But rage inspired by the fall of Paris had inspired her to work against the Germans, and she formulated a plan. She contacted the journalist and very belatedly accepted his offer. Once she was a member of the Abwehr, she figured, she would be able to pass information to the Allies, as well as misinformation to the Germans; her plan was reminiscent of Pujol's. Having been accepted by the Abwehr, she was sent for lengthy training in Berlin, before being told she could make her way to Britain. En route she contacted the British authorities in Madrid, who alerted B1a to her imminent arrival. All was set for Sergueiev to become a double agent, but she insisted that the British satisfy one condition before she left Gibraltar to work for them. Her beloved dog, Babs, which seems to have been a male dog in spite of its name, must be allowed to come with her to England.

There was a problem. Babs would first have to spend six months in quarantine in Gibraltar, but Sergueiev simply refused to accept this. Babs, she declared, had been vaccinated and had his rabies certificate. But, war or no war, Britain values its quarantine laws, and only after a series of emotional scenes was a solution reached. Sergueiev's US Air Force lover would smuggle the dog into Britain while MI5 looked the other way. And so a relieved Sergueiev finally flew into Whitchurch near Bristol. But her lover was to let her down. He never delivered Babs, who remained in a quarantine kennel in Gibraltar. And even though Sergueiev agreed to start work as a double agent – in February 1944 she travelled to Lisbon and returned with an Abwehr radio transmitter – the absent Babs would continue to dominate the case. In the end it was the simple fact that Sergueiev possessed a transmitter which persuaded the deceivers, who did not place much trust in her, to include her in their plans for Fortitude South.

There were a number of other agents who would play a part in Fortitude South – none of whom existed. In 1944 the Germans were being sold intelligence which they were told came from spies in the United Kingdom *other than those controlled by B1a*. The men selling the intelligence were two separate operators, Paul Fidrmuc, a Czech businessman in Spain, and Karl-Heinz Krämer, a German intelligence officer based in Sweden, who claimed to be in contact with these imaginary spies. All of this was dangerous as far as Fortitude was concerned because German Intelligence was apt to believe the reports, and there was a chance that Fidrmuc or Krämer, or both, might stumble on the real date and location of D-Day.

Fidrmuc, whose codename was *Ostro*, was effectively fooling the Germans into thinking that he had five real agents on British soil. In December 1943 Johnny Jebsen told MI6 that the Abwehr considered Fidrmuc to be 'a sort of prima donna who must not be ruffled' and that it sometimes sent him other agents' reports for evaluation. Fidrmuc was so highly regarded by the Germans that MI5 discussed methods of silencing him. These ranged from assassination (favoured at one point by MI6), to discrediting him (perhaps by an anonymous letter to the SD), to attempting to bring him under British control. John Gwyer of B1b proposed the last option, suggesting that Fidrmuc be approached and given the following warning: 'We have been watching you for some while. If you refuse our offer, you will be in great danger. You will be exposed to the same natural hazards as before – but we shall make it our business to expose you to the Abwehr.' But the problem with all of these options was that taking action against Fidrmuc could alert the enemy to the existence of Ultra. And so no action was taken.

The other man selling reports to the SD, Karl-Heinz Krämer, was an intelligence officer in Stockholm who had worked under Nikolaus Ritter in Hamburg during the days of Arthur Owens. Krämer had clearly learned how best to take advantage of his employers. His information was delivered under two codenames: *Josephine* for naval intelligence and *Hektor* for air intelligence. And it was gathered from various sources, including, it seems, the Hungarian legation in Stockholm, the Japanese military attaché, German Intelligence summaries (causing him to repeat material invented by the

British deceivers) and sheer guesswork. In time both Krämer and Fidrmuc would deliver information to the SD affecting Fortitude South. But in very different ways.

This, then, was the framework in existence as the double agents began delivering Fortitude South. Some agents seemed solid and trusted, others were primed explosives, threatening varying degrees of damage. The delivery would, at first, be a painstaking business, focusing on the notional Order of Battle and the movements of the FUSAG units to their concentration points in the south-east. And no sooner was it under way than the Johnny Jebsen crisis reached its climax.

In late April, Jebsen was called to Alois Schreiber's office, where his fears were finally realized. He was told that he was to be taken to Berlin – by force if necessary. He tried to run, but Schreiber overpowered him. Jebsen had no choice but to agree to be drugged, placed in a man-sized trunk and driven in the boot of Schreiber's car to Berlin. An MI5 report, written in June, explains that Jebsen 'was taken to Germany so that his financial dealings could be probed and for fear that he might *at a future date* come over to the Allies'. This explanation was contradicted by Walter Schellenberg, the chief of the Foreign Intelligence branch of the Reichssicherheitshauptamt (RSHA), the Reich Security Main Office, who told the Allies after the war that Jebsen was 'accused of working for Britain' after sending 'conflicting reports to different departments'. But, for whatever reason, it seems that Jebsen was subsequently sent to Oranienburg concentration camp. There he was recognized by a fellow inmate, Petra Vermehren. Jebsen arrived in the camp in July, Vermehren later recalled, and spent the next month in bed after his ribs were broken during an interrogation. She last saw him in February 1945, when he was taken away from the camp. Jebsen never returned, and he was never seen again.

Dusko Popov later recalled his final meeting with Jebsen in March. Jebsen must have realized that his time was nearly up. On parting he had begun to say 'AufWiedersehen', but paused on realizing its implications, settling instead on 'Goodbye'. Popov had said 'Goodbye' too, thankful for the ambiguity of the English phrase. And however brutal his interrogation, and wherever he finally met his death, it seems clear that Johnny Jebsen betrayed neither Popov nor Pujol. Nor did he reveal the existence of the Double Cross system to the SD. But the British deceivers had to assume the worst; they could not count on his silence. Working on the assumption that the SD would shortly be told the truth about Popov's network of agents, B1a acted quickly to close it down. Friedl Gaertner, Dickie Metcalfe, Eugen Sostaric, the Marquis Frano de Bona, Dusko Popov himself – every member of the team was retired from Double Cross service.

This potential disaster both for the Double Cross system, and for Operation Fortitude, confirmed the need to avoid any overt mention of the Pas de Calais as the Overlord objective until after D-Day, and to focus instead on building up the Order of Battle. This primarily meant passing information to the Germans about the movement of FUSAG units to their concentration points in south-east England. And so, on 1 May, Pujol's retiredWelsh seaman reported that the 28th US Infantry Division had arrived in Tenterden in Kent. He saw officers of that division in Folkestone and Dover, as well as troops bearing VIII Corps insignia in Folkestone. The following day the Treasurer of the Brothers in the Aryan World Order reported the 6th US Armoured Division in Ipswich. On 9 May, Roman Czerniawski located the 4th US Armoured Division and XX Corps in Bury St Edmunds. It was in this manner, piece by piece, that the Germans were handed the picture of an army group forming up in preparation for action.

And it was a picture that did not risk being contradicted by the Normandy landings.

While this was happening Lily Sergueiev began transmitting to the SD. She sent a message telling her handlers that the US First Army was under the command of General Montgomery's 21st Army Group. The purpose was to demonstrate that an American army could be under a British army group – as it would soon be suggested that US VIII Corps was under the First Canadian Army, which was under the First United States Army Group. But Sergueiev would not last much longer as a double agent. The wretched Babs had died in quarantine in Gibraltar and, on 17 May, Sergueiev informed her case officer that she had been concealing her security code since returning from Lisbon. She was apparently so upset by the dog's death that she had intended to take her revenge on the British by alerting the Germans to the fact that she was under control. On hearing this news 'Tar' Robertson brought her Double Cross career to a summary halt, although her channel was kept alive for a while using a Security Service wireless operator.

The Order of Battle deception continued. On 27 May, Pujol noticed lorries and vehicles belonging to the 83rd US Infantry Division in a car park near Dover. And, on the last day of May, Czerniawski began a major overview of information, intended to allow the Germans to place the units being fed to them into a context. He wired:

I am beginning a series of messages about First American Group of Armies, called FUSAG, C-in-C General Patton … from what I know, the Allied Expeditionary Force, commander General Eisenhower, is composed of FUSAG and the 21st Army Group, commander General Montgomery. One can conclude that FUSAG gives the impression of being ready to take part in active operations in the near future. FUSAG contains two armies: the First Canadian Army, Headquarters at Leatherhead, Commander General Crerar ... and the Third American Army, headquarters unknown ...

Czerniawski would send a series of similar consolidating messages a week later. And so, even as troops were coming ashore on D-Day, he was explaining the composition of the Third Army to the Germans.

One of the chief problems faced by the deceivers throughout Fortitude South arose from the fact that the demands of national security and those of deception appeared mutually contradictory. In the build-up to Overlord there was a huge amount of activity that clearly needed to be concealed. US formations were arriving, intensive training was being carried out, landing craft were being assembled, the Mulberry Harbours were being built and placed in position before being towed across the Channel, and the assault forces were being assembled. And while all of this and a great deal more was being done, the security authorities, unsurprisingly, took the view that drastic precautions were necessary to conceal it. It was up to the deceivers to point out that, unless these precautions were timed to fit in with their deception plans, the enemy would be accurately tipped off about the timing of the coming assault.

In the end a range of security measures was agreed upon by both the security and deception authorities. All military leave was suspended indefinitely from 6 April. The deceivers ensured that the suspension was in place very early so that, if the Germans heard about it, there was time for their suspicions to subside before the assault. Heavy restrictions were placed on movement within Britain and chief among these was a ban on entering coastal areas to a depth of ten miles, from Land's End to the Wash and from Arbroath to Dunbar in Scotland. In other words, the deceivers had ensured that the ban should cover the areas of Fortitude South and Fortitude North, as well as the area from which the real operation was to be mounted.

One area of concern related to the huge task of manufacturing and assembling the Mulberry Harbours. These were to be formed of massive concrete caissons – the largest 200 feet long, sixty feet wide and sixty feet high – which were to be towed across the Channel and sunk in line. They were designed, built and floated in just seven months – and all of this had to be done without the construction workers knowing what they were really building. They were told that they were making boom defence units. The secrecy was considered crucial: if the Germans learned that the British were building massive artificial harbours, then they would almost certainly correctly conclude that Operation Neptune's target was the Normandy beaches.

During the building process the minutes of a trade-union committee meeting which gave specific details of the harbour's construction were accidentally copied and distributed to addresses in Britain and one address in Eire. The copy addressed to Ireland was intercepted by the censors, and all the copies addressed to Britain were discreetly recovered. The incident was mentioned in a report on MI5's activity that was prepared by Anthony Blunt and seen by Winston Churchill every month from mid-1943 onwards. The fact that it was prepared by Blunt presumably ensured that a somewhat fuller version was also seen by Josef Stalin. Churchill's response to this particular incident was to write underneath in red ink, 'What action has been taken against the authors?' The prompt reply from the chief of MI5, Sir David Petrie, reads:

The Trades Union official responsible ... who is an official of many years standing, was in a state of great distress. He explained that his motive in raising the matter at the Committee Meeting had been to ensure that the work should proceed as smoothly as possible from the labour standpoint. He made no attempt to excuse his error in allowing the minutes to go out with his remarks reported in detail. He undertook that he would never be guilty of such an error of judgement again.

Petrie concluded his reply by suggesting that the taking of criminal proceedings against the official 'is considered inexpedient'. Underneath it Churchill wrote, again in red, 'I agree. All Clear!' And he ringed the typed words 'The Trades Union official responsible' and drew an arrow pointing to his final comment: 'Comfort him.'

As far as the deceivers were concerned, it was important that the harbours' construction did not give the enemy any clues as to where they would be used. And so Johnny Bevan's London Controlling Section managed to have them assembled at Dungeness and east of Selsey Bill – which would suggest their ultimate destination as being the Pas de Calais.

One measure that caused the deceivers some concern was an unprecedented ban imposed on diplomatic mail. Their problem was that the Foreign Office wanted the ban removed very quickly after D-day, a desire that they clearly did not share. LCS and SHAEF wanted to maintain the threat of a secondary invasion for as long as possible. In the end the deceivers won the argument and the ban was maintained until 20 June.

'All of this interference of deception into the realm of security,' writes Sir Ronald Wingate of LCS, 'was crucial. Failure in the smallest regard could have compromised everything.'

The agreed measures, which satisfied the needs of both security and deception, were actually far stricter than those initially proposed. Churchill, on seeing the original plans, described them as 'a pill to stop an earthquake' and insisted that they be redrafted to go 'high, wide, and handsome'. The measures described above were the result.

An interesting piece of deception carried out in the build-up to D-Day was one we encountered in the first chapter: the repatriation of German General Hans Cramer, prisoner of the British, who returned to Germany via Sweden on 23 May. It is worth adding one detail to the story. As well as being driven through south-west England, believing himself to be in the south-east, he was exposed to one further inspired hoodwink. He was invited to a dinner given in his honour by General Patton. During the dinner Patton was repeatedly described as the Commander-in-Chief of FUSAG and the conversation drifted more than once onto the subject of the Pas de Calais. It is little wonder that, on his return, Cramer scurried with alacrity to Rommel.

These, then, were the measures put in place by the deceivers in the lead-up to D-Day: a mixture of double-agent misinformation, physical deception, wireless traffic, misleading security measures and the odd maverick idea. But as D-Day grew closer, what were the Germans making of it?

So far as the physical deception was concerned, not very much. An FHW situation report in January stated that 'the Southern English ports are not able to be checked owing to the present lack of adequate air reconnaissance', and two months later the same source reports that, while a number of landing craft had been noted in various ports, 'the defective reconnaissance reports do not permit any deductions to be made as regards the distribution of landing craft'. The situation did not greatly improve. In fact, between 15 and 21 May no aerial reconnaissance of southern England was carried out at all.

As we have seen, the Germans were not fooled by Fortitude North into thinking that the major Allied offensive would come anywhere but across the Channel. They did not know exactly where, however, and opinion wavered in the months before D-Day. The weekly reports coming from the Commander-in-Chief West, Field Marshal Gerd von Rundstedt – known as 'Campaign Notes on the West' – were so vague as to be all but meaningless. A report of 24 April suggested that 'the focal point is still the Channel coast from the Scheld (inclusive) to Normandy or even to Brest (inclusive)'.

Hitler had long believed that the Pas de Calais would be the Allies' target. His Führer Directive of 3 November 1943 had stated as much. By late spring, however, his horizons seemed to be broadening. On 2 May, Walter Warlimont, Deputy Chief of Hitler's Operations Staff, informed Rundstedt that 'the Führer has today given an estimate of the situation in the West. Besides the Channel front, he regards the two peninsulas of Normandy and Brittany as primarily threatened.' Even a partial success by the Allies in the peninsulas, pointed out Warlimont, would tie down a large part of Rundstedt's forces, and he passed on the order that everything possible be done 'to reinforce the coastal defence with weapons, especially anti-tank weapons'. Rundstedt dutifully made arrangements for the reinforcement of Normandy and Brittany.

Rommel, who personally believed that the attack would come in the Pas de Calais, nevertheless made a request that 1 SS Panzer Corps be put under his command for the defence of Normandy and Brittany. Rundstedt objected; he could not agree 'to this premature commitment of his only, and best, operational reserves', when he was not yet sure where the attack would come. On 6 May, Jodl telephoned Rundstedt's chief of staff, Günther Blumentritt, to reassure him that 1 SS Panzer Corps would *not* be committed to Normandy.

Rommel's request was really a bid to deprive Rundstedt of the Panzer reserve units held in the Pas de Calais by the Oberkommando der Wehrmacht (OKW), the Supreme Command of the Armed Forces. He wanted them for himself. Rommel and Rundstedt had very different tactical approaches to dealing with the beachhead. Rommel believed that the invasion would have to be defeated on the beaches. 'Provided we succeed in bringing our mechanized divisions into action in the first few hours,' he wrote to Jodl, 'then I'm convinced that the enemy assault on our coast will be defeated on the very first day.' He wanted General Leo Geyr's Panzer divisions dug in at the water's edge, ready to repel the Allies as they came ashore.

Geyr, the commander of Panzer Group West, and Rundstedt had other ideas. As the Panzers' strength was their mobility, it made little sense to them to limit the tanks in such a way, particularly when it was not yet clear where the invasion would be mounted and there existed a risk of paratroop landings in the rear. The Panzer divisions, they argued, ought be kept in reserve to counter-attack where and when they were needed. 'If you leave the Panzer divisions in the rear,' countered Rommel furiously, 'they will never get forward. Once the invasion begins, enemy air power will stop everything moving.' In the end Hitler imposed a compromise. Three Panzer divisions were placed under Rommel's control, one of which, the 21st, a cobbled-together division containing many captured tanks, was moved near to the Normandy beaches at Caen.

The fact was that, as D-Day approached, the Germans were in a state of confusion about its timing, its location, how to deal with it, and whether it would be the main assault or a diversionary attack. The Allied strategic deceivers had so far held back on their use of double agents, employing them to build up the fake Order of Battle. They were about to receive confirmation from Hitler that their efforts were hitting the mark. They would soon be able to go for broke in their efforts to convince the Germans that the main assault was coming in the Pas de Calais. And there were still one or two other tricks to play before the sailing of the largest invasion fleet the world had ever seen.

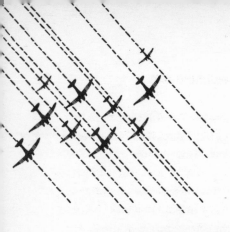

WARRIORS FOR THE WORKING DAY

A number of fake exercises simulated by wireless traffic were mounted in the build-up to D-Day. At the beginning of June, for example, Exercise Seesaw mimicked a landing exercise carried out by the US 28th Division in East Anglia. Such notional rehearsals were intended to supplement the genuine exercises which were being mounted on such a grand scale that they could not hope to be hidden from the enemy. One of the genuine exercises, Exercise Tiger at Slapton Sands in Devon on 26 April, went horribly wrong when it ran into German motor torpedo boats, resulting in the deaths of 638 servicemen.

Another of the genuine pre-invasion exercises, Fabius, mounted on 3 May, involved four real assault divisions and naval support. Its wireless traffic was intended to mimic the traffic of a real assault. The deceivers' plan was therefore to present Fabius as a first major landing exercise and Operation Neptune, when it came, as a second. An important supplement to the wireless traffic was 'Special Means', and so Juan Pujol and Tomás Harris set to work.

On 29 April the Gibraltarian waiter supposedly telephoned Pujol to arrange a meeting at Winchester Station the following day. At the meeting the waiter said that he had been posted to the canteen at Hiltingbury Camp near Southampton. The camp, located in the sealed coastal area, was genuinely occupied by the Canadian 3rd Infantry Division, a unit that was to take part in Neptune. The waiter told Pujol that the canteen had been preparing cold rations for the troops, who had been issued with vomit bags and lifebelts for a sea voyage. He was sure, therefore, that the invasion was imminent.

On 3 May, however, Pujol reported to the Germans that his lover, the secretary at the War Office, was telling him that an invasion was *not* imminent. The SD replied that he should not pay too much regard to her information, as she was probably being misled by the Ministry, or else had been warned not to reveal military intentions. The next day the waiter reported that the 3rd Division had set off from Hiltingbury towards Southampton with embarkation orders. He followed this information up with news that the camp was to be cleaned and prepared to receive a new batch of troops. 'This,' Pujol told the Germans, 'proves [the secretary's] lie because she suggested, naïvely, today that troops in the Southern area were on manoeuvres, information which has been disproved, as in this case troops would have returned.' The invasion, it seemed, was on.

Three days later Pujol was furious. The waiter, he wired, had demonstrated 'the ability of a simpleton'. Troops had indeed arrived at Hiltingbury, but they were the *same troops* who had previously left. According to the waiter, 'they have been in one of the many rehearsals which Churchill announced would be carried out before the Second Front was opened'. The 'rehearsal' was, of course, Fabius. Pujol reported to his handlers that the secretary had been quite correct in her interpretation and that he would never again be influenced by reports from the waiter, who had shown 'great stupidity'. His handlers were quick to defend the waiter. 'You should give him encouragement,' they wired, 'as, if not, it might happen that when the real invasion is about to take place he will not notify this owing to over-precaution.'

The Germans' top agent had thus confirmed his position. He had reported Fabius and the Germans had every confidence that he would also be able to report the real invasion. This suited B1a's intentions very well, because Harris and Pujol had come up with an ambitious plan that Pujol should appear to tip the Germans off about D-Day in advance. And the SD was left with two important impressions from Fabius: first, that Pujol's Ministry informants were worth listening to, and secondly, that an elaborate exercise was difficult to distinguish from a genuine assault, meaning that Neptune might be passed off as an exercise when the time came.

In the period leading up to D-Day a number of the deception plans laid down in Operation Bodyguard were implemented. Operation Ironside was an attempt to keep German forces – especially the 17th SS Panzergrenadier Division – in the south of France and thus away from Normandy. A notional two-division assault was to be made on Bordeaux from Britain, while four divisions were to sail to Bordeaux from the United States. Wulf Schmidt reported that a girlfriend, Mary, had returned from Washington, where she had learned that an expeditionary force was being assembled. In early June one of Pujol's Welsh nationalist sub-agents, a Swansea office worker whom the Catalan had already mentioned to the Germans as being a poor informant, supposedly reported to him that an American assault division was in Liverpool, ready to attack Bordeaux. Pujol and Harris were very keen to prevent Pujol's credibility being affected by a side issue such as Ironside, and so, in passing on the information, he warned the Germans that he was very sceptical about the report. Although the 17th SS Panzergrenadier Division was not immediately moved north after D-Day, it does not seem that the Germans took Ironside's threat to Bordeaux very seriously.

A colourful deception plan, Copperhead, was put into practice on 27 May. It owed its existence to Dudley Clarke's regular visits to the cinema. Early in the year, while watching a Billy Wilder film, *Five Graves to Cairo*, Clarke had been struck by the resemblance of one of the actors, Miles Mander, to General Montgomery. The film's plot revolved around the impersonation of one man by another and it occurred to Clarke that Mander could be just the chap to impersonate Montgomery in the run-up to Neptune. And there was no place on earth where an Allied personality was more likely to be spotted by the enemy than on the airfield at Gibraltar, as the Germans were known to keep a villa overlooking the aerodrome from which they observed passengers getting on and off BOAC flights. The relentless observation was why Pujol had not taken the scheduled flight to England in April 1942. But it could now be used to the Allies' advantage. If Mander, dressed as Montgomery, were to be spotted at Gibraltar shortly before D-Day, the Germans would surely assume that the landings were still some way off. They were unlikely to believe that an invasion was about to be launched in northwest Europe while one of its chief protagonists was elsewhere. It was an idea that was taken up with enthusiasm by London Controlling Section and Ops (B).

When discreet enquiries were made in Hollywood it was discovered that Miles Mander was several inches shorter than Montgomery. This did not scupper the plan, for it quickly became apparent that Monty had more than one double. But no sooner had another man been cast in the role than he broke his leg in a traffic accident. A third Monty was discovered by LCS while searching through the books of a Soho acting agency. This man was Meyrick Clifton James, currently a lieutenant in the Royal Army Pay Corps. Brought to the War Office in London for an audition, he was offered the part. He was sent off to meet Montgomery and spent some time studying his principal's mannerisms.

There was still a certain amount of work to be done before Clifton James could make his début. He had a finger missing as a result of his Great War service, so a prosthetic replacement was made. And it was discovered that had never flown before, so Dennis Wheatley arranged for him to be taken up before Copperhead began. To Wheatley's relief, Clifton James was not airsick. Had the Germans witnessed Monty throwing up on the tarmac at Gibraltar, they might have lost a measure of respect for the hero of El Alamein.

Montgomery himself was extremely keen on the plan, which was hardly surprising given that it was based, as Guy Liddell points out, 'on the theory that the Second Front cannot possibly start without him'. And so, in the early hours of 27 May, Clifton James, wearing Monty's battledress and famous beret, accompanied by a brigadier and an ADC, boarded an aircraft and took off from an airfield in southern England bound for Gibraltar. At the other end he was met by the Governor, Sir Ralph Eastwood. 'Hello, Monty, glad to see you!' Eastwood called out as Clifton James stepped off the plane. 'Hello, Rusty, how are you?' replied Clifton James. The deception was under way. It was hoped that the Germans were watching.

The party set off for breakfast at Government House, and shortly after ten Clifton James and the Governor walked to their cars for the short drive back to the airfield. This tiny stroll across a courtyard was the deception's *pièce de resistance* – thanks to the presence of a carefully chosen man in a room overlooking the courtyard. Ignacio Molina Pérez was liaison officer between the Spanish government and the British in

Gibraltar. But, far more importantly, he was a well-known German spy. He had been conveniently invited to the embassy that morning for a meeting with the Colonial Secretary, and his reaction to the sight of Montgomery was just as the planners had hoped. A report on Copperhead in the 'A' Force War Diary records Pérez's reaction:

> His interest in happening on this significant scene was far too great to hide. Eagerly he turned to the Colonial Secretary for further news, while the latter with well feigned embarrassment was forced to confess that the Commander-in-Chief was on his way to Algiers. On this the Spaniard hastened to his car, drove very fast to the Spanish town of La Linea, and there put through an urgent trunk call.

As Pérez hurried away to surprise the Germans with his news, Clifton James returned to the airfield, boarded his plane again, and took off for Algiers, where he was very publicly to meet General Maitland Wilson, the Supreme Allied Commander in the Mediterranean. On disembarking he walked past a passengers' enclosure full of British and American officers who spontaneously cheered him. The FANY who drove him from Maison Blanche airfield to a house in Algiers had previously driven Montgomery, but she failed to spot any change in her passenger's appearance, asking Wilson's military assistant if she could possibly have Monty's autograph. Having apparently convinced all comers that he was Monty, Clifton James could now come out of character. The next day he flew to Cairo where he lay low until Montgomery had publicly appeared in France.

It seems that the diffident Clifton James had not enjoyed the experience. The fact that he received Montgomery's pay, £10 per day, over the period that he was impersonating him was no compensation for the pressure, which left him taking solace in a bottle of whisky at the end of his performance. Wheatley, in his memoirs, is critical of the official attitude to Clifton James once his value was spent, considering that he was treated shabbily in that 'no recognition was given to him for the considerable service he had performed very efficiently'.

In 1954 Clifton James published a book about his experience entitled *I Was Monty's Double*, which four years later was made into a film starring John Mills. In the film Clifton James played both himself and Montgomery. And while the recognition he received was belated, it has endured. His wartime achievement is more widely acknowledged today than the achievements of all of B1a's double agents.

But did Copperhead achieve any results? There is no doubt that Montgomery's appearance in Gibraltar was reported to Berlin, because a number of double agents subsequently received questionnaires relating to the general's whereabouts. And while the meeting between Montgomery and General Wilson in Algiers was reported by FHW to Field Marshal Kesselring in Italy, it seems that it was not reported to Rundstedt.

The fact is that Copperhead ultimately seems to have had no effect on German attitudes towards the cross-Channel threat. Perhaps the deception was carried out too early: a flying visit to Gibraltar and Algiers by the commander of the 21st Army Group did not necessarily preclude a large-scale attack in north-west Europe ten days later. It is possible that a piece of utterly spurious intelligence sold to the Germans by Karl-Heinz Krämer, describing a meeting of senior staff officers in Gibraltar in mid-May, had pre-empted the deception. When Krämer's report was discovered by the Allies after the war, it was found to be marked with the question: 'Deception?', next to which Colonel Friedrich-Adolf Krummacher, the head of the OKW Intelligence Branch, had written in English: 'Who knows?' It seems that the Germans were so bombarded by conflicting reports, so confused about where and when an attack was coming, that there was little that Copperhead could add to the uncertainty.

One man, however, was not confused about Allied intentions: Adolf Hitler. On the same day that Meyrick Clifton James landed on the Rock, the Japanese ambassador to Berlin, Hiroshi Oshima, visited Hitler at the Berghof, his beloved retreat in the Bavarian Alps with sumptuous views over Berchtesgaden and Salzburg. The ambassador asked Hitler for his views on the Second Front. Hitler's confident replies were wired by the embassy to Tokyo, and duly intercepted and decrypted by the Americans. Barely had Hitler spoken than the Allies knew his opinions. He could not have made himself clearer had he placed a call to General Eisenhower at SHAEF headquarters.

Hitler began by assuring the ambassador that sooner or later the Allies would attempt an invasion. And he gave his estimate of Allied strength: 'I understand that the enemy has already assembled about eighty divisions in the British Isles.' This was over twice the true number, but since, as we have seen, Roenne, the head of Fremde Heere West, was scaling up the Allied Order of Battle by stressing every apparent enemy unit or partial unit, the deceivers had gained an inadvertent ally.

Hitler then set out his ideas as to how the invasion would be mounted. These ideas, he underlined, came from 'relatively clear portents', many of which had come from the deceivers. His view was that the Allies would first establish bridgeheads in Normandy and Brittany. Then, having sized up their prospects, 'they will come forward with an all-out second front across the straits of Dover'. This meant that he would not be able to strike a single blow against the Allies – as he would have wished. Instead, he said, the Allied forces would have to be finished off at several different bridgeheads.

Whatever Rundstedt or Rommel or any other German general, politician or staff officer believed did not ultimately matter. In Nazi Germany the only opinion that counted was Hitler's, and his view worried some within 21st Army Group. Six months earlier, after all, he had been predicting a single attack on the Pas de Calais, but now he was predicting a preliminary assault in Normandy and Brittany. But the deceivers were not worried. Hitler was still predicting that the main assault would occur in the Pas de Calais and stressing in the clearest terms that he would have to retain strong forces in this area to deal with the blow when it came. This tied in with the deceivers' own plans to keep German reserves in the Pas de Calais by mounting an all-out threat to the area after D-Day. They saw no reason to panic. On 1 June, Guy Liddell makes plain this view in his diary: 'The 21st Army Group are getting rather nervous about the number of divisions moved into the area south of the river and are suggesting we should put over some hot deception to get them out of the area. My own view and Tar's is we should continue as we are.'

Just before D-Day, Paul Fidrmuc, otherwise known as *Ostro*, the uncontrolled agent in Sweden, gave the Allies a scare. In his diary on 5 June, Liddell reports that Fidrmuc had correctly hit on the Neptune target area in a report to the Germans. Fidrmuc's information about the target area supposedly came from a colonel on Montgomery's staff. There was no such source – even if Fidrmuc's guess as to the target area was lucky. But Juan Pujol was about to play a more informed game. Just as he had sent the Germans a letter in November 1942 exposing the true target of Operation Torch as being North Africa, so he and Harris were now planning to send a message that would confirm the Germans' trust in him. He was going to warn them about D-Day.

Pujol had laid the groundwork with a message that Madrid should be listening at 3 a.m. on 6 June, as he was expecting a telephone call from his Greek seaman sub-agent concerning a build-up of troops around Glasgow. But the message he actually transmitted at that early hour had nothing to do with Scotland.

Earlier that night 'Tar' Robertson, Tomás Harris, Roger Hesketh and Juan Pujol had made their way to the MI5 safe house at Crespigny Road in Hendon. At 3 a.m., before the invasion force was in sight of the French coast, Pujol sent a message warning that it was on its way. What he actually wired was that the Gibraltarian waiter had gone AWOL from Hiltingbury Camp and had hurried to London with news. Once again, the waiter had observed cold rations and vomit bags being distributed to troops of the Canadian 3rd Division, who had then left the camp. But this time their place in the camp had been quickly taken by new American troops. In other words, the invasion must have started. Whereas Pujol's warning of Torch had arrived after the event, this warning was reaching the Germans *before* the invasion had hit the French coast – although too late for them to alter their preparations. And there was always the chance that they might interpret the message – for a short while at least – as an indication of another Fabius-like exercise.

In the event, Pujol's handlers in Madrid were not listening as instructed. Charles Haines, his wireless operator, made repeated efforts to send the message through, but Madrid did not reply. Only at eight that morning was it finally received, by which time the 3rd Division had been on French soil for eight minutes. Pujol subsequently expressed his fury at Madrid's failure: 'I am very disgusted in this struggle for life and death, I cannot accept excuses or negligence. Were it not for my ideals and faith, I would abandon this work.' In reply Madrid stressed 'our total recognition of your perfect and cherished work and I beg of you to continue with us in the supreme and decisive hours of the struggle for the future of Europe'. The message might not have been received in time, but Pujol had attempted to give advance warning.

And Madrid was right. These were indeed the decisive hours of the struggle for the future of Europe. While Pujol was sending his message, an armada was making its way across the Channel. In a reversal of the events of May and June 1940, when a fleet of ships had brought the British Expeditionary Force to safety from the clutches of advancing German forces, an astonishing armada of 6,483 vessels was now sailing towards the French coast to force the Germans back from the occupied lands. The fleet consisted of battleships, destroyers, liners and 4,000 landing craft containing the men of the 21st Army Group. The landing craft were to deliver the men onto five different Normandy beaches once dawn broke. The Americans were to land at the westernmost beaches, Omaha and Utah, the British at Gold and Sword, and the Canadians at Juno, in between the British beaches.

Operation Fortitude was not the only deception in support of this extraordinary undertaking. A number of tactical deceptions were also mounted. The Germans, it was realized, would be warned of the Allies' approach by the chain of radar stations built along the coast. A method was sought to blind them to the approach of the invasion force. There was a real danger, however, that jamming their radar would simply alert the Germans to the invasion. As a result something far more subtle was attempted which directly tied in to Fortitude: as the real invasion force approached Normandy, two other invasion forces were simulated, one approaching the mouth of the Seine, the other Boulogne.

Clearly real convoys could not be used for the deception. Every available vessel was needed for Neptune. Instead aircraft flying at 200 miles per hour attempted to fool enemy radar into thinking that they were task forces advancing at a handful of knots. They did this by dropping large quantities of radar-reflective tin-foil strips, known as 'window'. Four aircraft flew in line towards the French coast, with a gap of one-and-a-bit miles between each. Behind them flew another four aircraft in the same formation. All the aircraft dropped their foil strips at regular intervals. Then they turned and headed back towards England, before turning again and flying half a mile closer to France, at which point they dropped more foil strips. Each time the window was dropped, it showed up on German radar, with the result that the spoof fleet seemed to be approaching the French coast at a mean rate of five or six knots. The Stirlings of 218 Squadron carried out Operation Glimmer, flying towards Boulogne, and the Lancasters of 617 Squadron carried out Operation Taxable, flying towards the mouth of the Seine.

The men on board these aircraft had a difficult task. They had to synchronize their orbits exactly and drop their window at precise intervals. This work required such concentration that two pilots and two navigators flew in each aircraft, allowing the pairs to rotate. Special holes were cut in the nose of the aircraft out of which the window was dropped in solid blocks which scattered in the air – and this proved a great bonus to one member of 617 Squadron. A particular bomb aimer, according to Flight Lieutenant Arthur Poore of 617, was a small man with a small bladder, who invariably needed to relieve himself on a raid. The Lancaster was equipped with a chemical toilet at the rear, which meant that the bomb aimer had to clamber the length of the aircraft to carry out his mission, forcing the navigator to get up from his seat and lean over his table. The addition of a hole in the nose, says Poore, 'was a godsend to "X" who could spend a penny through that without disturbing anybody else'. Whether the 'penny' was an effective radar-reflector is not clear.

While the aircraft were at work, the effect was simultaneously compounded on the surface of the sea by small motor torpedo boats carrying echo systems. The echo systems delayed and amplified the impulse coming from the radar station, before radiating it back. This, too, gave the impression of a lot of ships approaching France.

At the same time as this deception was taking place, another was going on in conjunction with the airborne operations of D-Day. Operations Titanic I, II, III and IV were intended to simulate large-scale parachute drops behind German lines with the intention of attracting German forces away from the sites of the genuine airborne operations. Titanic II was ultimately cancelled owing to the amount of air traffic on a very busy night, but the other three went ahead. Titanic I involved the dropping near St Valéry of 200 dummy paratroopers, known as 'Paragons', and two small SAS teams equipped with Very light pistols and gramophones which would play bursts of small-arms fire interspersed with snatches of soldiers' conversations. Titanic III involved the dropping near Caen of fifty Paragons which were rigged to devices which would simulate the sounds of gunfire on landing. Titanic IV involved a drop of Paragons and two more SAS teams near Saint-Lô.

The historian Professor Michael Foot was, at the time, the Intelligence Officer of the Brigade, and he approached the commanding officer of 1st SAS Regiment, Lieutenant Colonel Paddy Mayne, with a request for the teams. Mayne asked what it was for. 'To do a very odd piece of deception work not too far from the battle line,' replied Foot. 'No!' said Mayne. Foot protested that he had received an order. 'It may be an order,' said Mayne, 'but I'm not going to obey it, and you can go back and tell your brigadier.' The SAS was clearly an unusual unit from its earliest days. Mayne explained his reasons: 'There was an early operation the regiment did in the desert, which was mixed up with beastly intelligence stuff, and when we got there the Italians were waiting for us, and very few of us came back. And I swore then that nobody in the SAS was going on a purely intelligence operation that I could stop. So get out!' Foot then approached Lieutenant Colonel Brian Franks, commanding officer of 2nd SAS Regiment, who proved more accommodating.

For Titanic IV, two teams were selected, each consisting of two lieutenants and two troopers. According to Captain Peter Tonkin of 1 SAS, all the old hands in the brigade were horrified by the apparently suicidal nature of the task these men faced, but tried to gee up the chosen subalterns, Lieutenants Fowles and Poole, both of whom were new to active service, by telling them that it was a marvellous job. When Titanic IV was briefly called off, the old hands admitted their true feelings – only for the operation to be put back on again. At this point the subalterns appeared 'as white as sheets'. Yet, despite the fact that they had the right to withdraw, both men chose to continue.

The Titanic IV teams were dropped near Saint-Lô just after midnight on D-Day. Initially the four troopers – Hurst, Merryweather, Dawson and Saunders – had to act on their own, as they could not locate the subalterns. They followed their orders and simulated a large-scale landing, before moving out of the area and hiding in a hedge. The next night they were found by a member of the local French Resistance, who moved them to the ruins of a nearby abbey before returning with Lieutenant Poole, who it transpired had knocked himself out on leaving the aircraft. Three days later the group was joined by Lieutenant Fowles, who had landed in a field away from the others and searched for them in vain. He had spent the past few days in hiding until he too was discovered by the Resistance. On the night of 8 July, while moving north in the hope of meeting the advancing Allies, the group was spotted by the Germans. Lieutenant Fowles and Troopers Hurst and Merryweather were wounded by German grenades and the entire party was taken prisoner – although the two wounded troopers fell into the hands of the Americans three weeks later when their military hospital in Rennes came under Allied control.

At the time, says Foot, the Titanic operations were considered 'a beastly disaster' by the SAS, but they actually seem to have achieved results. When the real airborne landings were initially reported, the subsequent report that dummy paratroopers had been found prompted General Hans Speidel, Rommel's chief of staff – who was effectively in charge of Army Group B while Rommel was in Germany – to doubt that an invasion was under way. And General Max Pemsel, the chief of staff to the commander of Seventh Army, who was also in effective charge as his chief, General Friedrich Dollman, was in Rennes, seems to have taken the apparent threat posed by Titanic IV seriously enough that he sent an entire brigade to look for the imaginary paratroopers who had been conjured up by Troopers Hurst, Merryweather, Dawson and Saunders.

It was against this background that the seaborne landings went ahead on the morning of 6 June. Leading the assault on Omaha Beach were the US 1st and 29th Infantry Divisions. Sub Lieutenant Jimmy Green was the commander of a landing-craft flotilla responsible for landing members of the 116th Regimental Combat Team. He left his men on a ridge about 300 yards from the German defenders. As he moved away, enemy machine guns opened up, killing every single man he had just landed. 'It's lived with me ever since,' he later recalled. 'I can still see those fresh-faced boys getting out of the boat.'

Omaha was the deadliest of the beaches. The defences had barely been touched by the air and sea bombardment which had preceded the attack, and Rommel had recently added a further infantry division in the area. The 352nd Infantry Division proceeded to defend the beach fiercely. In spite of the heavy Allied casualties – which caused offshore commanders to consider diverting the landing to Utah Beach – the infantry began to make slow progress. Finding a group of his men unable to move forward, Colonel George A. Taylor of the US 16th Infantry Regiment urged them on, saying, 'There are two kinds of people who are staying on this beach: those who are dead and those who are going to die. Now let's get the hell out of here!' Soldiers eventually started making their way off the beach through makeshift exits, heading inland and attacking German positions from the rear. Allied destroyers assisted them by sweeping dangerously close to shore and firing on the defenders. By the end of the day the beachhead was a mile and a half deep – and the Americans had suffered 2,400 casualties.

The Canadian 3rd Division, the men whom the Gibraltarian waiter had supposedly been serving in the canteen at Hiltingbury, came ashore on Juno Beach. The landing craft had to negotiate treacherous reefs as they advanced, and the resulting delay meant that they reached the shore as the tide was rising and had to contend with the submerged beach obstacles. Juno was defended by the German 736th Regiment, which took a heavy toll on the Canadians as they arrived on the beach. Only the Americans on Omaha Beach suffered heavier casualties. Private Frederick Perkins of the Royal Berkshire Regiment formed a 'body recovery party' after one wave had come ashore. 'It wasn't a very pretty sight,' he remembers, 'to see these men who'd gone a few yards and dropped down.' The bodies had to be cleared away. For one thing, tanks were continually arriving on the beach and running them over. For another, the sight would hardly encourage the next wave of troops. 'So we decided to get these people off the beach areas and lay them up and covered them over.' But once the survivors were off Juno Beach, they made quick progress inland. The 6th Canadian Armoured Regiment advanced ten miles, and though it ultimately had to turn back for lack of support, it achieved more ground than any other Allied unit on D-Day.

The assault on Utah Beach was made by the US 4th Infantry Division. Of all the beaches, the resistance at Utah was the weakest, and by the end of the day over 23,000 soldiers had landed, with around 200 casualties suffered. Tom Treanor, an American war correspondent with the *Los Angeles Times* and the NBC network, landed at Utah. As he came ashore the area was quiet, although German guns were clearly busy a few hundred yards away. He asked a soldier how the initial reception had been and was told that the defenders had waited until the landing craft had dropped their ramps before opening up with machine guns and high-velocity guns. It had been, said the man, 'a little hot at first', with heavy casualties in places, but the navy had gone to work on the German guns and things had soon calmed down. Treanor was struck by the lack of obvious fortifications at the spot where he had landed: the barbed wire blocking the beach exit consisted of just four single strands. A few minutes later he found himself on a path clogged with mines along which soldiers lay dead. As he stepped gingerly across the bodies, a voice said, 'Watch yourself, fella. That's a mine.' It belonged to a man lying by the path with half his foot blown off. He was waiting for the medics – but for the moment he was a valued pathfinder for the steady stream of men edging along the trail.

The British 50th Division came ashore on Gold Beach, which was defended by enemy forces in houses along the seafront, a coastal artillery battery, and by Kampfgruppe Meyer, a mechanized unit consisting mainly of eastern European troops. The first waves of troops met with fairly heavy resistance, but Kampfgruppe Meyer was out of action for much of the morning, having been sent to deal with the threat from airborne landings. Its absence meant that when British tanks eventually came ashore they were relatively unopposed and able to offer the infantry close support. Major Richard Gosling was a Forward Observation Officer with 147th Field Regiment who had never before experienced battle. As he came ashore that morning he heard a loud swarm of bees nearby. Only when he saw the sand kicking up in front of him did he realize that the sound was actually coming from German machine guns. He heard a bang and suddenly his legs were taken from under him. He felt as though he'd been tackled badly on a football pitch, but as he lay in the sand he saw that his leg was full of small pieces of shell splinter. He limped to the dunes, where he lay alongside others, including a corporal of the Royal Hampshire Regiment, who raised himself up to look over the dunes – and was shot straight through the chest. 'A little bit later,' Gosling recalls, 'I thought I should look over – I was the officer.' He crawled up the bank of sand and peered over the edge. On the other side, only yards away, was a German soldier. 'I didn't like the look of him, he didn't like the look of me, and I fired my revolver hopefully in his direction and then I slid back again.' When Gosling looked up again, the German was gone.

By the end of the day 25,000 men had come ashore on Gold Beach, at the cost of about 400 casualties. The 50th Division moved six miles inland and was able to link up with the Canadians who had come ashore on Juno Beach.

The most easterly of the five beaches was Sword, where the task of establishing a beachhead was allotted to the British 3rd Infantry Division. Resistance from the German 736th and 215th Regiments was heavy, their defensive positions having survived the bombardment. The attackers were also hampered by a coastal battery at Merville and heavy artillery at Le Havre. Corporal Jim Spearman, of 4 Commando, was initially shocked by the colour of the water and the number of bodies floating in it. He had the momentary impression of men drowning in their own blood; the sight filled him with determination to get off the beach. As Private William Lloyd of the East Yorkshire Regiment was waiting to come ashore on the left of the beach, two landing craft, one alongside his, the other directly behind, received direct hits from shells. The beach was gently sloping, with little cover, so he had no option but to keep running, always aware of the bullets that came at him like raindrops. 'You could hear them whistling and passing you,' he remembers, 'but you just kept going.' But even once the men were through the beach exits, safety was not assured. Sergeant Arthur Thompson of the East Yorkshire Regiment was wading through a flooded area when a soldier called to him for help. Thinking the man had fallen under the weight of his equipment, Thompson went to pick him up – and realized that he had lost both of his legs to a shell blast. He propped the man up against a tree and asked him if he wanted anything. A cigarette, the wounded man replied. 'So I lit him a cigarette, and had to leave him,' explains Thompson. 'He'd just die, you see.'

In total 29,000 men came ashore at Sword Beach, at a cost of 630 casualties.

While the mass slaughter that had been feared by some had not materialized, except perhaps on Omaha Beach, the horror of the day had seared itself into the minds of many of those who survived it. The Allied casualty figures for 6 June 1944 – including airborne troops – have been estimated at 10,000, although the true number may be considerably higher. And it is very easy to lose sight of the fact that these events represented Operation Fortitude's reason for being. Johnny Bevan, David Strangeways and the rest of the LCS, Ops (B) and 21st Army Group deceivers had not been working on a theoretical project. They had been working to minimize the risk to the men who went ashore on 6 June, and to assist them to achieve their objectives. Those objectives, scaled up, were the objectives of the Allied Expeditionary Force. Similarly 'Tar' Robertson, J. C. Masterman and the case officers of B1a had not spent years closeted with Welsh fantasists and Yugoslav playboys for their own diversion. They been working towards the grand deception which would help to change the course of the war. And D-Day was only the start. Fortitude would now have to assist these soldiers, and those yet to arrive, as they fought their way beyond the toehold now secured on continental Europe.

Erwin Rommel had stated his conviction that the invasion would have to be repulsed on the beaches if the Germans were to have any chance of resisting the Allies. That had not happened. However strong Rommel's Atlantic Wall, doubt about where the invasion would be launched had left the German defenders too thinly spread along the length of the coast to prevent it taking hold. Operation Fortitude had helped to propagate that doubt. The question now was whether the Germans would appreciate that this invasion was *the* invasion,

or whether they would anticipate that it was merely a preliminary to another assault. This would decide how quickly they
reinforced Normandy with the forces currently held in the Pas
de Calais. And the Allied deceivers had now to do all they
could to delay that happening. To this end, at 6 p.m. on D-Day
Roman Czerniawski reported that the invasion plainly only
involved units of the 21st Army Group. He continued: 'Am
surprised that the army groups, although independent, are
attacking separately. The general opinion at Wentworth was
that it should arrive simultaneously. FUSAG, as I reported,
was ready for an attack at any moment, but it is now evident
that it will be an independent action.'

This, then, was the start of an all-out attempt to keep the
German Fifteenth Army in the Pas de Calais.

At noon on 6 June, Winston Churchill had created an inadvertent headache for the deceivers. He had told the House of
Commons that 'the first of a series of landings in force upon
the European continent' had taken place. The Prime Minister
may have thought that this would lead the Germans to fear a
further assault, but it did not suit the deceivers' purposes.
They wanted the official line to be that there would be no
further landings – leaving the double agents to expose 'the
truth' about an attack on the Pas de Calais. Juan Pujol, in
particular, now faced a problem: he had been notionally working at the Political Warfare Executive and in this capacity had
learned of a fictional directive issued to public figures, including Churchill, stating that no reference should be made
publicly to further attacks. What would the Germans now
make of Churchill's speech? Would they assume that Pujol had
been lying and there had been no such directive? Might they
start to question his reliability? Desperate to undo the damage,
Pujol radioed Madrid at 8 p.m., saying that the PWE director
was dismayed that Churchill had not followed the directive,

but the fact was that Churchill had felt duty bound to tell the truth to his people – even at such obvious risk to national security. The SD did not take issue with this somewhat implausible explanation.

But the fact was that the Germans had greater problems. The invasion had taken them by complete surprise. According to Walter Warlimont, Deputy Chief of Hitler's Operations Staff, High Command had not had 'the slightest idea that the decisive events of the war were upon them'. In part he attributed this to the failure of the Luftwaffe in its reconnaissance role. But the problems went deeper. The immediate reaction to the invasion from those responsible for the defence of the West had been slow and uncertain.

During the early hours of 6 June, General Pemsel, Dollman's chief of staff of the Seventh Army, had spoken to General Speidel, Rommel's chief of staff, convinced that a major operation was being launched. Speidel, having been informed of the Titanic dummy paratroopers, remained unconvinced that Pemsel was right, believing this to be – at most – a local attack. He therefore hesitated to commit Rommel's Panzer Divisions. As the night wore on, and radar began to detect large numbers of ships arriving off the Normandy coast, Pemsel telephoned Speidel in desperation, but Speidel still failed to react. At 6 a.m. Pemsel telephoned General Hans von Salmuth, the commander of the Fifteenth Army, telling him that an offshore bombardment had been launched in Normandy, but was forced to admit that no invasion had yet begun. Salmuth went back to bed.

At the same time General Blumentritt, Rundstedt's chief of staff, was speaking on the telephone with Warlimont at High Command, reporting his belief that an invasion had arrived in Normandy. He urged on behalf of Rundstedt that the OKW Panzer reserves held near Paris be released to confront the attackers. Warlimont contacted General Jodl, who was not persuaded that the real invasion had arrived and refused to release the reserves. Whatever was happening in Normandy, Jodl felt, might well be merely a diversion before an attack on the Pas de Calais. He therefore declined to wake Hitler.

A little later Roenne, the chief of Fremde Herre West, telephoned Rommel's intelligence officer Colonel Anton Staubwasser and told him that Normandy was not to be the Allies' main landing point. Sure that another landing would take place in the Fifteenth Army area, Roenne stressed that no troops should be removed from the Pas de Calais.

In all this confusion and contradiction, various factors present themselves: first, the German belief that the main invasion was more likely to come in the Pas de Calais than in Normandy, and so a reluctance to commit too many forces too early to whatever was currently brewing. For this belief Fortitude South must take much credit. Secondly, the misfortune for the Germans that Rommel was currently away from his post; it is likely that he would have reacted with much greater urgency than his chief of staff Speidel. And, for that matter, had Rommel been allowed to dig his Panzer Divisions in behind the beaches, the invaders would have faced a far hotter reception. And thirdly, the fact that Hitler's subordinates were too scared of the Führer to wake him in case the information was mistaken. Better, they evidently felt, to let him sleep through the beginning of the end of the Thousand Year Reich.

When Hitler finally woke after 10 a.m., he was in a good mood. According to Warlimont, he stepped up to his maps, chuckled in a carefree manner, and said in unusually broad Austrian, 'So, we're off.' Relieved that the chance had finally arrived to confront the Western Allies in Europe, he expressed his certainty that the enemy would be swept into the sea. That afternoon Hitler agreed to Rundstedt's request that the Panzer reserves be released to mount a counter-attack. But the 12th SS Panzer 'Hitlerjugend' Division was not to arrive in Normandy until the following morning, and the Panzer Lehr not until the day after that. Both would be hampered by Allied air attacks. When Rommel finally returned to La Roche-Guyon in the late afternoon, he was told by Speidel that the 21st Panzer Division near Caen had not yet been released. Furious, he ordered the 21st and 2nd Panzer Divisions to attack. The Panzers were finally on the move – but many hours had been wasted, during which the Allies had been gaining their foothold.

On 8 June, German High Command proposed to start moving units of the Fifteenth Army to Normandy. Rommel, whose Army Group B was responsible for both the Fifteenth Army in the Pas de Calais and the Seventh Army in Normandy, was not happy about this level of intrusion. In a telephone conversation that evening, Jodl, whose view on the subject seems to have changed back and forth, told Rommel, 'I do not think we have to fear any second invasion in the west.' 'May I point out,' replied Rommel, 'that the enemy has so far only committed one of their two army groups, and this is precisely why we cannot afford to pull any forces out of Fifteenth Army's area.'

For the Allies this was a moment of great danger. The tender Allied bridgehead might be crushed by elements of the Fifteenth Army moving south to engage it. In the build-up to D-Day, General Eisenhower had said to the deceivers, 'Just keep Fifteenth Army out of my hair for two days. That's all I ask.' Now, in spite of Rommel's objections, OKW authorized the move of the powerful 1st SS Panzer Division, and the Panzer Regiment 'Grossdeutschland' of the 116th Panzer

Division, from the Pas de Calais to Normandy. The deceivers were to be put to a very severe test.

Until this point they had been careful – for the most part – to follow Dudley Clarke's blueprint by providing details of the Order of Battle in small pieces. Only Czerniawski, who was notionally working for FUSAG, had been allowed to draw FUSAG's elements together into a coherent picture. The strategy had evidently served its purpose: Hitler, Rundstedt and Rommel were all inclined to believe that the Normandy landings were merely an initial attack to pin down German forces. Now was the moment to hammer home the threat to the Pas de Calais. Tomás Harris, as we have seen, was of the opinion that it was not always sufficient to present the notional facts to the Germans; sometimes, he believed, they had to be spoon-fed with an agent's personal opinion in order to ensure a reaction. And who better to spoon-feed them than their most trusted agent, Juan Pujol?

And so, with Eisenhower's authorization, Pujol transmitted, in the words of Harris, 'the most important report of his career'. Beginning just after midnight, the message took two hours and two minutes to transmit. This was a dangerously long time for any agent to remain on air. Pujol began by stating that he had called his chief south coast sub-agents to London for a meeting: the retired Welsh seaman in Dover, 'Rags' the Indian poet in Brighton and the Aryan World Order treasurer in Harwich. They had, he said, delivered their reports in full. He went on to give the Germans a concentrated summary of all the real and notional formations in Kent, Sussex and East Anglia. In effect he was providing the Germans with a summary of the entire Fortitude South Order of Battle. He then went a step further. He provided his categorical opinion of what it all meant:

From the reports mentioned it is perfectly clear that the present attack is a large-scale operation but diversionary in character for the purpose of establishing a strong bridge-head in order to draw the maximum of our reserves to the area of operation to retain them there so as to be able to strike a blow somewhere else with ensured success. I never like to give my opinion unless I have strong reasons to justify my assurances. Thus the fact that these concentrations which are in the east and south east of the island are now inactive means that they must be held in reserve to be employed in the other large-scale operations. The constant aerial bombardment which the area of the Pas de Calais has suffered and the strategic disposition of these forces give reason to suspect an attack in that region of France which at the same time offers the shortest route for the final objective of their illusions, which is to say, Berlin.

Pujol went on to ask Madrid to be sure to pass his report to High Command because time was short and he was convinced that 'the whole of the present attack is set as a trap for the enemy to make us move all our reserves in a hurried strategical disposition which we would later regret'. The time had passed for allowing the Germans to draw their own conclusions. The Allies, through Pujol, were plainly telling the enemy not to send reinforcements to Normandy.

Madrid summarized the report and sent it on to Berlin. It was passed to Colonel Krummacher, the head of the OKW Intelligence Branch. At this point fortune played a part. That same day Krummacher had already received two pieces of intelligence which paved the way for Pujol's message. The first was an intercepted wireless message from London to the Belgian Resistance which German Intelligence believed might indicate an imminent assault, although Krummacher was not sufficiently impressed by it to pass it on to his superiors.

The second piece of intelligence received was a report from Karl-Heinz Krämer, the Stockholm-based intelligence officer, passing on information from an entirely fictitious British Air Force officer named 'Harrison'. 'In [Harrison's] opinion, and according to information from other sources,' Kramer revealed, 'a second main attack across the Channel directed against the Pas de Calais is to be expected.' Krämer, one of two uncontrolled agents providing German Intelligence with entirely fabricated reports, was, on this occasion, endorsing the Fortitude South story. It is likely that his source was material emanating from the Allied deceivers. Krummacher took the report seriously enough to bring it to Jodl's attention.

And so when Pujol's report arrived on Krummacher's desk the Intelligence chief was already in a very receptive mood. After studying it he wrote underneath in red pen, 'Confirms the view already held by us that a further attack is to be expected in another place (Belgium?).' He passed the report straight to Jodl, who underlined a number of words before placing it before Hitler. Field Marshal Wilhelm Keitel, the OKW chief of staff, then made a telephone call to the Commander-in-Chief West. And at 7.30 on the morning of 10 June, just a few hours after Pujol had finished sending his message, his request was complied with. Rundstedt declared a state of alarm for the Fifteenth Army in Belgium and northern France, and halted the move of the 1st Panzer Division (comprising over 21,000 troops) and the 'Grossdeutschland' Regiment, as well as the proposed move of the 85th Infantry Division and the 16th Luftwaffe Division. They would not be assisting with the defence of Normandy; instead they would be awaiting a notional invasion in the Pas de Calais. The 1st

SS Panzer Division would remain there for another week – by which time the bridgehead was secure.

In order to place Pujol's message into a realistic context, it is worth mentioning three factors. First, the 1st SS Panzer Division's passage to Normandy would have been badly affected by Allied bombing, a fact which may have influenced the countermanding order. Secondly, it can never be known to what extent these units would have altered the course of the battle, even had they arrived safely in Normandy. And thirdly, Pujol's message did not arrive in isolation; Karl-Heinz Krämer's report undoubtedly played a part in High Command's thinking. However, when Keitel was shown the text of Pujol's message during a post-war interrogation, he said, 'If I were writing a history, I would say, with ninety-nine per cent certainty, that that message provided the reason for the change of plan.' Ultimately it can be said with some confidence that an unprepossessing Portuguese chicken farmer, controlled by a half-Spanish art dealer, had made an extraordinary contribution to the success of the invasion. As had the other double agents who had combined to create the threat to the Pas de Calais in the first place.

Madrid was delighted with Pujol's contribution, particularly when it received the following reply from Berlin on 11 June: 'The report is credible. The reports received in the last week from the [*Garbo*] undertaking have been confirmed almost without exception and are to be described as especially valuable. The main line of investigation in future is to be the enemy group of forces in South-Eastern and Eastern England.'

General Eisenhower had asked for two days free from the forces of the Fifteenth Army; he was to receive many more thanks to Fortitude. An entire week after D-Day only one division had moved from its sector to Normandy. And German and Japanese sources for this period make clear how real the threat was perceived to be. On the same day that Berlin was reporting its approval of Pujol, an appreciation of the current situation by Rundstedt declared: 'One must realize that the enemy will still come at a second point; new reserves must then be there and further ones must be brought up.' A Führer Directive issued four days later stressed that the enemy's attempt to begin far-reaching operations from the bridgehead would have to be foiled by the strictest concentration of German forces in the area. To this end Hitler underlined that coastal fronts which have not been attacked would have to be weakened – 'with the exception of Fifteenth Army's'.

On 19 June the Japanese ambassador in Berlin reported to Tokyo that there were twenty-three Allied divisions still in Britain under General Patton. The original Allied plan, wired Oshima, had been to occupy Cherbourg and Le Havre with seventeen of Montgomery's divisions. But there was now evidence, he said, that Montgomery had already used twenty-five divisions in Normandy, of which two had been wiped out and several had suffered bad losses; it seemed, therefore, that his plans had gone awry. But the ambassador was very clear that the Germans were still expecting Patton to land between Dieppe and Boulogne.

Nine days later Guy Liddell wrote in his diary that a map issued by German Intelligence had been captured by British forces in Italy. The map showed Great Britain and most of Ireland, and on it was the supposed disposition of all Allied forces in the country as of 15 June 1944. It had been compiled using data received from Roenne's FHW, and it showed huge numbers of Allied units crammed into south-east England. As Liddell noted, 'It was almost identical with Plan Fortitude.'

The plain fact was that the Germans had believed what the Allied deceivers had been telling them, and were continuing to do so. And as the bridgehead was secured and the bitter and bloody battle for Normandy took hold, the deceivers – warriors for the working day – had now to keep the deception alive for as long as they possibly could. Their achievement had already exceeded expectations – but their work was not yet over.

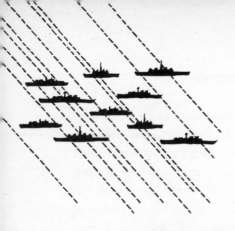

DOWN THE RABBIT HOLE

At the end of June 1944 the Germans were still convinced that another major cross-Channel expedition was planned, to be carried out by what they called Armeegruppe Patton. Twenty-two German divisions remained in the Pas de Calais to deal with the threat. A fortnight earlier the deceivers at Ops (B) had updated the Fortitude South plan. They were working on the basis that the deception would not be workable for much longer. After all, units notionally belonging to FUSAG were soon to start appearing in Normandy – as was General Patton himself, the living embodiment of the Pas de Calais threat. He was to arrive as commander of the United States Third Army. It was now time, the deceivers felt, to squeeze the last few drops from Fortitude South.

As it was expected that the majority of German reserves would be committed to Normandy by early July, the intention of the new plan was simply to slow down the reinforcement of the bridgehead. The Germans would be given the impression that the Normandy assault had been so successful that the Allies would now attempt to win an outright victory in Normandy before attacking in the Pas de Calais. This victory would be achieved by introducing FUSAG units into Normandy. And to replace these forces, a new Second United

States Army Group (SUSAG) would be formed in England which would eventually attack in the Pas de Calais.

There were problems with this plan. First, it would have been very plain to the Germans that Normandy was not going that well for the Allies. Secondly, by giving the impression that it was, the Allies would be encouraging the Germans to increase the rate of reinforcement. And thirdly, and most importantly, by the end of June it was clear that the Germans had not sent the majority of their reinforcements to Normandy. The plan was therefore built on a faulty premise.

David Strangeways, the man 'embedded in his own worth', stepped up once more. In late June he rewrote the plan to suit the circumstances. His new intention was not merely to slow down the rate of reinforcement, but actively to ensure that the Germans kept their forces in the Pas de Calais. This was a positive aim, in keeping with Dudley Clarke's rules. And it represented far more than an attempt to wring a few drops from a dry husk. Strangeways' story would now be that Normandy was not going as well as had been hoped, and therefore Eisenhower had decided to reinforce it with FUSAG units. These units would be reconstituted as the United States 12th Army Group under the command of General Omar Bradley. And no mention was to be made of SUSAG.

This put the double agents in a tricky position, however. By reporting that the old FUSAG units were embarking from the south-east of England for the bridgehead, they would be encouraging the Germans to reinforce Normandy. On the other hand, they would be expected to observe the movements; the units were soon to appear in France, after all. And so, to preserve their bona fides, Juan Pujol and Roman Czerniawski were both conveniently removed from the scene while the movements took place.

Pujol's fictional disappearance took the form of an arrest. Both the SD and MI5 were currently turning their thoughts to the Germans' V-1 bombing campaign, launched against Britain in the aftermath of the invasion. Pujol had been asked by Madrid to investigate the degree of damage inflicted by the flying bombs, and to verify a report from Paul Fidrmuc that central London was being ravaged. On 7 July, therefore, Pujol was notionally arrested in London for, according to Guy Liddell, 'poking his nose too deeply into buildings damaged by fly-bombs'. He was held in custody for a few days before being released on 12 July. On his release the Germans unwittingly played into Allied hands by urging him to lie low.

Posted at FUSAG, meanwhile, Czerniawski could hardly be expected to miss the transfer of units to Normandy and so, to avoid the unavoidable, he was notionally sent to Scotland for a week. He 'returned' from Scotland on 15 July and four days later began to send a series of messages, dishing out the complete story of the reorganization of FUSAG as it had been explained to him. The reorganization, he said, was due to the necessity of sending immediate reinforcements to Normandy, and Eisenhower had decided that the only troops immediately available were the FUSAG troops. He had therefore put these under the command of a new army group to be commanded by Bradley. FUSAG, Czerniawski continued, had been reconstituted to contain the British Fourth Army (the notional unit created for Fortitude North) and the Ninth and Fourteenth United States Armies, all of which were replacing the First Canadian Army and United States Third Army, FUSAG's original components. And so the Pole was making it very clear that the threat to the Pas de Calais still existed.

Czerniawski also mentioned that there had been a difference of opinion between Eisenhower and Patton over this course of action, resulting in Patton's dismissal as commander of FUSAG. Pujol had now been notionally released from custody and he wrote a long letter to Madrid giving the Germans the same information, although including a little more detail about the 'difference of opinion'. Pujol described Patton as 'a rough and brutal soldier' who had opposed any FUSAG troops being made available for Montgomery's 21st Army Group. When Eisenhower had told Montgomery that 'he could make use of all troops he required from FUSAG', Patton showed 'insubordination', leading Eisenhower to remove him from the command of FUSAG and give him instead the inferior command of the US Third Army.

With this information Pujol was preparing the Germans for Patton's appearance in Normandy in a relatively humble position. His letter went on to explain that FUSAG had remained without a commander for a few days, but that the position had now been filled by one of Eisenhower's favoured officers, Lieutenant General Leslie McNair. Pujol repeated Czerniawski's news about FUSAG's reorganization and finished by warning the Germans that the new FUSAG would not be any weaker than the old; in fact, thanks to the addition of the British Fourth Army, it would now consist of thirty divisions. All of this material was supposed to have come from the Catalan's sub-agent in the United States Army Service of Supply.

Once it had been sent, Pujol's letter came to the attention of Czerniawski's case officer, Hugh Astor, who was furious. Astor noted that the letter covered the same ground as Czerniawski's wireless message and at some points it tallied almost word for word. 'It seems to me preposterous,' he wrote, 'that two agents should have obtained such exactly similar details on so important and secret a matter. I do not know the notional position of *Garbo*'s [sub-agent], but I am surprised that he is able to obtain such a wealth of information about the organization of FUSAG.' Astor's indignation was fired by more than just professional jealousy: this was a rare example of B1a failing to coordinate its material. Just as had happened in the case of the pre-Neptune air exercise, double agents had passed over dangerously similar information. There was a real risk that the enemy would work out that both Pujol and Czerniawski were under control – although, in the event, no damage was done. In fact, the Germans read Pujol's letter as an important confirmation of Czerniawski's message, with the fortunate result that Fortitude South was kept alive. Nevertheless, the incident served as a warning to B1a against complacency.

In the meantime General McNair had been sent to Britain. Where Patton had once travelled around southern England pretending to lead FUSAG, McNair now did the same. But on 24 July, while visiting troops in Normandy, he was killed in a bombing raid carried out in error by Allied aircraft. The relentless deceivers were quick to exploit the incident. Czerniawski boosted his credibility by reporting McNair's death to the Germans long before the news reached them through other channels. McNair's place as FUSAG commander was taken by General John de Witt. De Witt is better known today as the commanding officer of American Western Defense Command, in which capacity he recommended the wartime internment of tens of thousands of United States citizens of Japanese origin. 'A Jap's a Jap. It makes no difference whether the Jap is a citizen or not,' he had said in 1942. Two years on, he was the commander of the First United States Army Group.

The scene was now set for the genuine arrival in Normandy of the units which had formerly constituted FUSAG. The twenty-third of July saw the formal activation of the First Canadian Army (now made up of II Canadian Corps and I British Corps), followed nine days later by the formal activation of the United States Third Army (made up of XX and XII Corps). Patton himself had been in Normandy since 6 July.

And it was a measure of the Germans' belief in the deception at this point that *Pariser Zeitung*, a newspaper of the German occupation, published the following article, entitled 'Patton's Army in the Bridgehead':

> In the Normandy peninsula it is noteworthy that amongst the enemy reinforcements which have been employed in the last few days are divisions which apparently no longer form part of Montgomery's Army Group but are already under Eisenhower's other Army Group, which is under the command of the American Patton. Whereas the enemy army group which has so far been fighting in the bridge-head was called the 'South-Western invasion army' because it was located in the South-West of England, these new divisions probably belong to the 'South-Eastern invasion army' and their employment shows to what extent the German defence in Normandy is depleting the enemy forces.

Apart from the failure to mention Patton's demotion, it would be hard to pen a more succinct synopsis of the Fortitude South cover story. And the cover story was still influencing the messages being intercepted by Allied signals intelligence. On 13 July the Japanese ambassador, Hiroshi Oshima, informed Tokyo that the Germans still believed that a further invasion would take place within an area stretching from the present bridgehead to the vicinity of Dieppe.

By 23 July, however, a measure of scepticism had finally crept into German thinking. While perceiving that the Germans were still ready to deal with another invasion, Oshima passed on the view of Ribbentrop, Germany's Foreign Minister, that the possibility of a landing in the near future 'had decreased'. This shift in opinion is reflected in an LCS summary of intercepted material which noted German opinion on 20 July: 'While possibility of Allied attacks north of Seine including Low Countries cannot be excluded, Allies may have abandoned immediate intention of setting bridgehead in this area.'

On 27 July, Rundstedt's weekly report accepted the probability that the Allies were 'contenting themselves with the landing in Normandy' and 'sending the forces still assembled in Great Britain into this area'. Over the next five days OKW released four divisions – 84th, 33rd, 89th and 85th – from the Fifteenth Army to the Seventh Army. For almost two months Hitler had been holding these divisions in an area that was never threatened. On 3 August, Patton's Third Army began its breakout, and by the end of the month the Fifteenth Army had been reduced to just seven divisions. The perceived threat from FUSAG was at an end.

Towards the end of August, Pujol wrote a letter to his handlers explaining why the invasion in the Pas de Calais had not happened. He had, he said, been speaking to his sub-agent in the US Army Service of Supply, who had provided him with 'the real story'. The invasion of the Pas de Calais had apparently been intended to go ahead around forty days after the Normandy landings, but it had been delayed by the reorganization of FUSAG and ultimately prevented by the desire of both the British and the Americans to steal the inevitable glory. Montgomery was determined that his assault on Normandy should come to be remembered as the principal operation, while the Americans were desperate to restrict the scope of his assault so that their attack on the Pas de Calais would provide a spectacular end to the war. This manoeuvring had finally been won by Montgomery, described by Pujol as an 'astute intriguer', who realized that he could claim the laurels by using his British and Canadian divisions to engage the German armoured forces in Normandy. He could then persuade Eisenhower to send the Americans into France through his hard-won bridgehead, from which they could advance with relative speed to the south and west. In this way the two operations would combine into one large operation – which was ultimately Montgomery's operation.

To anybody familiar with Montgomery's reputation for intrigue and ambition, as the Germans undoubtedly were, this story was eminently believable. And on 30 August 1944, three days after he wrote his letter, Pujol finally brought Operation Fortitude to an end. In a wireless message to Madrid he passed on news from his American sub-agent: the plan to attack the Pas de Calais with FUSAG forces had been finally and definitely cancelled.

Yet the extraordinary fact is that the Germans would *never* discover that the FUSAG threat had been a hollow one, or that a deception had been practised on them. According to Roger Hesketh, when Professor Percy Schramm, German High Command's war diarist, was interrogated by the Allies after the war, he asked, 'All this Patton business wasn't a trick, was it?' 'What do you mean by that?' asked his interrogator. 'What I mean is this. Were all those divisions sent to south-east England simply to hold our forces in the Pas de Calais?' 'I certainly imagine,' came the reply, 'that if you had denuded the Pas de Calais, they would have been used to attack that place, but since you did not do so, they were equally available to reinforce Montgomery.' 'Ah,' said Schramm, 'that is what we always thought.'

For Operation Fortitude to succeed, the enemy had to be unaware of its existence. Professor Schramm's words are overwhelming evidence of its success. Not only did the Germans accept the FUSAG Order of Battle, they also accepted FUSAG's supposed purpose. Of course, the Fortitude deception was only ever an adjunct to the bitter fighting on the beaches, inland, at sea and in the air. The efforts of the desk-bound deceivers were only given meaning and purpose by the labours and sacrifices of the fighting men. But this should not diminish the deceivers' achievement. Their work may have been quiet and secret and far removed from the battlefield, but it brought very real rewards, not least the safe return home of uncountable numbers of combatants.

Not that Fortitude was the only supporting factor in the success of Overlord. The Allies' aerial dominance offered a more immediately visible contribution. It allowed for a devastating Allied bombing campaign both before and after Neptune. Roads, railways and bridges were destroyed, making movement and communications difficult and dangerous for the German defenders. Supplies of fuel, weapons and ammunition were held up, and many infantry and armoured units were badly depleted by Allied bombing before even reaching Normandy.

But while Fortitude's part in Overlord's success was not quite so visible, it was no less real – and a picture of Fortitude's contribution exists in the German map of supposed Allied troop dispositions on 15 May 1944, reproduced in this book. The map gives an unparalleled picture of the extent to which the enemy accepted the deceivers' story. And it is a picture which owes its existence to the twin pillars of Fortitude: strategic deception and the Double Cross system.

During Fortitude South, Strangeways took the system developed by Clarke and ruthlessly and brilliantly adapted it to the prevailing circumstances. Strangeways had a clear idea of how he wanted Hitler to act – and the Führer duly obliged.

The Double Cross system, meanwhile, had turned out to be the only truly effective vehicle for passing over strategic deception. Its importance to Fortitude cannot be overstated. And given that the entire system had once amounted to a single transmitter in the hands of the pathologically unstable Arthur Owens, the role that it came to play bordered on the miraculous.

Those working within the system, however, were not surprised by its central role. At a meeting of the W Board on 10 May 1945, J. C. Masterman read the objectives of the system which he had first framed in December 1940. Last on the list was strategic deception, and Masterman now assumed the air of a vindicated prophet. 'It had always been the intention and object of our efforts,' he said, 'to have enough agents in place when the "great moment" came. This, it was anticipated, would be the return to Fortress Europe.' He then expressed the view that the work done in connection with Overlord had been 'extremely successful', and he paid particular tribute to Juan Pujol, Roman Czerniawski and Wulf Schmidt, none of whom had been blown by Fortitude. All had retained the trust of the Germans. He also spoke of the unfortunate collapse of the *Tricycle* group, 'who would, it was thought, be our most important channel'.

Wulf Schmidt made his last contact with Hamburg less than twenty-four hours before the city fell to the British on 3 May 1945. In spite of the dire situation, Schmidt's handlers were eager to reassure him that a suitcase containing valuables that he had left with them before he was parachuted into England was safe. Much had happened to Schmidt in the meantime, beginning with his arrest and subsequent interrogation at the hands of 'Tin Eye' Stephens. But Hamburg was aware of none of it: as they signed off for the last time they told Schmidt that they had delivered the suitcase to his sister, having destroyed any incriminating documents inside. Should it ever fall into the hands of the Allies, they wanted him to know, he would have nothing to fear. Their faith in him had never abated. But Schmidt, once so unwilling to betray his

German masters, had developed a liking for his adopted country. He remained in Britain after the war, becoming a photographer on the *Watford Observer* and a part-time judge of caged-bird competitions.

Juan Pujol moved after the war to Venezuela, where he lived under an assumed name, fearing retribution from the Nazis should they ever discover his betrayal. He was eventually tracked down in 1984 – not by the Nazis, but by the author Nigel West, who persuaded him to come to London, where he was reunited with old friends from MI5. He was also invited to Buckingham Palace and thanked by the Duke of Edinburgh for the service he had rendered the country.

But shortly after the end of the war Pujol had returned to Spain briefly for a very different sort of audience with his part-Jewish German handler, Karl-Erich Kühlenthal, who had been pleased to see him. In a report of the meeting Pujol wrote: 'In the matter of the Service, [Kühlenthal] thought me almost a God, saying that he still did not know what advice to give me "as I can assure you that no one could have carried out the tremendous work which you have brought to a conclusion and for which you have shown such a superior ability".'

Before the two men parted, Kühlenthal expressed his desire to travel to the United States, saying that he wished to leave all preparations for the journey in Pujol's hands and adding that he was ready to help him at any time and in any way that he possibly could. Needless to say, Pujol did not arrange for his handler's escape to America. But the episode is striking for the German's pathetic dependence on Pujol. Kühlenthal's life and career had depended on Pujol for so long that he could not possibly perceive him for what he really was. It is little wonder that handlers so often ignored clear signs that their agents were under control.

But not all of B1a's important double agents emerged from Fortitude unscathed. Dusko Popov, the head of the network which Masterman had expected to lead the deception, had been forced to break off contact with Lisbon in early May. After the war Popov moved to France, where he engaged in a variety of business activities, ranging from publishing to 'international finance'. He was to marry twice. At the age of 34 he married an 18-year-old French girl. Sixteen years later he married an 18-year-old Swedish girl. At the time of the first marriage, a B1a memo noted that the incorrigible Yugoslav's wife was 'apparently entering this matrimonial adventure with her eyes open'. The second marriage proved to be a happier one, although Popov did not mention his past as a double agent to his wife or their three sons until he published his memoirs in 1974. In the book he recounts the story of the Pearl Harbor questionnaire and his bitter clash with J. Edgar Hoover. The FBI attempted but failed to have the book banned. Popov died in the south of France in 1981, aged 69.

And so the tale of Fortitude, with its roots in Arthur Owens's visits to Hamburg and Dudley Clarke's posting to the Middle East, concluded with a wireless message sent by Juan Pujol to Madrid. A quote from a rousing speech by Churchill, Montgomery or Eisenhower – paying tribute to the deception and the deceivers – would be a fitting conclusion to the story. But no such speeches were made. Fortitude and the Double Cross system remained tightly guarded secrets long after the end of the war. As late as 1970, J.C. Masterman was refused permission in the United Kingdom to publish his account of the work of B1a and the Twenty Committee. Even ten years later, Margaret Thatcher refused to sanction publication of the official history of wartime strategic deception, written by Professor Sir Michael Howard, as he was to become.

OPERATION FORTITUDE

Since the late 1990s, Cabinet Office, War Office and Secret Service documents on which these works were based have been entering the public domain. We can finally meet the improbable cast of characters who came together to create an underground world of fakery and artifice. It contained, as we have seen, some characters predisposed to fantasy and melodrama, others who grew unable to separate the real from the imaginary, and others still who stubbornly brought their own certainty with them.

It was a world in which the German's wanted to believe. They came down the rabbit hole eagerly enough. Once inside, they rarely questioned their curious surroundings. And even when they did, they showed little desire to wake from their dream.

SELECT BIBLIOGRAPHY

Andrew, Christopher, *The Defence of the Realm: The Authorized History of MI5* (London: Allen Lane, 2009).

Barbier, Mary Kathryn, *D-Day Deception: Operation Fortitude and the Normandy Invasion* (Westport, CT: Praeger Security International, 2007).

Beevor, Antony, *D-Day: The Battle for Normandy* (London: Viking, 2009).

Brown, Anthony Cave, *Bodyguard of Lies* (London: W. H. Allen, 1975).

Bullock, Alan, *Hitler and Stalin: Parallel Lives* (London: HarperCollins, 1991).

Clarke, Dudley, *Seven Assignments* (London: Jonathan Cape, 1948).

Clifton James, Meyrick, *I Was Monty's Double* (London: Rider and Co., 1954).

Crowdy, Terry, *Deceiving Hitler: Double Cross and Deception in World War II* (Oxford: Osprey, 2008).

Cruikshank, Charles G., *Deception in World War II* (Oxford: Oxford University Press, 1979).

D'Este, Carlo, *A Genius for War: A Life of General George S. Patton* (London: HarperCollins, 1995).

Douglas-Home, Charles, *Rommel* (London: Weidenfeld & Nicolson, 1973).

Eisenhower, Dwight D., *Crusade in Europe* (London: Heinemann, 1948).

Farago, Ladislas, *The Game of the Foxes: British and German Intelligence Operations and Personalities which Changed the Course of the Second World War* (London: Hodder & Stoughton, 1972).

Farago, Ladislas, *Patton: Ordeal and Triumph* (London: Arthur Barker, 1966).

Handel, Michael (ed.), *Strategic and Operational Deception in the Second World War* (London: Frank Cass, 1990).

Harris, Tomás (introd. by Mark Seaman), *Garbo – The Spy Who Saved D-Day* (Richmond: Public Record Office, 2000).

Hart-Davis, Duff, *Peter Fleming: A Biography* (London: Cape, 1974).

Hastings, Max, *Overlord: D-Day and the Battle for Normandy 1944* (London: Michael Joseph, 1984).

Haswell, Jock, *The Intelligence and Deception of the D-Day Landings* (London: Batsford, 1979).

Hesketh, Roger, *Fortitude: The D-Day Deception Campaign* (London: St Ermin's Press, 1999).

Hinsley, F. H., and Simkins, C. A. G., *British Intelligence in the Second World War: Vol. 4: Security and Counter-Intelligence* (London: HMSO, 1990).

Holt, Thaddeus, *The Deceivers: Allied Military Deception in the Second World War* (London and New York: Scribner, 2004).

Howard, Michael, *British Intelligence in the Second World War: Vol. 5: Strategic Deception* (London: HMSO, 1990).

Imperial War Museum, Bailey, Roderick, *Forgotten Voices of D-Day* (London: Ebury Press, 2009).

Irving, David, *The Trail of The Fox: The Life of Field Marshal Erwin Rommel* (London: Weidenfeld & Nicolson, 1977).

Jones, R. V., *Most Secret War* (London: Hamish Hamilton, 1978).

Kahn, David, *Hitler's Spies: German Military Intelligence in World War II* (London: Hodder & Stoughton, 1978).

Kershaw, Ian, *Hitler 1936–1945: Nemesis* (London: Allen Lane, 2000).

Kershaw, Robert J., *Piercing the Atlantic Wall* (Shepperton: Ian Allan, 1993).

Latimer, Jon, *Deception in War* (London: John Murray, 2001).

Lycett, Andrew, *Ian Fleming* (London: Weidenfeld & Nicolson, 1995).

SELECT BIBLIOGRAPHY

Macintyre, Ben, *Operation Mincemeat: The True Spy Story that Changed the Course of World War II* (London: Bloomsbury, 2010).

Mackay, Francis, *Overture to Overlord: Special Operations in Preparation for D-Day* (Barnsley: Pen & Sword Books, 2005).

Maskelyne, Jasper, *Magic – Top Secret* (London: Stanley Paul and Co., 1949).

Masterman, J. C., *The Double-Cross System in the War of 1939 to 1945* (New Haven and London: Yale University Press, 1972).

Masterman J. C., *On the Chariot Wheel: An Autobiography* (London: Oxford University Press, 1975).

Miller, Russell, *Codename Tricycle: The True Story of the Second World War's Most Extraordinary Double Agent* (London: Secker & Warburg, 2004).

Montgomery, Viscount, *The Memoirs of Field-Marshal the Viscount Montgomery of Alamein, K.G.* (London: Collins, 1958).

Morgan, Sir Frederick, *Overture to Overlord* (London: Hodder & Stoughton, 1950).

Mure, David, *Master of Deception: Tangled Webs in London and the Middle East* (London: Kimber, 1980).

Niven, David, *The Moon's a Balloon* (London: Hamish Hamilton, 1971).

Owen, David, *Battle of Wits: A History of Psychology and Deception in Modern Warfare* (London: Cooper, 1978).

Pierrepoint, Albert, *Executioner Pierrepoint* (London: Harrap, 1974).

Popov, Dusko, *Spy/Counterspy* (London: Weidenfeld & Nicolson, 1974).

Pujol, Juan (with Nigel West), *Garbo* (London: Weidenfeld & Nicolson, 1985).

Rankin, Nicholas, *Churchill's Wizards: The British Genius for Deception 1914–1945* (London: Faber and Faber, 2008).

Rommel, Erwin, *The Rommel Papers,* ed. B. H. Liddell-Hart (London: Collins, 1953).

Royle, Trevor, *Patton: Old Blood and Guts* (London: Weidenfeld & Nicolson, 2005).

Ruge, Friedrich, *Rommel in Normandy: Reminiscences* (London: Macdonald and Jane's, 1979).

Scotland, Alexander, *The London Cage* (London: Evans Bros, 1957).

Sergueiev, Lily, *Secret Service Rendered* (London: Kimber, 1968).

Speidel, Hans, *We Defended Normandy* (London: Herbert Jenkins, 1951).

Stafford, David, *Ten Days to D-Day: Countdown to the Liberation of Europe* (London: Little Brown, 2003).

Stephens, Robin (ed. and introd. by Oliver Hoare), *Camp 020: MI5 and the Nazi Spies: the Official History of MI5's Interrogation Centre* (Richmond: Public Record Office, 2000).

Warlimont, Walter, *Inside Hitler's Headquarters* (London: Weidenfeld & Nicolson, 1964).

West, Nigel, *Counterfeit Spies: Genuine or Bogus? An Astonishing Investigation into Secret Agents of the Second World War* (London: St Ermin's Press, 1998).

West, Nigel, *MI5: British Security Service Operations 1909–1945* (London: Bodley Head, 1981).

Wheatley, Dennis, *The Deception Planners: My Secret War* (London: Hutchinson, 1980).

Wingate, Ronald, *Not in the Limelight: An Autobiography* (London: Hutchinson, 1959).

ACKNOWLEDGEMENTS AND SOURCES

This has been a fascinating book to write. It has taken me into a world closely related to, yet quite distinct from, the monumental operations of the Second World War. And so my greatest debt is to those who existed within this world, both the deceivers and the double agents. I was lucky enough to meet Mrs Peggy Harmer, the wife of B1a case officer and SHAEF liaison officer Christopher Harmer. Mrs Harmer, who was herself a secretary at B1a, is delightful company, and she was kind enough to share her memories with me. In addition she allowed me access to her late husband's papers, which contained his frank recollections of events in which he participated and of individuals with whom he worked. I was also fortunate to interview Christopher Mills, the son of Cyril Mills, the B1a man who codenamed Juan Pujol and who was responsible for the evacuation of double agents in the event of a German invasion. He was generous in sharing his father's memories with me.

The large number of previously classified documents now available to view in the National Archives in Kew have been central to the writing of this book. It could not have been attempted without them. Not only do they provide the essential facts of the story, but they give vivid insight into the attitudes and characters of those involved. I have also found much valuable information in the Imperial War Museum, in both the documents and the sound archives. As ever, the custodians of both have been generous with their time and assistance. The new research room at the Museum has proved a particularly valuable resource. I would like to express my deep gratitude to

Margaret Brooks, the head of Sound Records, who has very recently retired from the post.

So far as published sources are concerned, a number have been of particular value. Professor Sir Michael Howard's *Strategic Deception in the Second World War* is a succinct, wise and often witty record of wartime strategic deception from the British perspective. Thaddeus Holt's *The Deceivers* is a comprehensive account from a wider western Allied standpoint, which despite its encyclopedic detail, is extremely readable and paints vivid pictures of many of the personalities involved. Roger Hesketh's *Fortitude* is written by one of the central figures in the Fortitude deception, a man of whom Christopher Harmer writes, 'I have never encountered a tidier, more thorough, and more painstaking person.' The book accurately reflects these traits. It is a tightly reasoned, forensic, and extremely thorough account of the operation. J. C. Masterman's *The Double-Cross System* is a concise and enjoyable work. In addition to being an Oxford history don, Masterman was a popular crime novelist, and his account is both admirably clear and revealing about the problems encountered by those running the system. The reader is left with an impression of a small number of intelligent men grappling with complex logic puzzles as they attempt to second-guess the German Intelligence Service. *The Guy Liddell Diaries*, in two volumes edited by Nigel West, are indispensable to anybody with an interest in Double Cross. Liddell, the head of MI5's B Division, was not merely an assiduous chronicler of events, but also a wry commentator on them. I have referred to and quoted from Liddell's diaries throughout the present book, using the unedited originals as my source. These are held in twelve volumes, spanning the length of the war, in the National Archives. They can be downloaded digitally and their catalogue reference numbers run from KV 4/185 to KV 4/196. I have also found Terry Crowdy's recent work *Deceiving Hitler* to be very illuminating. It adds a good deal of colour to the existing literature, as well as offering very sound judgements.

A number of books concerning individual double agents have been of great value. *Garbo*, the memoirs of Juan Pujol, written in collaboration with Nigel West, takes the form of autobiographical chapters by Pujol interspersed with West's overview of the case. *Garbo: The Spy Who Saved D-Day* is a PRO publication. With an introduction by Mark Seaman, it consists of the official summary of the case written by Tomás Harris, Pujol's case officer. It is a long and detailed account of Pujol's career as a double agent, originally written as an internal report and therefore likely to be highly accurate. The original can be found at PRO KV 2/41 and the extensive Pujol files run from KV 2/39 to KV 2/42 and KV 2/63 to KV 2/71. Also relevant to Pujol are KV 2/101 (a file on his handler Friedrich Knappe-Ratey) and KV 2/102 (a file on his handler Karl-Erich Kühlenthal). My account in Chapter Fourteen of Pujol's rendezvous with Kühlenthal at the end of the war is based on documents found in the Kühlenthal file.

I have used two valuable books relating to Dusko Popov. One is Popov's autobiography, *Spy/Counterspy*, which reads better than most spy novels. The other is *Codename Tricycle*, a carefully researched and well-written biography by Russell Miller, published in 2004. The PRO files on Popov run from KV 2/845 to KV 2/866. The files begin with reports from December 1940 concerning Popov's initial approach to the British and his first trip to England. The German request for information relating to Pearl Harbor can be found in KV 2/849. The fallout from his time in the United States is discussed in KV 2/850, while material concerning the recruitment of Johnny Jebsen is in KV 2/854. Documents relating to the Jebsen crisis, his arrest, the possible repercussions for Fortitude, and the decision to discontinue the *Tricycle* network are in KV 2/858. The varying accounts offering clues as to Jebsen's ultimate fate are in KV 2/860.

Another autobiography of a double agent is that of Lily Sergueiev, entitled *Secret Service Rendered*. The tone of this book is set by its first sentence: 'Babs lifts up his shaggy, trufflelike nose and looks at me inquiringly.' Babs, it will be remembered, is the dog whose close bond with his mistress caused MI5 such anxiety. Sergueiev's files are to be found at KV 2/464 to KV 2/466. Another more interesting autobiography, which I found very helpful, is that of Dennis Wheatley. *The Deception Planners* is a superb read, as one might expect from such a successful and prolific novelist. Wheatley can take a novelist's licence with the odd fact, but his eye for small details is tremendous, as is his capacity for vivid description. His depiction of the birth and growth of the London Controlling Section is an ideal counterpoint to the less colourful accounts which exist elsewhere. Another extremely good account of wartime deception by a member of LCS exists in the National Archives. Sir Ronald Wingate's *Historical record of deception in the war against Germany and Italy* is at CAB 154/100 to 101. Wingate's detailed account of the Fortitude deception is at CAB 154/101. It ends entertainingly with accounts and analyses of six previous military deceptions, including those of Belisarius in AD 542 and Marlborough in 1704.

George Lane, originally Dyuri Länyi, the Commando who was taken to meet Rommel, recounted his story – and his conversation with the field marshal – to the Imperial War Museum Sound Archive in 1993. The interview is at Accession Number 13307. The tale is confirmed by Admiral Friedrich Ruge in his published reminiscences *Rommel in Normandy*.

Much of the material relating to Dudley Clarke was found in the Dudley Clarke papers at Box Reference 99/2/1-3 in the Imperial War Museum Documents Archive. I also referred to a biography of Clarke, *Master of Deception*, by David Mure. While Mure is reverential of Clarke, and of most things military, he is dismissive of MI5 and MI6, and utterly vitriolic about J. C. Masterman. One must be careful about relying too heavily on a book with unaccountable prejudices.

As I have suggested, the majority of Christopher Harmer's opinions and observations in this book have been gleaned from his private papers. Similarly the majority of Hugh Astor's contributions come from an interview with the IWM Sound Archive at Accession Number 18149. Occasionally, however, both men are quoted from a contemporaneous B1a document. Material relating to meetings of the Twenty Committee generally comes from PRO KV 4/63 to KV 4/69, while material relating to meetings of the W Board usually comes from KV 4/70. To take two examples from Chapter Two, Masterman's memo of December 1940 setting out the objects of the Double Cross system is at KV 4/63, while Wulf Schmidt's messages relating to the damage sustained by Coventry factories are at KV 4/70. A more detailed discussion of the problems concerning 'chickenfood' can be found in KV 4/213 and KV 4/214, files concerning the general policy regarding traffic for double agents.

The time has surely come for a biography of the arch-fantasist Arthur Owens. In the meantime his PRO files run from KV 2/444 to

KV 2/453. Material up to November 1937 is at KV 2/444. The interview between Owens and Edward Hinchley-Cooke is at KV 2/445. Material concerning the recruitment of Gwilym Williams, and the unmasking of Mathilde Krafft is at KV 2/446. The ill-fated trawler meeting with Nikolaus Ritter, as well as Sam McCarthy's subsequent trip to Lisbon, is at KV 2/448. The extraordinary events surrounding the trip made by Owens and Walter Dicketts to Lisbon are at KV 2/450 and KV 2/451 in the Owens files and KV 2/674 in the Dicketts file. This latter file also contains Dicketts's vivid account of his time spent walking the German streets. Ritter's account of the event, which seems to offer a solution to the riddle, is in *The Game of the Foxes* by Ladislas Farago.

The discussion of the Abwehr in Chapter Four quotes Hugh Trevor-Roper's 1945 report into the German Intelligence Service which can be found at CAB 154/105. Each of the 'Four Men in a Boat' has his own PRO file. Kieboom at KV 2/11, Meier at KV 2/12, Pons at KV 2/13, and Waldberg at KV 2/107. In addition there are court transcripts at KV 2/1452 and other papers relating to the trial at KV 2/1699 and KV 2/1700, including the letters written by the condemned men to their next of kin but never delivered. The IWM Sound Archive stories concerning the army officer in Barnet Hospital, the low-flying Dorniers, and the Reverend Nye can be found at Accession Numbers 12514, 19530, and 13724 respectively. Much of the material relating to the inimitable 'Tin Eye' Stephens is from his history of Camp 020, entitled *A Digest of Ham* (Ham being the camp's location near Richmond, Surrey). It is at KV 4/13 to KV 4/15, although it is available in book form, having been published by the PRO, entitled *Camp 020*, edited and with an introduction by Oliver Hoare. The edits are minor; the great majority of the original has made its way into the published version. So far as Alexander Scotland is concerned, the original unpublished draft of his book *The London Cage* can be found at WO 208/5381. Much of the information relating to the London Cage was originally uncovered by Ian Cobain in the *Guardian* on 12 November 2005.

Material relating to Gösta Caroli and Wulf Schmidt, including transcripts of their interrogations at Camp 020, can be found at KV 2/60 to KV 2/63. Further material relating to Caroli can be found in the Owens file KV 2/448. Farago's *The Game of the Foxes* contains information relating to the training of both men and their delivery into England. Much useful additional material, including the part played by Alexander Scotland and a detailed account of Caroli's attempted escape, comes from Guy Liddell. Nigel West's subsequent questioning of Schmidt is from his book *MI5: British Security Service Operations 1909–1945*. The B1a contingency plan, 'Mr Mills' Circus', is outlined at KV 4/211.

The spies who evaded the grasp – or attention – of the authorities, Albert Meems, Wilhelm Mörz, and Engelbertus Fukken, are to be found at KV 2/2428, KV 2/2106, and KV 2/114 respectively. The Josef Jakobs files, including his trial transcripts, are at KV 2/24 to KV 2/27. Karel Richter is at KV 2/30 and KV 2/31. The story of Richter's execution is in Albert Pierrepoint's *Executioner Pierrepoint* (p.138).

The files relating to Roman Czerniawski, including appreciations of his trustworthiness at different stages of his career, and problems concerning his court martial, are at KV 2/72 and KV 2/73. 'Tar' Robertson's memorandum relating to B1a's readiness to engage in strategic deception is at KV 4/70.

Plan Jael is at CAB 154/60 and Appendix Y at WO 205/3. The presentation of Bodyguard to the Chiefs of Staff is at CAB 80/77, while the original version of Fortitude is at WO 208/4374. The interview from which David Strangeways is quoted is in the IWM Sound Archive at Accession Number 16755. The material relating to the notional Fourth Army is primarily taken from a report by Colonel Macleod entitled *The Story of the Fourth Army and its part in the Deception Operation to Cover the Normandy Landings*. This report can be found in the IWM Documents Archive at Box Reference 82/33/1. The story of the dropping of a single wooden bomb onto a painstaking replica of an airfield is in Jon Latimer's *Deception in War* (p.188).

Hugh Clark's experiences of building and maintaining bigbobs, as well as the story of the skipper and crew of the sailing barge being taken into custody, are from *Hugh's Wartime Memoirs* at Box Reference 06/38/1 in the IWM Documents Archive. The quote relating to the 'coincidence' that three agents should all give the same explanation for the use of advanced bases is from Roger Hesketh's *Fortitude* (p.121). A first-hand account of the work of the wireless deceivers is given by N. J. Smith of the Royal Signals and can be found at Box Reference 99/61/1 in the IWM Documents Archive.

Much of the information relating to the security measures agreed upon by both the security and deception authorities appears in Sir Ronald Wingate's record of Fortitude at CAB 154/101. The story of Churchill ordering the Director of MI5 to comfort a trade-union official is from the reports on the activities of the Security Service, prepared by Anthony Blunt and forwarded every month to the Prime Minister. These are at KV 4/83.

'Campaign Notes on the West' are at CAB 146/332 to CAB 146/337, while a particularly good account of Rommel's difficulties in relation to Rundstedt and Geyr appears in David Irving's *The Trail of the Fox*. The story of Copperhead is from the 'A' Force War Diary at CAB 154/4. Files relating to Karl Heinz Krämer are at KV 2/144 to KV 2/154, while those relating to Paul Fidrmuc are at KV 2/196 to KV 2/201.

Richard Poore discusses Operation Taxable in an interview with the IWM Sound Archive at Accession Number 20261. Professor Michael Foot's account of his dealings with Paddy Mayne is at Accession Number 9788. Details of the Titanic IV raid are featured in *Overture to Overlord* by Francis Mackay. The personal accounts of the seaborne landings on 6 June 1944 are all from the IWM Sound Archive. They are: Jimmy Green – 28401, Frederick Perkins – 14252, Tom Treanor – 1630, Richard Gosling – 21290, Jim Spearman – 9796, William Lloyd – 13283, Arthur Thompson – 13370. The quote from the *Pariser Zeitung* is from Hesketh's *Fortitude* (p.267). The account of the May 1945 W Board meeting is at PRO KV 4/70.

Finally I would like to give my heartfelt thanks to a number of people. To Louise Stanley, Elen Jones, Iain MacGregor and Hannah MacDonald at HarperCollins. To Jim Gill at United Agents. To Santo Massine, who taught me a great deal about 'Tin Eye' Stephens and Camp 020. To Duncan Neale, who generously offered to look over the pictures. To Andrew Lycett, for his advice on Ian Fleming and Dusko Popov. To Chris Maton for fruitful discussions about Juan Pujol. To Peter Kirkham, opening batsman and expert on Karel Richter. To Marcus Cowper, who assisted hugely when time began to bear down on me. And to Claire Price for her loving support and enthusiasm. I am very grateful.

INDEX

INDEX